Praise for

BE SEEN

"*BE SEEN* will help you clarify your unique strengths and show you how to use them to build a one-of-a-kind brand that represents the highest and best of who you are."

> — **MARIE FORLEO**, #1 *New York Times* best-selling author of
> *Everything Is Figureoutable*

"I'm dedicated to optimizing our brain performance and health, so I deeply appreciate Jen's belief that anyone can overcome their past negative thinking and reach their highest potential. *BE SEEN* helps you defy expectations and achieve the visibility you seek."

> —**JIM KWIK**, *New York Times* best-selling author of *Limitless*,
> host of the *Kwik Brain* podcast, and the world's #1 brain coach

"You need this book! If you're looking for a book that will inspire you to get out of your own way and shine, look no further than *BE SEEN*. Through stories that draw you in and the honest wisdom of a friend, Jen Gottlieb shows you how to take action and get results. Whether you're an entrepreneur, a nine-to-fiver, or someone with a really good idea who doesn't know where to start, this book has got you covered with practical frameworks and step-by-step systems."

> —**JENNA KUTCHER**, *New York Times* best-selling author of
> *How Are You Really?* and host of the *Goal Digger* podcast

"A powerful read for anyone who has ever felt unseen, unheard, or unsure of themselves. With real-life stories, business strategies, and actionable tips, Jen's book will electrify you to reveal your true identity and leave an indelible mark on the world. Be seen, get what you deserve, and achieve the success that's waiting for you!"

> — **AMY PORTERFIELD**, *New York Times* best-selling author of
> *Two Weeks Notice* and host of top-rated podcast *Online Marketing Made Easy*

"Jen's sharp wit and strategies will help you overcome your fears and show up as your real self. Whether you're an entrepreneur, a creative, or simply someone who wants to make a difference, this book is for you. Read it, apply its wisdom, and get ready to shine!"

> — **KELLYANN PETRUCCI**, *New York Times* best-selling author
> and celebrity nutritionist

"*BE SEEN* is the must-have guide to claiming your power and embracing your unique gifts. Jen Gottlieb shares her personal triumphs and failures while offering achievable steps to help you uncover your voice, become visible, and attain the success you deserve."

— **TRENT SHELTON**, best-selling author and motivational speaker

"The bold, must-have guide to finally GETTING OUT THERE IN A BIG WAY that feels authentic—claiming your power and getting clear on your message to the world."

— **LORI HARDER**, best-selling author of *A Tribe Called Bliss*, founder of H2Glo, and host of the *Earn Your Happy* podcast

"*BE SEEN* is incredibly alluring and grabs you instantly. Her real-life, super-relatable, and ultra-vulnerable stories will inspire you to overcome your own fear, self-doubt, and comparison. . . . Jen's approach is refreshing, empowering, and transformative—just like her."

— **ALLI WEBB**, founder of Drybar and president of Canopy

"*BE SEEN* is a must-read for anyone who wants to succeed in the world of branding and marketing. Jen provides practical advice and essential insights to help you build an authentic and visible presence that will attract and engage your audience. I highly recommend it!"

— **NEIL PATEL**, *New York Times* best-selling author

"Jen got me featured on television shows, countless news articles, and even *ROLLING STONE* magazine!!! (Need I say more?)"

— **DAN FLEYSHMAN**, investor, best-selling author, and host of the top-rated podcast *The Money Mondays*

"There's a difference between wanting to build a personal brand and actually having a guide like *BE SEEN* to show you how to make it happen. When it comes to developing personal branding, confidence, and success, Jen Gottlieb is hard to beat. She is a trailblazer who has laid out a practical and inspiring approach for anyone who is looking to elevate their personal brand."

— **TIM STOREY**, best-selling author and motivational speaker

"If more good people read *BE SEEN*, we'd have a lot of personal dragons slayed. And the world would enjoy more inspiring stories of triumph."

— **TODD HERMAN**, *Wall Street Journal* best-selling author of *The Alter Ego Effect*

"*BE SEEN* is an inspiring read that will help you find your voice and step into your power."

— **DAVE MELTZER**, co-founder of Sports 1 Marketing,
host of *Office Hours* and *The Two Minute Drill*

"*BE SEEN* is the ultimate guide for anyone looking to build a loyal following and make a lasting impact in a crowded world. If you're ready to step into the spotlight, this is the book for you!"

— **NICOLE LAPIN**, *New York Times* best-selling author

"Your full potential can only be realized if you're visible. *BE SEEN* is your recipe. Read it, act on it, and leave your indelible mark on the world."

— **MIKE MICHALOWICZ**, author of *Profit First* and *Get Different*

"*BE SEEN* is the ultimate playbook for those seeking to elevate their personal brand and skyrocket their confidence. Jen equips you with the tools and insights to chase your dreams fearlessly and make a lasting impact."

— **KIM PERELL**, award-winning entrepreneur, investor,
and best-selling author of *JUMP*

BE SEEN

JEN GOTTLIEB

BE SEEN

**FIND YOUR VOICE.
BUILD YOUR BRAND.
LIVE YOUR DREAM.**

HAY HOUSE, INC.

Carlsbad, California • New York City
London • Sydney • New Delhi

Published in the United States by: Hay House, Inc.: www.hayhouse.com®
Published in Australia by: Hay House Australia Pty. Ltd.: www.hayhouse.com.au
Published in the United Kingdom by: Hay House UK, Ltd.: www.hayhouse.co.uk
Published in India by: Hay House Publishers India: www.hayhouse.co.in

Cover design: Works Well With Others Design Group • *Cover Art:* Partners in Crime
Interior design: Claudine Mansour Design • *Indexer:* J S Editorial, LLC
Author photo: Chris Eckert

A NOTE FROM LINDA (from *The Wedding Singer*)
Words and Music by CHAD BEGUELIN and MATTHEW SKLAR
© 2006 MATTHEW SKLAR MUSIC and CHAD BEGUELIN MUSIC
All Rights Administered by WC MUSIC CORP.
All Rights Reserved
Used by Permission of ALFRED MUSIC

Library of Congress Cataloging-in-Publication Data

Names: Gottlieb, Jen, author.
Title: Be seen : find your voice, build your brand, live your dream / Jen Gottlieb.
Description: 1st edition. | Carlsbad, California : Hay House, Inc., [2023] | Includes bibli-ographical references and index. Identifiers: LCCN 2023026125 | ISBN 9781401972585 (hardback) | ISBN 9781401972592 (ebook) Subjects: LCSH: Self-presentation. | Impression formation (Psychology) | Branding (Marketing) | Success. | Success in business.
Classification: LCC BF697.5.S44 G67 2023 | DDC 155.2—dc23/eng/20230623 LC record available at https://lccn.loc.gov/2023026125

Hardcover ISBN: 978-1-4019-7258-5
E-book ISBN: 978-1-4019-7259-2
Audiobook ISBN: 978-1-4019-7260-8

10 9 8 7 6 5 4 3 2 1
1st edition, October 2023
Printed in the United States of America

SUSTAINABLE
FORESTRY
INITIATIVE

Certified Chain of Custody
Promoting Sustainable Forestry
www.forests.org
SFI-01268

SFI label applies to the text stock

For Chris.
Thank you for always seeing me.

CONTENTS

FOREWORD

One day I'm on Instagram and I come across a serious scroll-stopper. There's this motivational speaker and she is totally knocking it out of the park.

Not only is she the cutest person ever . . . but she's also a bright light. Her high vibes and magnetic energy pour off the screen. I tap the follow button and spend 20 minutes getting lost in her content.

A few months later, Jen and I are introduced in real life, and—no surprise—she's as awesome in person as she is on my Instagram feed. We hit it off and become instant friends . . .

When it came time for Jen to write her first book, she came to me for advice.

"What does your audience want most?" I asked.

Without hesitation she replied, *"They want to feel seen."*

Hits home, right?

The need to feel seen is a core desire that can become a driving force in our life. So many of us grew up feeling inadequate, unlovable or not good enough. Whether we realize it or not, those beliefs affect every area of our life, particularly our career. Inside this book, Jen guides us to release the beliefs that hold us back from truly being seen—claiming our power—and stepping into our authentic self.

With practical steps and a healthy dose of no-bullshit-New-Yorker coaching, she shows you how to step into your greatness so that you can make a major impact in the world, by being authentically YOU. If you're ready to move into the spotlight and allow the world to see the real you, Jen will show you the way.

For nearly two decades, I've had the privilege of being at the forefront of the zeitgeist of women stepping into their power as wellness healers, coaches, and motivational speakers. It's been an amazing journey full of incredible women—but Jen stands out.

If you're ready to release the limitations holding you back and embrace how much you truly have to offer, there's no greater guide than Jen. Flip to the next page and prepare to Be Seen!

— **GABBY BERNSTEIN**,
#1 *New York Times* best-selling author of
The Universe Has Your Back

INTRODUCTION

"You're not *being seen,*" said the psychic, staring at me with deep knowing.

Her words hit me so hard, I flinched. In fact, I was so pissed off I almost grabbed my purse and stomped right out of Ms. Corina's "office."

I never should have done this.

Let's back up a few hours so I can let you in on how I got into this particular predicament. One thing that I always swear by is that taking a walk can solve most problems, bad moods, or arguments. Because of this, my husband, Chris, and I take lots (and I mean *lots*) of walks. Our long strolls around New York City aren't just our way of problem solving, they're also one of our favorite activities to do together. So when I was feeling a bit down on this particular Sunday and couldn't pinpoint why, Chris's immediate response was to "walk it out." As we sauntered down 14th Street toward Greenwich Avenue, we stumbled into a tiny hole-in-the-wall crystal shop owned by a psychic named Ms. Corina the Magical Medium. We dipped our hands into bowls of pretty rocks and browsed shelves packed with colorful candles, and when I spotted a sign near the register about tarot readings, I admitted to Chris that I'd never had one.

"I never want someone to tell me something bad about my future," I told him. "I just feel like I'll spend so much energy worrying about it that I'll manifest it into existence."

A smile grew on Chris's face, one I knew meant he wouldn't take no for an answer. "I dare you to get a reading."

One thing you're gonna learn about me real fast is that I take dares *very* seriously. So I Venmo'd Corina $200 (yes, it's true what they say about New York City prices) and prepared to face my fear of being told my future.

And of course it turned out the "psychic" was batshit bonkers. Not being seen? *Me? This* lady was crazy.

"Hold up," I said, stopping her midsentence. "I think you need to shuffle your cards better or something. I actually *teach* people how to be seen. That's my whole thing! That's what our *multimillion-dollar* company, Super Connector Media, does! We have a damn program called The Be Seen Accelerator, for god's sake! See?" I opened my phone and showed her our website, scrolling through testimonials of clients who had achieved massive success in their fields from what I'd taught them. I continued, "I'm like the definition of *seen*, so you probably just got the message confused."

Chris looked at me in shock as I yelled at this poor woman, but Ms. Corina sat as still as a statue and responded, "You're going to be wildly successful and help people on a global scale, but you will not reach your full potential until you allow yourself to fully be seen."

"That's it!? That's all you've got?"

"'Be seen' is what's coming to me. That's the message." She shrugged, clearly used to her customers accusing her of bullshit and just as clearly not caring. She gathered the cards that were laid out on the table and escorted us to the door.

"Can you believe it?" I asked Chris, still fuming hours later, back home, as we got ready for bed. "Be seen?! What a waste of money."

It was well past midnight, and I still couldn't sleep when it finally hit me—as much as I didn't want to admit it, Corina was right. I wasn't fully being seen. The crazy ironic thing was, what I'd told her was also right: I knew *how* to be seen. I mean, I'd built a successful PR company from the ground up and sold it so I could teach thousands of people to be seen through my boot camps, courses, masterminds, and events. I helped them leverage media appearances to create viral TikToks, publish books, and land major speaking engagements. I was helping other people go from FOMO to famous in their industry by encouraging them to lay it all on the field and step into the limelight. And it was working for them! My clients were building massive platforms, powerful brands, and profitable businesses, but I was sitting comfortably in the wings like a stage mom as my students took the spotlight.

Sure, I had come a long way from where I started. I had social media accounts with hundreds of thousands of followers, but each time I posted a highly curated photo with perfect lighting and a full face of makeup, I knew in my heart I wasn't letting people see the real me. I was hitting a wall with a lot of my goals and, just as I thought (and feared), Ms. Corina the Magical Fucking Medium had hit the nail on the head as to why. I wasn't truly being seen because there was something hiding inside of me that I still wasn't sharing with the world, and I was ignoring the whisper deep within my subconscious mind telling me it was time.

Then, as the neon numbers on the clock next to my bed flashed 3 A.M. and I flipped my pillow for what felt like the 85th time, that whisper turned to a roar. If you've ever heard that voice from within, you will totally get it when I tell you that if you don't listen to it, it cranks the volume from background music to a loudspeaker on repeat.

"Jen, it's your responsibility to be seen," said the voice. "Fully, authentically, messily, imperfectly *seen*."

I knew what I had to do.

I got up that morning, turned to Chris with a big lump of fear in my throat, and said, "I'm writing a book."

I knew if I told my lifetime accountability partner this news, there was no turning back. Chris would never let me go back on my word, so the moment I said it, I was in it to win it. I *had* to follow through. For even more accountability, I knew I had to put my money where my mouth was, so I went online and bought the web domain for the title I thought I was going to use. For a cool $3,287, I now had double accountability. I was clearly in what Tony Robbins, one of the top motivational speakers in the world, calls "peak state." Tony says that's the best time to build momentum, so I ran straight back into my bed, pulled out my notebook, and handwrote a (really shitty) introduction to a book that's definitely *not* the one you're reading right now. But that messy, totally crappy start was just that—a start. My tiny action step was like turning on a faucet, and before I knew it, the drip turned to a steady flow.

After about two years and a hell of a lot of rejection, rewrites, prayers, uncomfortable asks for help, and the use of all the methods I'm about to teach you, you now hold in your hands a real-life manifestation of my response to Ms. Corina's message to me from beyond. *BE SEEN*.

My guess is you picked up this book because something about the title struck a chord in you just like it did for me that day in the West Village. Maybe you feel like the best-kept secret in your field and know you aren't shining as brightly as you're capable of, or you've been trying everything you know to build an audience but still feel stuck. Maybe you spend way too much time scrolling social media and watching other people in your niche speak to a huge audience of raving fans, with waitlists to buy their products or services, and you're done thinking, *That should be me.* Maybe you've been holding back because, despite your desire to be the recognized expert for what you do, no one in your life gets it. Or maybe you've been showing up publicly as someone you're not, and you know in your heart you need to let the world see the real you. If you resonate with one of those, or if you're still just trying to figure out who you are and what you want, I've so got you.

I know without a shadow of a doubt that by the time you close this book, you'll have everything you need to create the fulfillment, alignment, visibility, and success you dream of by stepping into your very own spotlight and allowing the world to see you. Really see you.

I took Corina's words to heart and held nothing back while writing this book. Inside these pages are personal stories I've never told publicly and actual strategies I've used to completely transform not just my life but also the lives, brands, and businesses of my clients. I should probably tell you up front that this isn't going to be your typical business book. I'm not going to sell you anything at the end, and I'm not going give you a gazillion examples of my successful clients so you can FOMO your way to purchasing my courses.

Throughout our journey together, we will walk through a four-part process that will help you start to gain the clarity and confidence we both know you need to start shining as bright as we both know you can. I've named this the Be Seen System, and it's broken up into these four sections:

1. Be Courageous

2. Be Creative

3. Be Connected

4. Be Visible

Let's talk about Part I, shall we? Have you ever felt like you were living a life that someone else planned for you? Or maybe you woke up one morning and thought, *How the hell did I get here?* The realization that you've built a life, brand, or business that's so full of "shoulds" and other people's ideas of success can stop you in your tracks, because it comes tied to another common realization—you've lost touch with who you really are. In this first part of the book, Be Courageous, you're going to learn all about how to look in the mirror and be seen *as* you, *by* you, in a more real and true way than you could ever imagine, because you're a total badass, my friend, and I can't wait to show you why. Part I will teach you to start recognizing and dealing with the fears that hold you back from growing your brand, and how to build confidence until it's practically shining out your ass. I'm going to give you a simple strategy that will help bring you back into alignment with your true self, because if you can't see and appreciate yourself for who you really are, how will others be able to?

That will bring us to Part II, Be Creative, where I'll show you how to take Real You and start leveling up to You 2.0 by getting clear on what you really want. Who do you want to be seen as? What do you want to be seen doing? Do you want to be seen as the person somebody else created, or as the person *you* created, mixed with a splash of the incredible human you reconnected with in Part I? Here in Part II is where we're going to decide that together, because in these chapters you'll be outlining your goals and creating the future you want to see, one daring step at a time. Yes, you heard me, you'll be making your own magic in Part II, and I've got the receipts to back me so you'll know it works. I'm going to show you the exact system I used to land my dream role in a Broadway national tour, meet the love of my life, and go from losing it all to building a super successful business from the ground up. Believe me when I say the keys I'm going to hand over to you will start the engine of the time machine that's going to take you right to the exact future you want.

In Part III, Be Connected, we'll take the blueprints for that future and start to open your eyes to all the people who are going to be there with you as you construct it into reality—the people who are there already, the ones who you might want to offload, and the ones you haven't found yet—with time-tested networking techniques and hacks to help you get over the sting of rejection and harness your network to both give and get value on your way to your goals. We're going to brush off your connection skills with some easy, bite-sized techniques that can make even the shyest introvert the star of a room, and show you how to actually get over yourself when you need to ask for help. In order to be seen, it takes people who support and love you to see you, and once you've got a squad of supporters fanning the flame for you instead of putting it out, all the tactics I'll be teaching you in the next part will feel easy peasy.

By the time you reach Part IV, you'll know who you are and what you really want, and you'll have an amazing network of people who will lift you up as you get there. Now you're going to discover how to build and engage with your audience and start to truly shine and be seen as the version of yourself you were always meant to be by the people who need you most. In Part IV, you'll learn all the steps and tools I use to create a profitable brand, including how to tell your story in a way that captivates people, how to create compelling and engaging content, how to leverage your own credibility and influence to amplify your wins and get into the media, and how to follow the path laid down by your biggest, most successful idols.

Throughout all four parts, each of the chapters in this book will end by breaking down what you've just learned into bite-sized, easily digestible pieces. After a short recap of some of the chapter's mic drop moments to remind you what's important, I'll give you a quick win—otherwise known as a way you can easily take action on what you've just learned. I'll also include a section called "Put It on a Post-It," which will contain a tidbit of advice, an affirmation, or a friendly reminder that I want you to jot down on a sticky note so you can keep it on your bathroom mirror, your fridge, your dashboard, or the edge of your computer monitor. I'm serious—grab a stack of sticky notes to keep by your side while you're reading. Soon, you'll create a small collection of reminders all over your home, office, and life that will keep you accountable so you can really start to commit to being seen.

If you couldn't already tell, I've anointed myself your new "no BS" New Yorker girlfriend, and I'm gonna start you off with some tough-love truths: if you haven't found who you really are and what type of future you want to create, you're going to build an inauthentic brand and a disconnected audience, and believe me, because I can tell you (from a whole lot of personal experiences that you're about to read about) that that's the fastest way to eventually start to hate what you do. I had to learn the hard way that when you're not in alignment with yourself, your goals, and a community that really sees you, you will probably go back into hiding and have to start all over again. My hope is this book will feel like we're sitting across the table shooting the shit at your favorite cafe. I'm about to dish plenty of impactful—and occasionally cringeworthy—stories from my own life and the people I've worked with. As you work your way through the four parts in this book—each of which includes tactical *action*—I'll be 100 percent genuine, honest, and supportive of your growth. By the time you reach the end of Part 4, you'll have done the work to finally go out into the world and be seen by the clients and audiences who need you the most.

This book is a little bit personal growth and a little bit business strategy, sprinkled with lots of my real-life stories that will make you laugh, cry, lean in, and hopefully give you goose bumps that help you to believe that whatever you're dreaming about is possible. I'm gonna give you all the goods. My most embarrassing faceplants, biggest failures, personal realizations, real-life fears, and biggest successes. They're all in here, along with the lessons I've learned through them all. Please add them to your toolkit of life and allow me to be your guinea pig as you find your voice and build a brand you love. If you're someone who loves frameworks and tactical step-by-step systems, I've included all of the actual methods I've used to grow a ride-or-die community of supporters and customers who consistently buy my products and services.

If I could take a step back and zoom out on my own life—a pretty wild ride that you'll hear more about in the chapters ahead—I'd tell you I would never have been able to create the life, love, and career I envisioned for myself if I hadn't stopped pretending to be someone I wasn't and started allowing the woman I lovingly call "Real Jen" to start being seen. Once Real Jen started driving the bus instead of the version of me I thought I was supposed to be, it became a lot easier to get clear on the life I *really* wanted to create, connect with the community of people that could help me get there, and speak directly to the audience I was meant to serve. So whether you're an entrepreneur growing your customer base, a nine-to-fiver who is capable of so much more than your boss sees for you, a budding influencer taking your first steps to build your brand, or a human with a dream who doesn't know how to start living it, I've got you. It's time to stop hiding and start being seen for the magical uniqueness that is you. The one and *only* real you.

When I was at my lowest point, I sat on the floor of a Barnes & Noble reading books by people who were doing what I wanted to do, and it inspired me to change my life. Those authors became the "friends in my head" who helped me reconnect and build a relationship with Real Jen. They told me I had something more to give, and I used them and their virtual support to get to where I am today. With this book, I want to give that back. You know deep in your heart that you have something *more* to give, or you wouldn't have cracked open this cover. I wrote this book so you can read it and think, *If Jen can do it, I can do it too.*

And I know, if you follow the path I've laid out in this book, you truly can.

My last ask before you dive in is to please use this book imperfectly. Let it be messy. Let it be scary. Embrace the feelings that come along the way. They are there to help you discover who you are and what you're capable of so you can build the unshakeable confidence that's always been inside of you. And don't forget, I'm with you every step of the way!

Thank you for seeing me through these pages, new friend. Please know that I wrote every one of these words with so much love and gratitude for you. Yes, *you*. I see you.

Let's dive in!

Xo,
JEN

P.S.: Some names, dates, and timelines have been gently altered throughout the book not only to enhance the resonance of these stories, but also to respect and protect the individuals involved, while maintaining the integrity and spirit of each event.

PART I

. . . .

BE COURAGEOUS

. . . .

CHAPTER 1

SEEING YOU

"Come on out, Jennifer!"

The bleachers full of studded-dog-collar-wearing metalheads went wild in anticipation. Just as I had hundreds of times before, I took a deep breath, adjusted my pushup bra, and grabbed the big black box full of CDs and T-shirts known as my "Box of Junk." Pasting a smile on my face, I started my hip-swinging strut onto the Warner Bros. soundstage toward the winner of *That Metal Show*'s trivia game, "Stump the Trunk." Looking like someone who just won the lottery, the superfan reached his hands into my "Box of Junk" and excitedly pulled out a Metallica beer koozie. I winked, said congratulations, and carried the 40-pound box off-camera where my makeup team powdered me so I could repeat the process for the next four winners.

As soon as the game ended, our producer called, "Cut!" I made my way backstage, closed the door to my dressing room, and collapsed into a puddle of uncontrollable tears. That morning, before shooting the first episode of season 10 for VH1's *That Metal Show*, I had discovered that my boyfriend of three years was cheating on me with one of our friends. I tried to fake a smile as I walked onto set, but beneath the surface, a panic attack brewed as I came to terms with the fact that the "perfect" future I had so carefully planned for myself was crumbling.

By now in my life and career, I was an expert at ignoring my feelings by hiding behind my safety mask, which consisted of dark burgundy lips and massive false lashes. So that's exactly what I did. I teased my hair, squeezed into my pleather leggings, and used the cheering of the in-studio audience to numb the debilitating fear and rejection that radiated through me. As long as I was being seen as Miss Box of Junk—who was loved and adored by her raving fans—I didn't have to be Real Jen, who had no idea what the hell she was going to do with her life when the producer called, "That's a wrap!"

If you'd looked at my Instagram that day, you would have thought I was living the dream. That's exactly what I wanted everyone to think. You see, I'd carefully curated my social media to look like a never-ending highlight reel of the happiest, sexiest, blondest, tannest "rocker chick" ever. One who oozed badassery and lived for heavy metal music. She spent her time jet-setting from NYC to LA to film a TV show, while her tall, rich, and handsome hedge-fund-trader boyfriend waited for her in their Upper West Side penthouse apartment. She took selfies with celebs, wore fingerless leather gloves, and partied like a rockstar.

But she was only a character I played. I had been living a lie, and it was unraveling right before my eyes. I was in a constant argument with my true self, doing everything I could to hide behind the facade of who I thought everyone else wanted me to be. I knew deep down that I was meant to be more than just a sex symbol online or arm candy to a successful guy. Sometimes I thought about leaving the entertainment industry and starting my own business or dyeing my hair back to its natural brown. But every time, I was faced with the debilitating fear of what I would even do with my life if not this. I felt unworthy of being anything more than "the hot chick," and that, along with the peanut gallery of people who surrounded me, led by my boyfriend Rob, put me back in my place.

"Just be pretty," they said. "And let people give you money for it." Easy enough, right? The problem with this specific life hack was that it only works if you believe you're pretty, which I had a hard time doing on most days. Years of being in an industry where your worth is often dictated by your bust size, hair color, and hip-to-waist ratio both tore down my self-esteem *and* helped me create the belief that I wasn't capable of building the "picture-perfect" life a working actress was supposed to have without relying on my looks and a rich boyfriend. So I doubled down on trying to be a successful "hot chick," both in my work and in my social circle. But something deep within me wasn't totally sold on this being it for me. That voice kept getting louder and louder, and the internal battle soon became absolutely exhausting. Being in a relationship with a guy who perpetuated the toxic tape I played in my mind about my self-worth definitely didn't help. So why the hell didn't I just leave him? Why did I stay? I look back and ask myself that all the time. The truth was, I was petrified of being alone and had zero trust and belief in myself that I could make it in life without someone taking care of me. I let those fears control me until I felt lost in a cave and couldn't see any light that would lead to an exit. Rather than facing my fear and finding my way out, I pitched a tent and hid alone in the dark, hoping for someone or something to save me.

YOU'RE NEVER FULLY DRESSED WITHOUT A SMILE (AND A SOUNDTRACK)

To understand where my rescue eventually came from, I need you to step back in time with me, to a tiny frizzy-haired Jen circa 1989 to 1995, dressed in a giant Chicago Bulls T-shirt, ferociously belting out "Tomorrow" from *Annie* in my parents' basement. Every afternoon, from the moment my dad pressed Play on our 1984 edition Revox sound system from Switzerland (my dad made sure I added that detail for you!), I was immediately swept away into a fantasy world. In a matter of minutes, I would go from my hard-knock life with Miss Hannigan to being under the sea with Ariel and Sebastian to skipping down the yellow brick road in the land of Oz to shuffling through the cemetery with zombie Michael Jackson. All while making sure Dad's video camera was capturing every hair flip and jump split. Remembering these daily jam sessions still brings on the happy tears and, without fail, reconnects me to my truest, purest version of myself. The me that was tapped in to her unfiltered joy, unapologetic enthusiasm, and contagious optimism. The me that definitely didn't fear what other people thought of her off-pitch singing or ridiculous dance moves. The me that didn't feel like she needed to fit in and be perfect at all costs. The me that allowed herself to be seen in all her glory. Today I lovingly call this little person "Real Jen," and I didn't know it for a long time, but she was the person I always needed to be.

I'm sure it's no shocker that I decided to spend the next 20-plus years chasing the high that performing gave me. I studied musical theater in college and then dropped out after a semester to move to New York City and pursue acting full time, where I booked my dream role on the U.S. Broadway national tour of *The Wedding Singer.* Then the universe shook shit up in a big way and sent me the life-changing opportunity to have a long-time part on VH1's *That Metal Show,* which, if you haven't gotten the vibe by now, was a talk show all about heavy metal music. The latest Black Sabbath single was definitely never one of the tracks Dad and I danced to, but it was a gig that changed my life, for better or worse, and it all went great—until it didn't.

That awful day, as I lay curled in a ball in a puddle of snotty black mascara tears, I could no longer ignore how lost I had become. Miss Box of Junk couldn't have been further from who I really was. Throughout my years on the show, I found myself portraying her all the time to stay relevant to fans and get likes on social media. I was being seen, sure, but I was doing it by being inauthentic, and the sharks could smell it from miles away. It wasn't long before I found myself deleting mean tweets from fans of the show saying I was a fake. They were right—I was. But I was so far disconnected from what was real that faking it felt like the only option.

If you picked up this book, I would bet that you're well aware of the overwhelming amount of faking it that people do when they're trying to build an audience. It's all too easy to hide behind a version of yourself that you think you need to be in order to be seen. Nowadays, most of us spend a very large amount of time consuming highly curated content that companies, brands, and "influencers" carefully create to make us feel, think, and act a certain way. Spending so much time in this filtered reality makes it reeeeally easy to forget that we're only ever looking at a highlight reel. So many of the influencers and creators we follow hide behind carefully Facetuned and filtered views of their high points, pretending they have a life that contains none of the flaws or obstacles we all deal with. And seeing it every day puts so much pressure on us to do the same. Haven't you ever looked at someone else's post and thought, *Ugh, I wish I had that life. I wish I could travel all the time. I wish my kid would sit still and smile for photos. I wish I could quit my day job and run my own business full time. I wish I wish I wish . . .*

It's okay to admit it—in fact, 60 percent of Americans have said that social media has a negative impact on their self-esteem. And can you blame us, when we're surrounded with all this polished, overly curated content? A lot of us might even change the way we're acting in our own content to try to seem more put together and with it than we are. Dress for the job you want, right? But all we're doing is feeding into the lie that we need to be someone we aren't to build our brand when it's actually the opposite! Here's a tweetable thought that will change the game for you: You attract what you *are*, not what you want. So if you're portraying a version of you that's into metal music and mosh pits (just for example), your audience will look more like the one at Ozzfest. The fastest way to create a life that feels stuck and untrue to you is to be seen as someone you're not. Example: the past few pages of my real-life faceplants.

I don't want this for you. In fact, let's take this cringey screenshot of me on the floor in my dressing room and draw a big red X through it. The Jen in that dressing room was only listening to what other people wanted from her—she was being seen as who she *thought* they wanted to see.

The totally ironic thing is that I'd already learned the lesson that I needed to be myself. In fact, it was what had gotten me the job in the first place! Let me explain . . .

NOT A (METAL) GIRL, NOT YET A WOMAN

In the Broadway National Tour of *The Wedding Singer* (yes, based on the Adam Sandler classic!), I'd played the role of rocker-chick-wannabe Linda—who was basically Pat Benatar, Blondie, and "Like a Virgin" Madonna all wrapped up into one super-sexed-up ditz from Jersey. So when I snagged an audition to play a "sexy metal girl" on VH1's *That Metal Show*, I felt like I had the gig in the bag! The day before the audition, my boyfriend—yep, the cheater I told you about earlier, though this was way before I knew that—took me shopping at Bloomingdale's, where we saw a Van Halen T-shirt on the rack. You know, one of those overpriced fake rocker T-shirts that no real fan would ever actually wear? That shirt was the key. I needed to transform into the girl who lived for metal, and the actress in me knew this was the costume that would bring my character to life.

I turned to Rob and said, "If I buy this T-shirt, I'm going to get this job tomorrow." I think he actually believed me, because within seconds he had walked up to the register and handed his Platinum Amex to the woman behind the counter. I walked out of that store with $120 worth of polyester blend and took my first steps on a path that would forever change my entire identity as I knew it.

I went home and spent the night studying. Despite the rocker-chick character I'd embodied for 10 shows a week in *The Wedding Singer* and the, like, *totally* authentic shirt I would be wearing the next day, I knew as much about heavy metal as I did about quantum physics. Which is to say, nothing at all. I loved Lady Gaga and Christina Aguilera, not Iron Maiden and Pantera, but the folks in the casting room at *That Metal Show* didn't need to know that. I decided to invent a new Jen—let's call her Heavy Metal Jennifer—who loved metal and knew everything about all the biggest rock stars on the scene. I would be a Van Halen and Black Sabbath expert. I would walk into that room and say "Master of Puppets" by Metallica was my favorite song. (I still have never listened to it in its entirety.) Like a good little actress, I was ready to forget who I was and pretend to be someone else entirely.

The next morning, I put on thigh-high leather boots, a Victoria's Secret Very Sexy Push-Up Bra, and my new Van Halen tee. I teased my blond hair until it had more volume than a nightclub speaker system, threw on some black eyeliner, and headed for the audition. I sat in the waiting room and did what all aspiring actresses do in casting rooms: sized up the competition. The room was flooded with girls who had huge fake boobs in studded leather bustiers and tiny miniskirts that were definitely *not* from Bloomingdale's. It seemed like everyone in the room had a tattoo—or 10. Just as I started to seriously question if this was the right move for me, they called my name.

"Jennifer Leah Gottlieb? You're next!"

I took a deep breath, handed over my headshot, and walked into the room, scared stiff. A nagging in my gut said there was something not right about this whole situation, and that something was me. I didn't belong here. When they started asking me questions, I completely forgot most of what I'd studied the night before.

"What's your favorite band?"

Crap. I knew this one had been coming. I'd studied this! *Come on, Heavy Metal Jennifer! What kind of music do you listen to?* The questions wouldn't get any easier than this.

"Well," I said, desperately trying to formulate a response, "as far as music goes, I like everything from Beyoncé to, um, Black Sabbath. Like, I was jamming out to, uh, 'Paranoid' in my room this morning, and my neighbors knocked on the door to ask me to turn it down." The producers laughed politely, and I continued. "I like eighties rock music, I like Poison, I like Guns N' Roses . . ." Crap. *How come I can't think of any other bands?*

I could feel the fake energy in my voice and wondered if they could too. I was wearing the right costume and saying the right words, but it was clear that I wasn't Heavy Metal Jennifer, not really. All the overpriced band tees in the world couldn't turn me into one of the metal-obsessed girls with nose rings right outside the door because that just wasn't me. I felt the opportunity slipping through my fingers.

And then, at the end of the audition, something happened that taught me one of the greatest life lessons I've ever received. One of the producers asked, "Can we see your Britney?"

I'd almost forgotten the little detail at the bottom of my resume about my Britney Spears impression. I'd left it on there just for fun, but never in a million years had I thought they'd actually ask to see it! *Oh, shit.*

Even though Real Jen loved Britney and could do a spot-on impersonation of the pop princess, I was supposed to be Heavy Metal Jennifer. This would definitely take the audition in the wrong direction! But they'd asked, so I steeled myself and shoved away the metal persona I'd tried to build. I pretended I was at home in front of my bedroom mirror or out with my friends being silly, and let Real Jen take the reins. I sang Britney Spears's pop ballad "I'm Not a Girl, Not Yet a Woman" to the room full of producers. (What a song choice though, right? Was I *trying* to tell myself I had some serious personal growth to do?)

Two weeks later, I booked the gig, and the producer said, "You know, it was the Britney impression that got you the job. We auditioned a lot of girls, but you were the one that we all could see ourselves hanging out with on set!"

I was floored. I had tried so hard to be who I thought they wanted me to be, but in the end, I stood out when I shared who I really was. It didn't matter if I was "metal enough"—they chose me because I made them laugh with something that only *I* could do.

I wish I could say that this was an aha moment for me, but unfortunately, it was a lesson I would need to learn about a bajillion more times before it actually sank in. I've since learned that recognizing the *real you* and letting that part of you lead the way will always be the key to making powerful relationships, creating lasting impressions, and unlocking opportunities that will bring you a lifetime of delicious "in the pocket" moments (we will talk about what that means in a bit).

THE REAL SECRET TO BEING SEEN

Before we continue, I need to press Pause and give you an important reminder. Even though this book is called *Be Seen*, I'm not giving you a quick-fix how-to guide to becoming the prom queen of every networking event or holiday party (though that might be an amazing side effect). I *will* give you strategies to make yourself memorable and leave everyone you talk to feeling better because that's a big part of creating success and opportunity. But what this book is really about is *the power of being seen as your authentic self* so you can build a brand that attracts and deeply connects with your ideal audience. First and foremost, it's about reconnecting to Real You. The beautifully unapologetic, perfectly imperfect human that's been hiding behind the masks of what everyone else has wanted you to be.

I've spent years getting myself to a point where I'm comfortable being seen as Real Jen, and I've had more than a few ups and downs. Here at the beginning of our adventure together, it's important to make it clear that the end goal of our journey isn't about being famous or getting likes on Instagram. Yes, I have helped thousands of people get on television and into major publications, become guests on top podcasts, and grace the covers of magazines, but that's all just a by-product. Behind the scenes at Super Connector Media, we actually consider ourselves a personal development company. We teach entrepreneurs and thought leaders how to use brand visibility as the gateway to connection, transformation, and self-actualization. While they come to us for the business and brand building strategy, what our clients and mastermind members *stay* for is the mega-bonus of confidence and clarity we give them. Nobody gets away from us without discovering who they *really* are, what they *really* want, and the impact they are capable of making in the world.

The secret to standing out from the crowd and building an audience of raving fans isn't being the perfect version of yourself that you think everyone wants you to be. It's leveraging your number-one superpower: Being the real you! There's a reason you are who you are, love what you love, and dream what you dream. It's because this is what the world needs from you and only you! But until you take off the filter and start being seen as your true self, you can't make visible the message you're here to deliver, create the brand you're meant to build, or attract the people who need your support.

Let's take a detour back to my rock-bottom moment, shall we? Remember that girl completely losing her shit on the floor of her dressing room? Yeah, let's check in on her again.

Here's a spoiler for you that I wish I could have given to that girl drowning in her puddle of tears: It got better. A lot better. I eventually found Real Jen again. I learned to be seen as myself, and it paid off in a big way. I wish I could tell that girl on the floor about all the opportunities she had coming to her, opportunities she never thought possible.

- I built a successful career as a celebrity fitness trainer, tripled my business revenue, and created an entirely remote company so I could work from anywhere.

- I met and fell in love with my now-husband, Chris "the Super Connector" Winfield.

- I formed deep connections and friendships with many of the influencers, authors, and celebrities who were formerly just "friends in my head."

- Together, Chris and I built and sold a multimillion-dollar, award-winning PR agency.

- We created a mentorship platform where we help thousands of business owners build profitable, impactful brands.

- I started speaking on stages in front of thousands of people all over the world.

- I began waking up each day with hope, enthusiasm, and gratitude for what was—and what was coming—because I was proving to myself that creating my dream life was possible.

- I connected even more deeply to Real Jen and started to build the momentum that led me to where I am today: sharing this book with you, and helping you see and be seen for your truest potential too!

I didn't do it all at once, and I certainly didn't do it without a ton of fear and self-doubt. (Don't you worry, we'll get into all that soon!) But the more I pushed past my discomfort and truly allowed myself and others to see the Real Me, the more I grew—and the more doors started to swing open. Turns out there's an actual science to being seen. And there's good news for you, since you and I are pretty much besties now (you can't tell someone about your crying-on-the-floor low point and your all-consuming love for Britney Spears without reaching BFF-tier, in my humble opinion): I'm about to teach you the exact system, tools, and strategies I used to get here.

I want to show you how to create a life even beyond what you've imagined for yourself. Whether you identify with my specific journey—an eating disorder, messy breakups, and periods of depression—or your personal brand of breakdown looks totally different, I assure you that you're in the right place. All you have to do to get started is to be willing to look in the mirror and see yourself—your true self—clearly.

GETTING IN THE POCKET

After rewatching my *That Metal Show* audition at least 100 times (you can find it on YouTube!), it became very clear that the reason my Britney impression worked so well was because I allowed the people around me to see me at my realest. I was in the zone when I sang for those producers, and my self-consciousness from waiting with all those metal girls and trying to answer pop-quiz questions about rock stars had evaporated. I've since learned that the trick to accessing that state of mind and being myself comes from moments exactly like these, when I feel the most "me." I like to call moments like these being in the pocket.

In music, the phrase *in the pocket* refers to being perfectly on beat and in tune, never missing a note. It's about precision, timing, and listening to the other musicians you're working with. It's a term I use for what positive psychologist Mihaly Csikszentmihalyi coined as being *in flow*. It's that moment when you're so completely in your zone of genius that you feel like time has stopped and you could go on forever. Thinking back on your in-the-pocket moments will probably give you an emotional response, like a smile or even a little misty-eyed joy.

Learning to recognize and capture in-the-pocket moments, and then *being* in the pocket during your speaking engagements, media segments, social media content, and even personal interactions like difficult conversations, is going to make a huge difference. You'll present yourself differently and feel a *lot* more confident and focused because you'll be Real You, and all your realest goals and realest intentions will be right there center stage with you. When you are in the pocket, nerves disappear. You are fully in the moment, and you can shine without worrying what anyone else is thinking of you. It's one of the best ways to quickly connect with Real You, and the trick is figuring out how to turn that feeling on and off like a light switch.

I didn't realize this at the time, but I learned how to get in the pocket during acting school. We spent what felt like hundreds of hours practicing the skill of reigniting actual feelings from our past so we could bring them into our scenes and experience them in the present. This technique is known as method acting. When I began my entrepreneurial journey, I started using this tool (with a twist) to bring me back into the pocket when fear took over and disconnected me from Real Jen. I found that if I could tap into the feelings I felt when I was the most *me*, every task suddenly became easier. I could instantly connect with my true self and her badassery when I needed her most.

I'm going to teach you the four steps that I use to get in the pocket and reconnect with Real Jen before I speak onstage, write pages of this book (yes, I used this system to write the words I'm typing right now!), or even have hard talks with my team, family, or friends. Once you master this system, you will be able to get into the pocket quickly so you can step into the spotlight as the real you.

SETTING THE S-E-E-N

> SENSE
> EXPERIENCE
> EMBODY
> NAVIGATE

Before we dive into step one, I want you to think back to a moment in your life when you were truly in the pocket. This will be your trigger thought going forward. When was the last time you felt this way? Was it when you ran that marathon last year? When you taught your kids to make chocolate chip cookies a few weekends ago? Or maybe it was when you were crushing it onstage speaking at an event? Was it in school, at work, or at home with your family? Don't get discouraged if it doesn't immediately come to you. It's okay to take your time, journal, and even do some research to help you find it! I love to look back at photos on social media or in old albums to rekindle my in-the-pocket moments. A good sign that a memory is from a time when you were in the pocket is if you have an emotional response to it. For this specific exercise, make sure your response is one of joy, pride, excitement, or gratitude because those are the feelings that we want to reconnect to. Once you have a memory locked in, you can move to the first step.

1. Sense

Our senses are constantly taking in stimuli from the world around us. Not everything we see, hear, taste, smell, and touch automatically gets stored in our long-term memory, but those senses *are* the key to unlocking memories—even subconscious ones we've almost forgotten. Haven't you ever smelled the hint of your grandmother's perfume in a garden breeze or tasted a dish that brought you right back to a vacation you took years ago? That one sensory trigger unleashes a flood of information, and suddenly you're picturing your grandmother's face clearly in your mind and hearing her voice for the first time in years, or you're reliving your entire dinner conversation from that long-ago vacation. This phenomenon, especially when triggered by our sense of smell, has a name—the Proust Effect—and scientists believe it's because inside our brains, our olfactory system and memory hub are basically next-door neighbors who can hear each other's conversations through the thin walls.[1]

We are going to use our senses to bring back memories and feelings from when we were our most real, in flow, and in-the-pocket versions of ourselves so we can reconnect with them and eventually embody that version of ourselves. If your in-the-pocket moment was in college, listen to a playlist of songs you loved during that time. If you haven't felt in the pocket since you were a child, light a candle that smells like the lilacs in your grandparents' garden. If you had red velvet cake at your wedding and that's when you felt the most you, go grab a slice from a local bakery and take a bite while watching a clip of your first dance. Look at old photos, read old journals, or watch old videos.

2. Experience

As you draw on the smells, sounds, physical sensations, or tastes of that memory, go back to that time in your mind's eye as if you were watching a movie starring Real You. Start to tap into a feeling of gratitude for that moment and allow your body to relax into the experience in detail. Fun fact: when you get good at this part, this can be as exciting and joyful as the real moment! As you relive this time and start to re-experience the emotions, take a moment and remember who that person was—in case you need the Spark-Notes, remember, it's *Real You*! Start to explore what it's like to move through life the way the truest version of you does. What does Real You really desire? How does Real You view the world? What really lights Real You up? Milk these emotions and allow yourself to sit in the fullest expression of gratitude, flow, and joy. Allow yourself to smile, laugh, and even cry.

3. Embody

Now it's time to bring those experiences and sensations to the present moment and allow yourself to actually become the person you are watching in your mind's eye. How does that version of you stand? How do you hold your head? Do you smile more? Do you walk a little faster and with a little more spunk? Once you've sensed and experienced the moment as a visualization, I want you to take a lap around the room or even go for a walk outside embodying the person you just saw. I highly recommend you connect this with step one, if possible, by listening to a song connected to that experience as you walk, dance, exercise, or just softly maneuver around as that version of yourself.

4. Navigate

Once you've practiced embodying the real you, I want you to start navigating through your life with Real You leading the way, using a tool I call Wonder Walks.

Back when I was an actress, the only way I was able to memorize lines was if I was out walking, because it was an easy way to connect my body to my brain. I quickly learned that I could take it a step further if I pretended to actually be my character while I was out on these walks. How would that character move throughout the world? How would they hold their body as they put one foot in front of the other? How would they react if someone bumped into them on the sidewalk?

These powerful moments of navigation mean really learning what it would be like to live your life as Real You. Did you walk differently when you were in the pocket? Start to walk that way when you walk through the grocery store. Have a big decision to make? Make it through the lens of the Real You that you've been embodying and visualizing. Try taking what I now call a "Wonder Walk." Go for a walk—down the street, in the woods, at a park, on a treadmill—and practice how you would move through the world during a time when you were the most in the pocket. What would it feel like to actually be that version of yourself? See who you want to be, experience what that looks like, feel what it's like to actually be that person, and, through taking a Wonder Walk, navigate the world as Real You.

Believe me when I say you're going to start seeing—and being seen as—the person you want to be before you know it. The more you take action utilizing the body and energy of Real You, the more clearly you will start to see them, be them, and eventually be seen as them by others.

STARTING WITH THE YOU IN THE MIRROR

After you successfully learn how to set the SEEN, you will most likely start to realize that Real You is one badass human who has a lot of wisdom that's probably been stored away for quite some time. Now I'm going to give you an exercise to help you get coaching on the daily from this brilliant being that is Real You. Ready for some magic? Here we go!

Pull out a notebook or open the notes app on your phone and write a letter from your Real Self to your Present Self. What would your Real Self say to you? What would your Real Self, whether it's you a month ago or 20 years ago, think about where you are now? And most importantly, what would they want you to know? What would they want to remind you about yourself? What advice would they give you?

Don't judge your own words. Be open and allow your thoughts to flow into your letter in a stream-of-consciousness style. Write everything that comes to you without self-censoring. It doesn't have to be perfect—it just has to exist. Remember, no one has to read this but you.

If you need help, here's a little fill-in-the-blank letter to get you started.

> *Dear Present Me,*
> *Congratulations! Today is the first day of the rest of your life!*
> *Don't forget that you only get this day once, and when it's over,*

you can never get it back. So let's shine and make it count! I'm so proud of you for getting to this moment—you've become an amazing person along the way. Remember that your super-power is _____ and it's been given to you specifically because it's your responsibility to share it with the world. Don't for-get that you're truly in the pocket and feel the most joy when you're doing _____. Be sure to make time for some of that today, especially if you feel stuck. You are capable, powerful, and _____. Your only job is to show up in a way that will make you proud when you put your head on the pillow tonight. That might mean being a little afraid, uncomfortable, or uncertain, but that's okay because discomfort is temporary, and what you get on the other side of that is growth, which is permanent! Never forget that you always have everything you need, and you're exactly where you're supposed to be. I'll be here in your heart cheering you on.

You've got this. I love you.

— Real Me

The most important relationship you'll ever have is the one you create with Real You. Whenever you need to tap into that part of yourself and find your way back into the pocket, read your let-ter from yourself. You might not always believe everything Real You said in your letter, but that's okay. Confidence in yourself is something you have to build, and it's something we'll discuss a lot more in Chapter 3.

One of my mentors shared this quote with me: "When you love yourself as much as you care what people think, you will change your life." Throughout the rest of this book, we'll remember what it's like to start to truly love Real You and all that comes with it. The good, the bad, the perfectly imperfectness that makes you the only *you* there is. When you begin with genuine self-love, you will allow that version of yourself to be seen by your community and your audience. But it all starts here—it all starts with this:

Look in the mirror. Who do you see?

MIC DROP MOMENTS

- The fastest way to create a life that feels stuck and untrue to you is to be inauthentic.

- The secret to standing out from the crowd and building an audience of raving fans isn't being the perfect version of yourself that you think everyone wants you to be. It's leveraging your number-one superpower: Being the real you!

- Unpack your box of junk and abandon the sense of "should" that follows you everywhere in your life.

- Get into the pocket and connect with the truest version of yourself. Remember that Real You will lead you to higher highs than Fake You ever could.

- Remember the last time you felt truly you.

 A QUICK WIN

- Set the SEEN to get "in the pocket" and take a Wonder Walk around the block as the badass that you are.

PUT IT ON A POST-IT

- Be you, Boo!

CHAPTER 2

GIVE FEAR
THE FINGER

Ever have one of those moments when you open social media to see pics of your cousin's new baby or your bestie's birthday party and suddenly 45 minutes have gone by and you feel like you need to redecorate your home, redo your website, get Botox, totally change your business model, and stop eating carbs completely? If you are giving me a little "hand raise" emoji right now, I feel you! Every single day we are bombarded with images and ideas of what perfection should look like, and it's super easy to start to compare your reality (which is perfectly imperfect by design!) to someone's highly curated showcase on social media. It's all too common to suddenly feel like you need to do whatever it takes to be seen as perfect too.

Here's some really real talk for you: When I start to scroll, I often catch myself feeling exactly the way I felt back in the *That Metal Show* audition room thinking I needed to run out and get a few piercings to land the job. Even though nose rings and lower back tattoos are no longer on the list of things I think will move the needle for me, I still have moments when I feel like I can't share pics that aren't Facetuned or I have to buy the perfect out-fit for every single video I make. If my TMS audition experience taught me anything, though, it's that being Real Jen is key. The producers saw hundreds of girls who were metal goddess perfection, but when I came along and gave them something different, they leaned all the way in!

The same goes for you when you're connecting with your audience, customers, and community. Perfect is boring, unrelatable, and—let's be real—unachievable. The reason people choose to follow you, listen to you, buy from you, or spend their time with you is because *you* have something special and different that they can't get from anyone else. Your community and clients could hear the exact same information from other people, but *you* are the one they resonate with. We'll talk a lot more about this in Part IV!

The beautifully messy uniqueness that makes you stand out from the crowd is something only Real You possesses. If you continue trying to fit into a box that you think others need you to be in, you're going to find yourself with a business, brand, or life that is stuck in the "almost there" phase. You may find financial success, sure, but I know for certain that as long as you live a life that isn't true to who you are, you will always have a nagging feeling in your gut. You know, the feeling deep inside that's telling you that *this* isn't quite it? That you are meant for more?

If you hear me, but the idea of finally being seen for who you really are while creating a life doing what you really want makes your belly do a backflip, I get it! Why does it feel so much safer and easier to filter our real lives and follow the path that others want for us instead of chasing our heart's calling? Why does pursuing someone else's dream feel so much easier and less terrifying than stepping into what we are really passionate about?

I have one word for you: one very real, very debilitating experience that floods our bodies and minds just when we are about to take a step into unknown territory. Have you guessed it yet? If you are thinking about our good ol' frenemy *fear*, then you are right!

Fear is one destructive force, and it shows up wearing a lot of different hats. Fear of success. Fear of the unknown. Fear of what "they" will think. (And who are "they" anyway?) Fear is kind of like an ex-lover who reemerges to suck you back in every time you start to move on, entering the picture at the most inopportune moments to tell you all sorts of lies about why you shouldn't change. Why you shouldn't take any risks. It begs and pleads with you to stay exactly the same, because fear knows that as long as you aren't stretching and growing, you will never reach your true north.

The truth is that fear is a dirty liar, and all those nasty little whispers in our ear serve fear's one true goal: to stop us from taking action.

I'm not ready yet.

I don't have the money.

I don't have the time.

I'm already doing too much.

So many of fear's lies are about being overwhelmed. I often catch myself saying, "I don't have time!" But then I have to check myself because I have plenty of time to watch *90-Day Fiancé* on Netflix. I'm simply prioritizing Netflix-and-Chill time over my goals. And that's okay if that's my choice, but it means I can't complain that I'm too busy. When we're overwhelmed, it's because we're making a choice to put more on our plate than we can handle, whether it's conscious or not (most of the time it's not!). We do this because being overwhelmed gives us a handy excuse to avoid doing things we don't want to do and, especially, things that scare us. I'm sure you're reading this remembering the last time you said the words, "I can't right now. I'm just too busy!" By now you should know I'm gonna give it to you straight, so let me get real with you. Sometimes we find ourselves with what feels like "too much" on our plate, and that's when it's time to reevaluate our priorities so we can gain back time for the stuff we truly care about. I invite you to really take inventory of how you're using your time each day— is being "too busy" just an excuse not to do something you know will move you toward your goals? If you choose to not prioritize the action steps you need and you use being "too overwhelmed" as an excuse, fear is winning. It's in control! It's doing exactly what it came to do, which is to keep you from growing.

Look, you *will* experience fear as you begin to be seen as your Real Self. Anyone who tells you fear isn't real, or that you need to be fearless, is a good candidate for permanent deletion from your brain. If you carry around a belief that you shouldn't feel fear or that only weak people get scared, you are setting yourself up for big-time disappointment. Because I have some news: the human experience is a twisty-turny road with plenty of ups and downs. We slip up, mess up, but the important thing is that we *get back up*. Every time we do, and we finish what we started, we become stronger, all while learning new ways to snap back even faster next time. If you are a human, you will pretty much always experience some form of fear as you navigate these ups and downs, and that's a good thing! Yes, I said that. Feeling fear is a mega-win! Let me explain.

I've had the opportunity to speak to some of the most successful and famous people in the world, and one thing many of them have shared with me is that no matter how successful you become, fear never goes away. In fact, the more you grow into your full potential, the more fear will rear its ugly head. Oscar De La Hoya, one of the greatest boxers of all time, told me that he loves when he feels scared because it means he's headed in the right direction. It means he's about to do something that will make him stronger once he's conquered it. He then explained that if you never feel fear, it means you aren't stretching yourself enough to experience any sort of growth.

What I'm about to share with you is one major difference between successful people and those who never make it: successful people lean *in to* their fear. They don't expect it to totally go away. Instead, they embrace it and allow it to come along for the ride.

Think about it: fear's entire job is to enter the picture when we are about to step into "dangerous" unknown territory. It was initially installed into the human experience to keep us from jumping off cliffs, sticking our hands into a blazing fire, or doing anything else that could cause us harm.[1] Unfortunately, the mind views judgment, failure, uncertainty, and even success as major threats. This is because they fall into the category of the unknown, and to our lizard brains UNKNOWN = SCARY. Our instincts delegate fear to barge in and stop us from taking risks that might hurt us down the line . . . even if the potential reward could be something incredible.

THE SIX SYMPTOMS OF FEAR

It's easy to acknowledge fear when it presents itself in the form of heart flutters while you're watching a scary movie or belly flips when you're about to crest that first big hill on a roller coaster, but it's trickier to recognize when it sneaks up on you disguised as other emotions that prevent you from taking action.

I've found there are a few distinct ways that fear likes to creep in and keep us from accomplishing our goals. I call them the Six Symptoms of Fear, and once we learn to recognize them, we can start to remove the power they have over us. As we go through these symptoms, remember—the goal isn't to banish fear, it's to recognize it, call it out, and then embrace it, because fear is done driving this car. It's time for you to banish it to the passenger seat and take back the wheel.

1. FOMO (Fear of Missed Opportunity)

The first symptom of fear is one you've probably heard of, but instead of "fear of missing out," I call it "fear of missed opportunity." You know, when you see one of your peers doing something great—maybe a former college classmate is absolutely killing it with their new company, or a business rival is publishing a book—and you think, *That should be ME. I should be the one doing that!* FOMO gets to us all at one time or another, especially when we feel like our dreams aren't progressing as fast as we'd like.

We've got a whole chapter on FOMO coming up in Part IV, but for now, I'll say this: you can let your FOMO take you down a rabbit hole of jealousy and bitterness and stop you from taking action, or you can use it as fuel to supercharge your success. First thing's first (and pay attention, because you're going to hear this a lot), you'll need to acknowledge your FOMO and recognize that it's just a symptom of fear. After you've acknowledged what you're feeling, ask yourself, *What is this fear really trying to show me? What about this opportunity I'm missing out on is something I want for myself? Now, how do I get there?*

Boom. Suddenly your fear is turning into an actionable plan that will lead to results and momentum. How about that?

2. Comparisonitis

We live in a social media world where it's easier than ever to "should" all over ourselves. Have you ever gone down the scroll hole on social media and found yourself thinking, *I should dress more like them, I should run my business like theirs, I should create content like that, I wish my brand was as profitable as theirs, I should decorate my home like that*? If we don't live up to the "shoulds," these highlight reels plant inside our brain (and spoiler, we *won't*) we can start to catch a case of very real, very serious comparisonitis. (I did not invent this word. It is actually in the dictionary!)

As long as you're comparing yourself to other people, you're not taking action on what you want. You're simply wallowing in indecision and self-doubt, which all lead to being *stuck* and not taking action. Another point on the scoreboard for fear!

Here's the thing to remember when you catch a case of comparisonitis: you're on a different journey *and* at a different milestone than everyone else on the planet. That person you keep comparing yourself to because they have 120,000 followers and you only have 120? They've been at this for years, and they probably failed and plateaued and worked hard without results for a long time before they found success. So don't compare your Chapter 1 to someone else's Chapter 20. We often forget that everyone (even megastars like Rihanna, Michael Jordan, Oprah, and Michelle Obama) started at zero! You are exactly where you are supposed to be at the exact right time. The more you "should" on yourself, compare, and focus on the other guy, the longer it will take you to get to where you want to be.

3. Analysis Paralysis

Are you the type of person who needs to ask at least six people what you should do before you do it? Have you ever spent an hour in a fitting room debating between two shirts and then walked out of the store with nothing because you couldn't make up your mind? If so, then you have experienced our third symptom of fear, analysis paralysis. I'm over here raising my hand so high with you because this used to be me (and still is sometimes!). When I was building my first business, I had such bad analysis paralysis that tasks that should have taken me a few hours took me *weeks*, sometimes even *months*!

Fast decision-making is one of the most important skills you can develop, especially if your goal is to build something or lead people. Being in indecision for too long is just another way to stay stuck. And since fear's whole job is to keep us from taking action, it shows up disguised as "I can't decide" all the damn time. Take social media. It's so easy to overthink everything about posting on social. *Do I use this filter or that one? Is this caption stupid? What do I even have to offer here? Should I be doing it like that other person instead?* Pretty soon, you're on the road to overwhelm, which often leads to one definitive conclusion: *I'm just not going to do it.*

Here's the super cool thing to remember—there's no such thing as a wrong decision. It's all about your perspective. Every decision you make (yup, even the fuckups) will lead you toward something you needed to learn in order to grow into the person you are becoming. I wouldn't be where I am today without my chaotic, insincere past or all my "wrong" decisions. Just like you'll never get where you're going (and believe me, I *know* you're going to go far) without all the beautiful, messy truths and mistakes that make you who you are. Think back on an experience or situation from your past that felt like the end of the world at the time. Can you reframe it? Try this: "That was actually the best thing that ever happened to me. Because if that never happened, _____ wouldn't have happened."

Thank god I didn't get that part because if I did, I wouldn't be here right now, writing this book.

Thank god I didn't go out with that guy because then I never would have met the love of my life.

If you're consistently stepping into unknown territory in order to grow, failure is inevitable. However, it can be one of the greatest gifts if you embrace the lessons that come with it. So just make a decision. It might not get you the outcome you want in the moment; in fact, it might totally bomb. But I promise you that eventually the bomb will blow a hole in the roof of your fear and allow the sun to start shining right through it.

4. Perfectionism

To all my perfectionists out there (and I know you know who you are), I need you to sit for this, because you're not going to like it.

Are you sitting down? Good. Now say this with me: *Nothing is ever perfect. And that's okay.*

I know, I know, but I'm not sorry. Perfectionism is another symptom of fear that stops us from moving forward. When you refuse to take action until something is perfect, then you will never press Go, because perfect doesn't exist! Some people walk around wearing their perfectionism like a badge of honor, but saying you're a perfectionist really just tells me you're a professional procrastinator. Putting this symptom of fear into the passenger seat means allowing yourself to use one of my favorite mantras: *Better done than perfect.*

Don't get me wrong, you always want to strive to put out your best work, but I can promise you you'll never find what works best if you don't allow yourself to be imperfect while figuring it out. I consistently get DM's from my followers telling me they relate the most to my less "overly produced" content. It's the realness that makes people want to follow me or subscribe, because nobody's perfect, and being able to glimpse the messier, rawer side of life makes me relatable!

5. Imposter Syndrome

Do you ever feel like a fraud? Or have you ever had a moment of debilitating fear of being "found out" as undeserving for a position, job, or responsibility? If so, you are not alone. This feeling of unworthiness, called imposter syndrome, is something that 70 percent of people experience at some point in their lives, *especially* high-achieving individuals. This symptom of fear is the persistent inability to believe that your success is deserved or has been legitimately achieved as a result of your own efforts or skills. When I was on *That Metal Show*, I learned that I was not alone in my fear of not being good enough. Every single rock star we interviewed (especially the most famous ones) experienced imposter syndrome

right before my eyes! They would all come off set after their interview and ask me the same set of questions, to the point where I
could probably have recited along with them!

"Was that good enough?"

"Did you get what you needed?"

"How was I?"

My mind was blown by this. The biggest rock stars in the world
felt like they needed *my* approval. If you ever stop yourself from
stepping into unknown territory or find yourself not owning your
badassery because you feel that twinge of fear saying *you're not
good enough*, I need you to listen to me here, and listen carefully:
you are enough.

Don't believe me? Read on, because I'm going to give you a
tool that's going to help you give imposter syndrome the boot in
Chapter 4.

6. Disease to Please

The disease to please can disguise itself as "good manners" or being humble. This symptom of fear shows up when we downplay
our accomplishments and deflect compliments, dimming our
light because we don't want to make those around us uncomfortable. Having the disease to please is also known as being a people
pleaser. You know the type—they try to make everyone else happy
even if it means not taking care of themselves. If this is you, listen
up, because it's holding you back more than you even realize!

First and foremost, you're not alone. A survey that was published the year I wrote this book suggested that as many as half of
Americans identify as people pleasers, and 90 percent of people sur-
veyed identified with at least one of the nine behaviors attributed
to people pleasing.[2] (The survey also found that women are way
more likely to experience this than men, so ladies, pay attention
to what I'm about to tell you!) Maybe you don't want to seem like
you're bragging or you're worried a friend will react poorly if you
tell her about your new promotion. A lot of women, me included,
have experienced this to debilitating levels because we're taught
so young that we need to make people like us. We worry that if we

shine too bright, the people around us will get jealous or angry. But this often comes from an even deeper-rooted fear of stepping into our fullest potential. Allowing ourselves to take off the mask, fully go for it, and then start to shine can be terrifying because it opens us up to being judged and rejected. But staying small with this "perfectly valid" excuse of not wanting to upset people or make them feel bad means hurtling toward a moment in 20 years when we wake up with regret for never going for it.

When I step into the people-pleasing zone, I like to remind myself that playing small doesn't serve the world. The more brightly you allow yourself to shine, the more you give other people permission to shine their lights too. We'll chat a lot more about this in Part III, but for now, remember that the people who get jealous or angry about your success are the people whose microphones you need to mute.

. . . .

It's safe to say that fear will manifest every time you're making big moves, but it's important to remember that the more these symptoms show themselves, and the more you don't give in to their pleas to pause, the more you will grow. Believe me, I know that moving through fear isn't fun. It's *so* much easier to give in and go back to binging *Breaking Bad* for the fifth time instead of taking a risk with your side hustle or having that tough conversation with your team member, but the only way to grow is to get out of that comfort zone and experience some pain, uncertainty, and, of course, fear. Every time you do and you make it to the other side, you get that more courageous.

CAN'T STOP THE FEELING

One of the events Super Connector Media used to run was called Unfair Advantage Live (UAL), where we taught entrepreneurs, coaches, and experts how to connect with the media so they could become the recognized expert in their niche. Over the course of three days, attendees learned marketing techniques that would rocket-boost their sales, how to pitch themselves to mainstream media gatekeepers, and mindset tools to step outside their comfort zone and finally allow themselves to show up and be seen. Most importantly, our attendees (who we lovingly call our UAL family) left the event with life-changing connections to other like-minded entrepreneurs who could help them unlock their full potential and build businesses, brands, and lifestyles that are truly fulfilling.

I honestly have a hard time describing the magic that took place at UAL, and on a personal level, nothing felt better and more aligned than being on that stage with Chris and my team. But (and this is a big fat but), it definitely didn't always feel that way. If you stalk my Insta now and look at the photos of our recent events, you will see me in my full glory up on the UAL stage dancing my heart out, in the pocket and totally confident. Please know that what you are looking at is a much later chapter of a bumpy, fear-filled story that started with a pretty mortifying Chapter 1.

When Chris and I decided to build Super Connector Media together, I was still new to the whole teaching thing. I had all the knowledge I needed, but I was experiencing every single symptom of fear on the regular. Some days it was imposter syndrome with a dash of analysis paralysis, the next day it was massive perfectionism with a side of comparisonitis. With each step into the unknown territory of leading a company alongside my powerful, talented, brilliant boyfriend came new manifestations of fear that screamed at me to get off the bus. Chris had previously hosted UAL (which he created from scratch) by himself, so everyone knew him as the face of the brand. He's also a total star onstage and had way more experience than I did in speaking, sales, marketing, branding, social media, and—let's be real—business in general. While I knew deep in my gut I had what it took to be up on that stage, I also understood that I needed to earn my stripes before people could take me seriously in this industry. Chris didn't know this at the time, but at the very first event we did together, I was completely petrified. Imposter syndrome threw a rager in my mind every time I had to stand on a stage next to him. I'm talking sweaty palms, nervous laugh, fake smile slapped onto my face—I

was sure everyone could see right through to the total fraud beneath my facade. I stood behind him a little bit, letting him be the
center of attention because, of course, I wasn't worthy of it.

He always knows what to say. It's better this way.

I'm not good enough to be up here.

*Look at those people out there. What must they think of me? They're
going to think I'm just his girlfriend. Arm candy. A pretty face. Just like
on VH1.*

I'm not good enough to be up here.

I so badly wanted to prove to Chris and everyone in that room
that I deserved to be there, but this avalanche of negative self-
talk combined with my desperate desire for the team to take me
seriously as a leader snowballed into debilitating fear with all of
its symptoms. I couldn't even make myself open my mouth to
add to what Chris was saying. Imposter syndrome was driving the
car, and it was driving me right off a damn cliff. Chris took the
lead, and I nodded along like a dashboard bobblehead on a bumpy
road, terrified to speak up or say the wrong thing.

Unfair Advantage Live was a huge revenue generator for SCM.
Not just through ticket sales, but because we also sold a higher-
priced mentorship program right from the stage. At that point, 90
percent of our revenue came from these events—meaning there
was always a lot of pressure for the pitch to be stellar so we could
make our sales goal. My second time co-hosting UAL with Chris,
the team agreed that I should give the pitch. I agreed. How hard
could it possibly be?

If you'd asked me the night before, I'd have told you it was
going to be easy. *I'm just gonna read the slides*, I thought. *It's going
to be fine.*

But when Chris took a step back and I started to share about
the program, telling our audience exactly why they should spend
thousands of dollars on us, I realized, ooh boy, I did *not* know how
to sell from a stage. Hell, I didn't know how to sell anything from
anywhere at that point. It wasn't until the moment I took the stage
that I thought, *Maybe I should have practiced this.*

To put it nicely, I completely shit the bed. I stumbled over my words and skipped over important slides because I didn't know how to work the clicker. I even tripped over my own foot at one point. The whole time, fear hissed at me with its venomous mantra: *You're not good enough to be up here.* When I finally reached the end of the torture I was putting our attendees and team members through, I awkwardly gestured to the table of gift bags onstage.

"Okay," I said. "Now everybody who wants to sign up, come onstage and grab your gift bag!" This was the moment everyone was supposed to swarm the stage and excitedly grab their bag while proclaiming that they would be signing up!

Crickets.

Nobody moved.

Not a single person.

You could tell the whole room felt bad for me. I could see Chris at the edge of my vision, and my cheeks burned with humiliation. I'd just tanked our business, I knew it. Chris was going to break up with me, and everything I'd started building for myself, every bit of success and progress I'd made, was flushing down the drain with a terrible echoing finality I could feel to my toes.

Our Chief Publicity Officer got on stage and desperately pleaded with the audience. "Please sign up," she begged, sounding nearly as pathetic as I felt. "Please."

It was so bad. I cringe thinking about it, even now. I walked off that stage and headed to the green room with my tail between my legs. My coat and purse called to me. I could just leave. It would be better for everyone. Chris was way better at all this than I was, and he could salvage the situation if I wasn't there to remind everyone of how badly I'd screwed up. With shaking hands, I grabbed a bottle of water and leaned against the wall, staring at nothing, lost in my thoughts.

I'd proven myself right, I realized—I *was* just an imposter. A fraud. A fake. I wasn't good enough to be there. My limiting beliefs had turned to prophecy, and now I'd let everyone down. I'd created that negative belief in my mind, and my brain was doing everything it possibly could to prove me right. I told myself I wasn't good enough over and over again, and eventually, I really started to believe it.

And that realization made me *angry.*

I blinked away my shame and took a deep breath. The way I saw it, I had two options before me:

1. I could leave.
2. I could continue on.

Number one was tempting as hell, I'm not gonna lie. If I left, I would save myself the embarrassment of having to go back on-stage in front of hundreds of people who had just watched me completely flop. I could avoid Chris's disappointment for a little while longer. But—and this was a huge but—I would also be proving to myself and everyone else beyond a doubt that my nasty little prophecy was 100 percent correct: I *wasn't* good enough.

Well, crap, because number two didn't sound so fun either. I'd have to get out there again and face those people, and I did *not* want to do that. Then I thought about the day Chris and I committed to being partners in this business. I had confidently told him I could do this, that I didn't want to be in the background, that I would step into the spotlight and shine even if I was scared. That I wouldn't give up! *That* Jen was the real version, screaming to get out from beneath the avalanche of negativity where I'd trapped her.

So I shifted my energy, and I tapped into Real Jen.

Real Jen was fun, she was confident, and she belonged on that stage just as much as anyone else.

"All right." I asked her, "What do we do?"

Real Jen responded with another question. *What are you afraid of, Jenny?*

I wanted to laugh and cry at the same time as I admitted, "I'm scared I don't belong up there. I'm scared that I'm not as good as Chris."

I could feel Real Jen's amusement, and then the answer hit me like a freight train. *You're never going to belong up there if all you're doing is trying to be Chris—because you're* not *Chris. You're Jen. Be Jen.* I thought back to the *That Metal Show* audition room, when I realized being the real me was my superpower.

Holy shit.

Real Jen acknowledged my fears, and then she showed me what they were trying to teach me. Then she firmly shoved those fears out of the driver's seat so she could take the wheel.

Because Real Jen had an idea, and damn, Real Jen could *drive*.

I left the green room with my head held high and my eyes flashing bright with determination. Real Jen told me, *We can do this.* And I needed to believe her.

I found the DJ in the back of the room and pointedly ignored his sympathetic smile and the pitying way he said, "Heeyyy."

"Listen," I said, handing him my phone. "When we come back from lunch, I want you to play this song all the way through, and I want you to play it really loud."

"Um," said the DJ, openly puzzled. "Okay?"

"No, seriously," I said. "Play it like we're at a wedding and you're trying to get everyone on the dance floor. Just trust me."

He didn't trust me, I could tell, and honestly, I didn't blame him. The Jen who had gotten offstage not 15 minutes ago was absolutely not the kind of person whose harebrained ideas you'd listen to. But I channeled Real Jen, who was starting to be able to see some sunlight as she dug her way out of that avalanche, and convinced him.

The rest of lunch was awkward. No one wanted to talk to me, and Chris was pissed and just trying to figure out how the hell we were going to salvage the event. The audience filed back into the room, taking their seats, and I got back onstage, giving the DJ the signal.

Justin Timberlake's "Can't Stop the Feeling!" flooded the speakers, filling the room with noise. *Fuck it, I've got nothing else to lose,* I thought, and held up the mic.

"All right, everybody!" I moved my hips to the music and summoned every ounce of enthusiasm I could possibly wring from myself. "Get on your feet!"

I danced my way through the audience, pretending the entire morning had never happened, and encouraged everyone up out of their seats. It was awkward for a few seconds, I'll admit. But before long, I had this room of business professionals on their feet, dancing. People were climbing on tables, busting out moves I'd never have guessed they had in them. And as for me? I was back to being that little girl dancing in front of my dad's camera. My mind left my body and I forgot about my embarrassment and insecurities and the category five disaster that had been the morning. I gave in to Real Jen, and she allowed herself to be seen.

We had the best time dancing to the entire song, and our midday dance party completely shifted the energy of the event. Once I let Real Jen drive the car, we ended up getting back on track and made over a million dollars in sales from the rest of that event.

This story tells the birth of one of our favorite traditions—the midday dance party, which has since become a time-honored and much-anticipated part of all of our events—even the ones on Zoom! But it's more than that. It's what gave me permission to step into who I was. Me. Not Chris, not Heavy Metal Jennifer, but *Real Jen.*

I didn't need to be like Chris because I was never going to be Chris. All I could be was me, and the me who runs these events now brings the fun, the connection, the energy, and the enthusiasm that our audiences have come to expect. And for the record, I have since mastered the sales pitch and now teach our Super Connector Mastermind members how to make seven figures from both in-person and virtual events—using a lot of what I learned from failing miserably.

My failures, faceplants, and run-ins with fear have always ended up being *for* me, but I'm not telling you that you need to throw dance parties for hundreds of people to reconnect to your true self and give fear the finger. Flipping off fear might look like quitting your crappy job or hitting Post on your first TikTok video. But what I *am* telling you is that you need to have the courage to be seen as your real self in order to unlock the opportunities that will connect you to your fullest potential and most fulfilling future.

HOW TO TALK TO FEAR

I know you're thinking, *But Jen, how do I take action when fear is giving me all the excuses in the world to stop?* Right here, right now, I'm going to teach you how to talk to fear. Just like a potential client on a sales call or your unruly two-year-old in a toy store, fear needs to be schmoozed and then put firmly in its place. Here's how you do it:

1. Acknowledge your fear. Say, "What's up, Fear? I see you, I hear you, and I get it. You're trying to keep me safe, and I love you for it. But I'm not in any real danger here other than the risk of not living up to my highest potential. And honestly, you are getting in the way of that right now, so it's time for you to shut it."

2. Put fear in the passenger seat. In her book *Big Magic*, Elizabeth Gilbert writes about taking a road trip with your fear, and it's no wonder the metaphor works so well! Fear is there for the ride whether you like it or not, but it's more than just a special-occasion kind of trip; in fact, it's a lot more like a daily commute. The trick is to envision getting into a car with fear while giving it specific instructions: "Okay, Fear, we are going for a drive together. I know you need to come along, but it's my turn to drive, so your ass is riding shotgun. Here are the rules: you can't control the A/C, you can't touch the steering wheel, and you can't even sing along when I play a song you love. You just have to sit there and be quiet. I'm in charge here."

You and your fear are always going to be carpool buddies. It's not going anywhere, so you're going to have to get used to taking action with it sitting right there beside you. But remember—*you* are the one in charge. Once you can become the boss of fear and all its sneaky symptoms and stop letting its road rage take over your life, you will start to realize that if you look closely, it's trying to show you something. Because that's all fear is—an opportunity for growth! Learning to use your fear as a tool will give you power beyond measure, a power you can use to harness your Real Self and hold on tight so you never lose yourself again. Remember, your fear is always *for you*.

🎤 MIC DROP MOMENTS

- Fear is a natural human response to new situations.

- Fear's entire job is to stop you from taking action and keep you safely hidden away in your comfort zone, instead of being seen as Real You.

- But believe it or not, fear is an opportunity for growth, and if you can start to recognize its symptoms, you'll learn to take away its power.

- The six symptoms of fear:

  - FOMO

  - Comparisonitis

  - Analysis Paralysis

  - Perfectionism

  - Imposter Syndrome

  - Disease to Please

👏 A QUICK WIN

- Acknowledge which symptoms of fear are showing up for you right now and have a conversation with that biyatch. Tell it you're grateful for the guidance, but you can take the wheel from here!

✍️ PUT IT ON A POST-IT

- Successful people lean *in* to their fear. They don't expect it to totally go away. Instead, they embrace it and allow it to come along for the ride.

KEYS TO THE CONFIDENCE CONTINUUM

All too often, clients will tell me about their fears and discomfort when it comes to networking or allowing themselves to be seen on social media, and then say to me, "But you probably don't have that problem because you're super confident."

It stops me in my tracks every time because let me tell you something: at my core, I am probably one of the most introverted people you've ever met. Yes, I can speak with authority in front of a crowd of business professionals, and yes, I'm a trained actress who can transform into characters onstage. But would I prefer to be at home on my couch with my dogs, binge-watching *The Great British Baking Show* and speaking to absolutely no one other than my husband? Also yes! All of these things can be true at once. Being an introvert definitely doesn't mean that you are shit out of luck when it comes to building confidence. And losing your confidence—no matter how—doesn't mean it's gone forever. Seriously, take it from me. I'm living proof.

SKATING ON THIN ICE

Hey there, lovely reader, just wanted to give you a little heads-up before you dive into the next section of this chapter. It covers some content related to eating disorders, and I know that can be a sensitive topic for some of us. So I just want to remind you to take care of yourself and proceed with caution if you feel like it might be triggering for you.

. . . .

I started taking figure skating lessons at 12, which is basically grandma status in the figure skating world. Even though I absolutely loved skating, I was no Tara Lipinksi. As a thicker girl with very developed D cups and a little extra fluff around my midsection, I also didn't have the typical "skater body," so I wore double tights to try to flatten my belly in my spandex dresses. This winning combo of feeling too old and too fat meant I never felt confident in the rink among the tinier, younger girls, who were all way more capable of actually "making it" than me. Even after reaching competitive status, I never got as much attention from my cold Russian coach, Vera, as they did, so when she told me one day, "You look so skinny! Have you lost weight?" dopamine lit up my 14-year-old brain like a Christmas tree. "Great job, Jenny!"

In that moment, basking in Vera's approval, my brain made a connection: *skinny = love.*

I felt like I had cracked the code, and I was determined to keep it going.

Earlier that year, my parents got divorced and my dad was diagnosed with multiple sclerosis. Just like that, I was no longer the center of my parents' universe. They were doing the best they could, but they had their own issues and drama to deal with. We lived in Florida at the time and my mom had a new boyfriend who lived in New York, so my brother and I were left to our own devices when she traveled to visit him. I didn't realize it at the time, but the less I felt seen by my parents, the more my confidence plummeted. I quickly went from a super outgoing little spitfire to a reserved shell of myself, searching for validation. And, like a lot of 14-year-olds, I found it in all the wrong places.

I began to make it my mission to be accepted by the "popular" girls at school. If they approved of me, I thought, I would feel better about my situation at home. So when I finally got a seat at the lunch table next to Courtney, the "queen bee" of the cool kids, I swapped my overalls for low-cut V-necks and super-short shorts with the waistband rolled twice so my butt cheeks would show. I slathered my eyelids with sparkly Urban Decay eyeshadow and thick black eyeliner. I even started speaking differently. The more I morphed into a mini mean girl, the more I was accepted into the group. But with each coat of dark-brown lip gloss and each day in the cafeteria next to Courtney, I lost more and more confidence in being good enough just as I was. Real Jen—confident, fun-loving, silly, unapologetic—was nowhere to be found.

One day, the cool girls collectively decided to go on a "diet." We ordered pre-packaged salads from the cafeteria, picked out the croutons, and threw away the dressing. To be clear, all there was on the salad was croutons and a side of ranch, so lunch became dry lettuce and a Diet Coke. I *loved* food, but my desire to feel part of the group at school and gain approval from Vera at the rink was so strong that I was willing to experience a little bit of hunger. After a few weeks of lettuce for lunch and 100 crunches each night before dinner, I transformed my voluptuous body into a leaner physique. I relished how loose my jeans felt and how my fingers touched when I put my hands around my thigh. But even more, I loved the newfound attention I was getting.

Though family drama consumed my household, the one conversation that everyone loved to have was about how great I looked. The 15 pounds of extra "fluff" that came off me turned a cute little girl into a strikingly beautiful young woman. Men on the street turned their heads when I walked by. Courtney and her friends invited me to all their parties and even passed me their heart-shaped folded notes in between classes. From then on, it was officially official: skinny = love, and I wanted nothing to do with any other version of me.

The world around me was chaotic, but pushing away dessert or picking every grain of salt off of the one pretzel I ate for a snack made me feel powerful. I felt accomplished whenever my stomach made noises. The thinner I got, the more Vera smiled at me during skating practice, and the more in control I felt.

I'd begun to pretend that a sense of control and approval from others could be a good substitute for my lost confidence, and the consequences of that lie soon became dangerous as my diet turned into full-blown anorexia.

My poor little body was working overtime. I was going to school and training on the ice for hours every day on little to no calories. One day I came home from school in a daze. The room was spinning, my hands were freezing, and I could hardly think straight. I walked into the kitchen to grab my afterschool snack— a Diet Coke—when I spotted a box of Famous Amos cookies on the counter.

The moments that followed are a bit of a blur, but the next memory I have is of staring at the empty box with a painfully distended belly and a feeling of utter disgust and massive panic. *What did I just do? How can I take it back?* My heart was pounding, and tears welled up in my eyes. I had failed at the one thing that made me feel worthy of love and attention. I'd have done anything to erase that moment.

Anything.

By this point, I had lost all confidence in myself, my worthiness, and my ability to control my actions. I mean, I couldn't even stop myself from inhaling a box of chocolate chip cookies! Before this moment, I'd never been able to understand why anyone would want to make themselves throw up. I hated throwing up. It hurt a lot and it was gross. But having the power to reverse the sin I had just committed felt like hopping onto the last lifeboat before the *Titanic* sank beneath the icy waves. I could save myself from this debilitating shame if I wanted to. All I had to do was throw up.

So I did.

That day, Real Jen completely peaced out and her understudy officially stepped in. This version of me was shy, insecure, full of doubt, and obsessed with her appearance. Always nervous that she wouldn't be good enough, skinny enough, or in control enough to be accepted. It was the beginning of a 20-year eating disorder that would impact the way I viewed food, control, love, and self-acceptance for the rest of my life.

I've never told this story before, but I'm telling it now because I want you to know that if you have previously or are currently struggling with any form of disordered eating, body image issues, or feelings of unworthiness, you are not alone.

Let me repeat that for you in case you didn't hear me: You. Are. Not. Alone.

Research suggests that as many as 30 million Americans will suffer from an eating disorder during their lifetime,[1] and more than 50 percent of Americans feel pressured to have a specific body type.[2] I'm one of them, on both counts. And while I'm definitely not a psychologist, therapist, or trained mental health expert, I am living, breathing proof that you *can* re-create confidence and rediscover your worth, even if it's been lost for a long time. I am going to teach you strategies I've personally implemented to become more confident and create opportunities for my life, brand, and business that I used to only dream about, but please note that this book is *not* intended to be a replacement for professional help from a trained mental health practitioner. So if body image and disordered eating is something you are struggling with, please seek help from a pro and use this book as your extra cheer squad alongside your healing journey. I'm here for you. I see you.

It took me years to build back the confidence I lost in my teen years, but there's one thing I want to make perfectly clear: whether it's caused by an eating disorder or a bully or a negative comment on Instagram, you *can* build it back, and I want to make sure you know just how important it is that you do. When allowing yourself to fully be seen, and navigating around with one or more of the six symptoms of fear, a big part of what you need is confidence. And thankfully, confidence can be created, so we're not just shit outta luck if we feel like we've lost our mojo.

WHAT'S CONFIDENCE GOT TO DO WITH IT?

I'll admit, I'm *waaay* more confident these days than I used to be. I've come a long way from that teenage girl who starved herself to feel some semblance of control or the budding entrepreneur who was petrified to speak onstage next to her boyfriend at his event. Here's the cool news for you: I didn't become more confident magically or by accident. I worked really hard to make myself that way, and you can too!

So what is confidence made of anyway, and how do we get more of it? My (very unofficial, non-technical) definition of confidence is that it's the stuff that turns thoughts into actions. And since actions are what turn thoughts into things, some amount of self-confidence is essential if you want to create anything. If I were to ask you to think of a "confident person" in your life, I would bet the person who immediately comes to mind is that friend who's always the first one on the dance floor and the last one to leave the party. That bright light of a human who easily floats around the room like a celebrity on the red carpet, kissing babies and taking selfies. If you feel like you're screwed in the confidence department because you can't see yourself ever being anything like that person, that's okay. You don't have to be a super outgoing, mega-extroverted prom queen to deploy the superpower of self-confidence and become more successful. I know many people who have what I like to call "quiet confidence," which, in my opinion, is way more powerful than pose-for-the-paparazzi poise.

Another way of thinking about confidence is to consider it as an undeniable trust you have in yourself and your ability to follow through no matter how uncomfortable or difficult something is. You know that person who walks into a room and shifts the energy without having to say a word? They possess a sense of "knowing." They *know* they're the type of person who sticks to their commitments and doesn't give up when it gets hard. They *know* they have what it takes and don't feel like they have to prove anything to anyone. People flock to them and want to do business with them just because of the magnetic energy that they possess. That kind of quiet confidence is some superhuman shit that will undeniably change your life. The good news is, with practice, we can *create* confidence (quiet confidence and/or red-carpet swagger) over time, and I'm really excited to teach you how.

Let's not forget that we are all born super confident. All of us. Even if you were one of those kids who hid behind Mom's legs, hear me out. When we're kids, we aren't conditioned to care what anyone thinks of us yet. We're not afraid to ask for what we want. We run around naked, throw tantrums when we don't get our way, wear dress-up costumes to the grocery store, and fearlessly ask for hugs and kisses when we want them. We innately trust ourselves and don't second guess our feelings and desires. But then, somewhere along the way, we learn about rejection, judgment, and the importance of fitting in, and we lose that unapologetic confidence. Basically, we let fear get into the driver's seat because we stop believing that we have what it takes to get to the final destination by being who we really are.

When I was 10, I was part of a touring children's theater group called Starmakers, and every performance, I was in my element— loud, proud, unafraid, and thrilled to be onstage. I remember standing there in bedazzled denim overalls with the lights shining on my cheeks and thinking, *There is nothing better than this.*

There was a point in the show when we each introduced ourselves to the audience and said what we wanted to be when we grew up. I remember taking three steps forward, sticking out my chest, and proudly announcing, "Hi, I'm Jennifer Gottlieb, and when I grow up, I want to be a Broadway star!" I wasn't scared to declare what my goal was because I didn't fear what they would think if I failed. Failure didn't even enter my mind. I just wanted to perform because that's what set my soul on fire.

Later, with the help of "role models" like my skating coach and the popular girls in my grade, I began to see the importance of fitting into society in order to feel accepted, acknowledged, and even loved. Maybe it happened earlier for you, or later. But what we all have in common is that at some point, we became conditioned to act the "right" way and want the "right" things. Maybe for you this manifested as choosing a career path because it was what your parents wanted or marrying someone who was totally not your match though they looked perfect on paper. For me, this desperate desire to fit in created a deep fear that locked away the courageous little girl on the Starmakers stage. I still wanted to sing and dance in front of anyone and everyone, but I dimmed that light for fear that I wasn't "good enough" or "perfect enough," and I started to believe the lies that fear was telling me.

WORK YOUR CONFIDENCE MUSCLES

Even today, though the universe has given me many experiences that proved that being Real Jen is always the vehicle to success, I still have moments where I forget and slip back into hiding. I'll be the first to raise my hand and tell you that fear gets the best of me every once in a while. Hell, this book is full of stories where I've entered the boxing ring with fear and it has given me a serious run for my money! But the important part is that if I go down, I go down swinging. And these days, 99 percent of the time, I come out ahead, even if I feel battered and bruised by the fight. Why? Because I don't give up. I'm worth more than that, and so are you.

Repeat after me: confidence comes from consistently sticking with the commitments you've made with yourself—*especially* when those commitments are uncomfortable. Every time you tell yourself you're going to do something and you follow through, you put a penny in your confidence bank. *Cha-ching!* This creates a little more motivation to take action the next time. But beware, my friend, because the same sort of thing happens in the other direction too. Every time you commit to something and quit when it gets a little tough, scary, boring, uncomfortable, or painful, you're telling your subconscious mind that you can't trust yourself. You just made a withdrawal from your confidence bank, meaning you won't be as confident the next time you try to take action in the face of fear. Remember that sense of knowing we talked about? Consistently quitting before you reach the final destination diminishes that knowing over time. It makes you unsure, insecure, and disempowered. As we discussed in the previous chapter, the one thing that keeps us from following through with our commitments is our good ol' frenemy fear and its six annoying symptoms.

Confidence and fear are intimately connected in a toxic relationship; if we don't have the confidence to take the steering wheel, guess who hops right back in and demands to drive?

Just like the muscles in your body need exercise in order to build strength, you have to work your confidence muscles consistently to build stronger self-confidence. That means repeatedly practicing the follow-through part of the equation, even when you get uncomfortable. When you repeatedly put those reps in, you start to get results, and then you start to create the amazing, delicious feeling we all love called motivation!

Let's talk motivation for a sec. Have you ever found yourself saying, "I'm waiting for the motivation to hit me"? I'm with you, buddy. I sat around for years, waiting for motivation to magically strike so I could change my life. I waited . . . and waited . . . and . . . no dice. I'm sorry to ruin your fantasy of one day waking up and having it all figured out, but there is no "motivation fairy" that bops around hitting people with glitter bombs of confidence and inspiration. Motivation is created by *winning*!

One of our clients, Pamela, has an amazing niche business as a sex therapist. She started noticing that some of her competitors were having great success building an audience on TikTok. She knew the benefits getting on the platform could have for her brand, but she just couldn't get the motivation to make that first video. She kept saying she would make a TikTok "one day" when she "felt ready," but that day never came, and she continued to have FOMO watching other people in her space grow their following and get new business on the app. Finally, with some coaching from us and a social media expert we brought in to speak to our members, she decided to put fear in the passenger seat and finally make her first video. That video ended up going viral, getting hundreds of thousands of views! As I'm sure you can imagine, Pamela was now motivated to make more videos on TikTok, but it wasn't because the "right time" finally came. It was because she took action anyway and got a win. She used the motivation from that win to make another video, which got her an even bigger win. Soon enough, her channel grew to over one million followers! That big win was what she needed to launch her into massive momentum.

THE CONFIDENCE CONTINUUM

As you can see, motivation is built by taking action, creating something, and collecting a win on the other side. Those little wins add up, making you want to do it again. When you do, you'll find you're building momentum—that juicy, amazing feeling of going and going like the Energizer Bunny—and feeling great about it. Throughout the cycle, you are sticking with your commitments and practicing taking action, which continuously builds more and more confidence!

I have a name for this phenomenon: the Confidence Continuum. It's one of the key strategies I've used to train myself to consistently build more confidence, but it doesn't come all at once. The Confidence Continuum has its own framework, a six-step "workout" for those confidence muscles that will help you quickly and effectively rebuild your confidence to get you to that action. I call them the six Cs.

1. Clarity

An unclear mind pauses momentum. So the first C of the Confidence Continuum workout is clarity. Before you take action, it's important that you know your desired outcome. Your goals. Your intention. When I was an actress, any time I went into an audition with a clear objective—*What does this character want? What are her goals within the story?*—9 times out of 10, I'd kick ass and book the part. But when I felt muddled on that *why*, I didn't do so well.

One of the biggest reasons people get stuck in the "I can't gain clarity" vortex is because they get caught up in the how. But you don't need to know all the steps on *how* you're going to get across that finish line yet. Instead, I want you to focus on the *what* and the *why*. What's the end goal and why do you want it to happen? Patricia's *what* was gaining clients from TikTok, and her *why* was building her business and ultimately helping people have better sex. She didn't know that the *how* was going to be a very specific post going viral. She just knew what she wanted and tried a bunch of different ways to get there. One worked, and that became the *how* piece of the puzzle! Once you have clarity with your intention, you're gonna have way more confidence when it comes time to take action toward that goal.

2. Community

Let's face it, there aren't many things that feel better than someone you love cheering for you! When I have friends and loved ones celebrating me when I succeed, I feel confident AF! If you're about to do a presentation at work and your friends and co-workers are texting you—*You've got this! Go crush it! Let us know how it goes!*— then I bet you'll walk into that conference room with a spring to your step, ready to take on the world. But it's important to surround yourself with the *right* people, and that's key. Stay tuned for much more on how to find those people in Part III.

I recently did a talk for a prestigious mastermind in front of a group of seven- and eight-figure CEOs, and I was nervous as hell, to put it lightly. The entire time, Chris and his daughter, Vivienne, were cheering me on via text.

Don't let them forget who you are!

I'm so excited for you!

You've got this!

You are gonna blow their minds!

Those texts kept me going, and their voices were so much louder than the voice of my fear. Their support gave me the confidence to absolutely crush it onstage. When I got home, there was a sign on my front door: *Welcome home, world's greatest speaker!* I felt so loved and had a little more swagger in my step the next time I spoke in front of a group like that because I knew my people had my back!

When you have a community of people in your life who celebrate your achievements, their confidence in you will give you an extra boost to finish strong, just like a pre-workout supplement before a cycling class.

3. Commitment

Now that we've chatted about community, tell me: Who is the one person you can always count on? Your partner? A co-worker? Your best friend?

Wrong, wrong, and wrong.

The one person you can always count on, no matter what, is *you*.

When you make a commitment to someone else, it can be powerful and motivating, but as we discussed earlier in this chapter, confidence comes from consistently sticking to the commitments we make with ourselves. Why? Because we become confident that no matter how hard or scary something might be, we've got it! It's about building that trust within yourself and creating a deep belief that you are the type of person who follows through on what you say you are going to do. So the next time a cool opportunity comes your way, it's exciting instead of terrifying because you have a deep knowing that you'll make it happen. You can take action even knowing the result might be imperfect. And when you can build that relationship with yourself (with Real You!), it will become one of the most powerful tools in your arsenal.

4. Creation

If you don't prove to yourself that you are capable of taking action and creating things, then you can't get that delicious dopamine rush that comes with the win. So you have to create to gain confidence. You gotta do the damn thing! Say you're about to go live on social media for the first time, and you're petrified to be on camera. The first time I made a livestream video, I sat in front of the camera for 30 minutes before finally hitting Record and then spent the first 45 seconds talking about how awkward I felt doing a Facebook Live video. Even now, looking back on it, that video is a hot mess, but I am *so* proud of it, and do you know why? Because it exists. I took action and hit that Record button. I *created* something, and I got to the other side.

Each moment of creation produces a little win. You know what I'm talking about—that little sense of accomplishment, that little surge of dopamine and serotonin. Like, *I did the thing. I didn't die. It's all okay.* Start collecting those little wins and you will generate motivation, which will urge you forward to do it again.

The next time I made a video, it only took me five minutes to hit Record. (And I *still* talked about how awkward I felt, but for a little less time!) Each time, it got a little less scary, and now, when I hit Record on any social media platform, I'm confident AF! But getting there takes consistency, which we'll talk about next!

5. Consistency

It's easy to do something hard once, and here's what I've noticed about entrepreneurs who find themselves unable to grow past a certain level: they *love* to do new things one time and then move on to the next "shiny object" or strategy if that thing doesn't produce immediate results. This is a bad habit that will most likely keep you in a constant state of stuckness.

Confidence is built over time. It's created by climbing the mountain again. And again. And again. Each time, you're getting stronger. Each time, you're trusting yourself a little more. Each time, you're learning something new that makes that next trek to the top a little bit easier.

Consistency means that every time you do something hard, every time you step out of your comfort zone, you're making an investment in your confidence bank. Eventually, those confidence coins will add up. But remember: *not* sticking to your commitments will *cost* you money from that bank. So keep showing up, keep being consistent, and you'll be rich in confidence in no time.

6. Celebration

So often, we want something so bad and work so hard at it, and when we get the win, we think, *Okay, what's next?*

But wait, slow down! Why are you moving on so quickly? If you don't celebrate, you're missing out on all the goodness that comes from that win, which means you're missing your chance to gain confidence, motivation, and momentum. Milk your win. Revel in it. I'm giving you permission. Reach out to your friends (that community you've built!) and tell them, *Oh my god, I did it!* Let them be proud of you, and remember to be proud of yourself. Take yourself out for a massage or a fancy lunch. Buy yourself a new outfit or have a date night with your partner. Indulge. Treat yo'self. Remember how great it feels to succeed, and then *use* that memory to fuel your confidence for the next time you try something new.

Here's a challenge for you: every night before you go to bed, write down your wins for the day, big or small.

I woke up without having to press Snooze today.

I went to the gym today.

I made dinner instead of ordering takeout.
I spoke up during a meeting at work.

Collecting little wins will help you celebrate your commitments to yourself, start to love on yourself, and build your confidence, adding more and more confidence coins to that bank until you've got enough momentum to keep the ball rolling. When you collect those little wins and learn to mentally catalog your successes throughout each day, you'll learn to find all the validation you need from *you* without needing to seek it from an outside source.

THE RULE OF 51 PERCENT

The Confidence Continuum can help you achieve any win, big or small, but sometimes it takes time, and that's because we're not all starting from the same place. Chris taught me an amazing method that freed me from inaction due to fear, and I'd love to share it with you here.

A lot of people are going to tell you that, in life, it's important to believe in yourself 100 percent. You have to go all out. Believe in yourself and anything is possible.

I'm here to tell you that is a big load of bullshit.

If I waited to take action until I believed in myself 100 percent, I would never get anything done. Ever. Even with fear in the passenger seat, it's still in the car, right? It's still present, and it's still trying to chip away at my confidence.

Life is too short to wait for 100 percent.

Chris changed my life when he reminded me that all we need to do, really, is believe in ourselves a little bit more than we don't.

Fifty-one percent.

That's all it takes. That's all the magic you need to kickstart that Confidence Continuum. If you can convince yourself to take a tiny action, just the littlest baby step toward your goal, you're going to collect that win, celebrate, and add some dough to your confidence bank. Suddenly, you're at 52 percent and ready to act again. Before you know it, you're at 60 percent . . . 65 percent . . . 75 percent. One day, you might find you're up to 97 percent, and the next day you might drop back to 80. But the rule of 51 percent is all about knowing that's okay. It's about knowing where you are and giving yourself the grace to move forward, use your knowledge of that spectrum to keep your momentum going, and take action today to support your dream tomorrow.

But what if you're not at 51 percent? What if you're all the way down at 8 percent or 5 percent, and you just don't feel any belief in yourself? Well, it's time to start adding to your confidence bank. Start with something easy. Start by doing *something. Anything.* It doesn't even have to have anything to do with your overall goal. Remember, not all wins need to be big. For example, if you find yourself stuck while working on your website for your business, tell yourself, "I am committing to taking a walk around the block today." Remember, walks have the power to fix every problem! And then—and here's the key part—do it.

Boom. Coin in the bank.

Maybe you put on your workout clothes or sign up for a gym membership. You don't need to touch those weights yet; just put on the clothes. That's it. That's your win. The next day, commit to walking on the treadmill for five minutes. That's penny after penny—5 percent up to 6 percent, just like that.

The more you create that win cycle, the more motivation and momentum you're going to build. And once you get that number up over 50 percent, you'll be unstoppable.

QUICK CONFIDENCE BOOSTERS

But no matter where you are on that spectrum of belief, that first action step can still be hard to take.

People often ask me, "How do I take action when I'm still so scared?" And it *is* kinda like a double-edged sword, isn't it? You have to take action to gain confidence, but you also need some confidence to take action. Luckily, I've got a few quick confidence boosters and techniques that will get you confident in the moment so you can take that scary action.

Get Camera Ready

You know how great you feel when you take a moment to do your hair and put on an outfit that makes you feel powerful? Like you're ready to take on the world, right? Next time you're feeling scared, go get camera ready. Throw on a few swipes of mascara or that power suit someone complimented you on last week. For me, being camera ready means a full face of makeup and a blowout, but for you, it might be your comfiest pair of sweatpants where the camera won't see and a nice, professional shirt on top. Maybe it's your lucky T-shirt or your favorite player's jersey, or taking a minute to fix the frizzy flyaways around your face. When you're camera ready, you not only look different, you feel different. You walk differently. You hold yourself differently. It's like taking a shortcut to the most confident, powerful version of yourself.

Turn Up the Tunes

Okay, so we've already established how much of a role music plays in helping me find Real Jen, but now it's your turn. Put on some music before you do something scary. Play a song you love, or one that makes you want to dance and sing along. Get in the pocket. Loosen up.

When I was on tour with *The Wedding Singer*, I used to do my warm-up to a couple of songs by Lita Ford. She felt so sexy and powerful to me, and I used her song "Kiss Me Deadly" to get into character before every show. Eventually, the song became a quick way for me to quickly transform into the badass rocker chick I needed to be onstage.

Find your Lita Ford. Tap into your confident self.

Tune In to Your Alter Ego

Did you know Beyoncé is secretly shy? She famously taps into her alter-ego, Sasha Fierce, when she goes onstage.[3] Embodying that alter ego helps her be the Beyoncé we all know and love. Other celebrities, like Adele, have admitted to doing the same. It's what my friend Todd Herman calls "the alter ego effect,"[4] and what scientists have referred to as "the Batman effect."[5]

What it comes down to is self-distancing. Studies have proven that stepping away from ourselves and being able to look at our actions from an outsider's perspective can allow us to see ourselves more dispassionately. Once we separate our emotional self from what we're doing, it can become that much easier to think rationally about the scenario and take action on challenging tasks.

Consult Your Badass List

This last booster is my favorite, and it's something we're going to explore much more deeply in the next chapter. For now, I'll let you in on this little secret: you are *way* cooler than you think you are, and reminding yourself why that is can be a powerful tool to boost your confidence on the fly. If you're ready to find out exactly why you're so amazing and learn to harness your badassery for success, stay tuned as we dive into Chapter 4.

MIC DROP MOMENTS

- We're all born confident, but somewhere along the line we start to dim our light.

- Being an introvert does not mean you're shit out of luck when it comes to building confidence.

- Follow the rule of 51 percent—you don't need to believe in yourself 100 percent, you just need to believe a little more than you don't.

- Every time you take action and get a tiny win, you're putting a coin in the confidence bank, upping that 51 percent to 52 percent, and so on.

A QUICK WIN

- Do one thing today that you wouldn't typically do, and celebrate that win to pay yourself some confidence cash!

PUT IT ON A POST-IT

- Confidence comes from consistently sticking to the commitments you make with yourself.

THIS ONE LITTLE LIST WILL CHANGE YOUR LIFE

"I'm pulling the plug. I can't launch this."

The one person I thought had all her shit together was breaking down, and all I could do was hold the phone to my ear in shock. "What do you mean?"

"No one is going to buy it, and I'm going to look like a failure."

The woman on the other end of the line was Tory, my best friend, mentor, and accountability buddy. Tory and I initially connected so deeply because we were both former New York City actresses who were now building coaching businesses online. We had met at the first personal development event I ever attended and had been having weekly check-in calls about our goals ever since. When I first social media–stalked Tory, I was in complete awe of what she had already accomplished all by herself. She had a gorgeous personal brand and website that she built and designed with no help. She had an e-mail list and knew how to use a special software to keep in touch with everyone on it. She even had online programs and retreats for her clients and was making real money! She was doing everything I wanted to do, and I couldn't believe the universe sent me a friend like her to learn from. Our weekly calls were one of the most powerful needle movers for me during that time in my life. She helped me launch my first online program, and she even singlehandedly designed my first e-book! (I think I paid her $500 and it took her about 500 hours. Thank you, Tory!)

So I'm sure you totally get why I was in complete shock when my already successful and totally brilliant bestie called me in tears, too scared to launch her latest course. She was knee-deep in imposter syndrome, and fear wasn't just driving her car, it had hijacked it and was speeding uncontrollably down the freeway. Tory had always been one of the most phenomenal people I know, but she wasn't seeing herself that way. I took a beat and thought, *Okay, Jen, this is your time to shine as a friend. You need to help Tory realize how amazing she is and that fear is just telling her all sorts of lies right now.* The pressure was on to be Super Friend!

"Tory," I said, firmly derailing her pity train. "Can you just hit Pause for a second? You're completely forgetting how incredible you are. You need to see what I see and what everyone else sees. You are a badass!"

Silence.

"No, I'm serious," I said. "You're such a badass. I could list five reasons off the top of my head right now."

More silence.

I don't think that helped, I thought, taking a deep breath. An idea took root, and I let it grow. *Let me try again . . .*

"Do me a favor," I said. "Do you have a pen nearby?"

Tory sounded confused. "Yes . . ."

"Okay, great. Get some paper, 'cause we're doing this. Right now. Let's list out all of the badass things you've done in your life."

"I don't know, Jen . . ."

"No, no deflecting. Come on." I wasn't going to let her get away with thinking this way about my friend. She was the *best*, and I wanted her to see it as clearly as I did! "I'll go first: You're a badass because you started your own business without any support, and it's still going, even if it's sometimes scary as fuck."

Tory laughed. "I guess."

"So what else?"

"I've had my face on a billboard," she said slowly. "I guess that's pretty badass."

"Yes! This is exactly what I'm talking about! What else?"

She cleared her throat, blew her nose, and started listing off her accomplishments as she scribbled them down. "I moved to New York alone when I was nineteen . . . I was in a music video . . . I ran the New York City Marathon . . ."

"Yes, yes, yes! I love all of this," I told her. "You're such a badass."

"You really think so?" She still didn't sound convinced. "None of this stuff is going to help me make this launch a success, though."

I couldn't believe it. I'd just listened to her tell me half a dozen stories that were mind-blowingly powerful and impressive—when she made her first six-figure deal, for example, or when she launched her podcast—but she still didn't seem to think so! *If only she could see herself the way I see her!* That gave me another idea.

"Okay, let's change tactics here. I want you to look at your list and read it out loud like you're reading it about someone else who's not you." I clarified, "Pretend you're reading it about someone you are comparing yourself to on social media."

As Tory recalled each moment with this mindset, her voice finally began to lose its shakiness. Finally, she stopped sounding like she was just humoring me! As she read me her list, pretending it was about someone else, she became a little more empowered with each item. *There* was my confident friend!

Midway through number 23, I stopped her. "Okay, woman, do you think that person you're talking about is worthy of launching and selling this course? Would you pay money to learn from them?"

"Holy shit, Jen," Tory said. "You're right! Yes, I would."

"You're a badass, and you've got this!"

I could hear her smile through the phone as she echoed back, "I *am* a badass, and I've got this!" By the end of our call, we were both laughing at how ridiculous it was that she was even doubting herself for a minute!

When I got off the phone that day, I realized we'd created a tool that we could use to combat imposter syndrome every time it tried to stand in the way of our dreams. Tory taped her list to her wall near her desk, and we called it the Badass List. That evening,

I created my own list on my phone. Since that day, I've taught thousands of people how to use the Badass List to bust through imposter syndrome and allow themselves to be seen.

ASSEMBLE YOUR HIGHLIGHT REEL

We all have these moments in our lives when we were a complete and total badass. Don't you dare shake your head at me—you know it's true. Think of a moment when you crushed it onstage or when you guided one of your clients to the biggest *aha* moment of their entire career and you thought, *This is exactly why I do what I do.* Maybe it's not work related—maybe it's when you walked down the aisle at your wedding and saw your partner's eyes well up with tears, when your first child was born, when you finally came out to your parents, or when you emerged healthy from an illness you didn't think you could beat. In moments like these, you feel unstoppable, with a distinct realization that you are so unbelievably powerful. They're the moments that make you want to drop everything and call your best friend immediately to say, "Oh my god, I did it."

We have so many of them, but we're so close to them that sometimes we forget how cool they are. How cool *we* are. I do it all the time, downplaying my accomplishments and forgetting about how absolutely amazing they made me feel. "Eh, it's not that cool," I'll say, trying to brush off someone's praise. "It's not a big deal."

Um, *wrong*!

Don't you dare dim your light. You and me, we're family now, and this family is in the business of shining and allowing ourselves to fully *see* our greatness so it can then be seen by the people we can help. So here's what I want you to do: I want you to write out every moment you can remember—every single one—of when you were a complete and total badass. (If you need a little help, think back on those in-the-pocket moments you uncovered in Chapter 1.)

No, I'm serious, do it right now. I'll wait. *Find* your moments when you felt like you could rule the world. If you need to, ask someone who loves you to help get you started. I'm sure they've got a million ideas ready to share. And whenever you're feeling like an imposter, like you're not worthy or good enough, I want you to pull out your Badass List and read it. But here's the trick, because you can't just read it. You need to read it like you're reading about someone else—someone you are FOMOing over on social media. Read it like you're looking at *their* highlight reel.

Take a moment and get a little jealous of that person. That person is pretty fucking cool, aren't they? And then take another moment to remember: that person is *you*. Allow your personal highlight reel to be seen by *yourself*.

If you can do all those things on that list, then come on, you're more than worthy of doing whatever is scaring you, whether it's launching your first business, strengthening your brand, or finally asking that super cute guy from the gym for his number.

You can write out a whole story for each entry, or use just a few key words and phrases to ignite that in-the-pocket feeling. Your list can be 2 items or 20, so long as whatever is there helps trigger your memory and your sense of total badassery. This list is going to be one of your most powerful tools. I use my Badass List every time I feel self-doubt creeping in. Before going onstage to speak at an event, before walking into a room at a mastermind, or before doing an interview, I take a moment to read my Badass List and remind myself who I am. I keep my list on my phone so I always have it on me, and I add to it every time I achieve something I'm proud of. Remember, we gotta celebrate those wins to build momentum!

Here's mine, so you can see what I mean:

- Landing my dream role in the Broadway tour of *The Wedding Singer* and performing as Linda in front of an audience for the first time

- Going to my first personal development event all by myself and making a whole new group of friends

- Getting engaged to Chris in my favorite place in the world

- Moving into the *exact* apartment that was on my vision board

- Being the first woman to speak at 100 MME Mastermind, Avengers Mastermind, the Power Room Mastermind, and Scale and Escape Summit

- Getting my book deal with the perfect publisher for me (love you, Hay House!)

- Launching my podcast, *I Dare You*

- Shutting down my successful personal training business to partner with Chris and create Super Connector Media

- The day my grandpa Gene told me he was proud of me

- Chris's daughter, Vivienne, saying, "I love you" to me for the first time

- The moment I told Vivienne that Chris and I were getting married and her bursting into happy tears

- Being able to donate the Louis Vuitton bag that Rob bought for me to charity and walk into the store and buy my own for the first time

- My first photoshoot with Annebet Duvall and Chris Eckert's famous editorial team, when I felt like a movie star

- Booking my job on *That Metal Show* and being on it for almost five years

- Becoming a personal trainer at Reebok Sports Club and helping people transform their bodies

- Helping Brenda go from almost taking her life to building a successful business and a life that she loves (using this Badass List method!)

- Helping over 30,000 entrepreneurs be visible and transform their businesses during the pandemic with our Be on TV Bootcamp and Be Seen Accelerator

- The first time I got paid five figures to speak on a stage

- Gracing the cover of *Strong* fitness magazine

- Seeing myself on a billboard in Times Square

- Being interviewed on Hallmark Channel's *Home & Family*

- Being featured in *Forbes*

- Being featured in Goop as one of the top 11 coaches helping people find successful careers

- Having a 20-minute interview on the *Elvis Duran and the Morning Show* on Z100

- Bouncing back from losing everything and creating the life that I used to dream of

- Walking back into Equinox and being able to easily afford a membership that had once nearly bankrupted me

- The day our PR agency was acquired

- The moment my dad walked me down the aisle at my wedding

- Being named one of the Top 50 Speakers in the World by *Real Leaders* magazine

- Being named #2 of the Top 10 Entrepreneurs and Business Experts of 2022 by *Maxim* magazine

- Turning in my finished manuscript of this book!

Some of these moments I've told you about already, and some of them you'll read about in future chapters. Now that I think about it, this book is full of my Badass List moments because even my failures make for great entries once I turn them around and figure out why they were for me. The important thing is, every one of these moments brings a smile to my face when I think back on it, even the rough ones. Every one of them makes me feel accomplished, and strong, and capable, and worthy. They're moments when I felt in the pocket, with a strong sense of pride and flow.

And look, I realize I just showed you a list of my accomplishments, and I'm not gonna lie, I felt a little queasy typing it. In fact, I even deleted it completely and convinced myself that it shouldn't go in the book because showcasing my list of badass moments was way too "braggy." But then I took a step back and reminded myself that the whole point of writing this book is to tear down the wall and show you that I, too, need to use the tools I'm teaching you in order to move through my own symptoms of fear when they show up (which is quite often!). I promised you that I'd give you all the goods, and that means showing you things like my personal Badass List. I realize there is a chance you might compare your list to mine, and I want to catch you before you step foot in that nasty comparisonitis trap. Your Badass List is for nobody but you. The moments you list out might seem "small" to someone else, but they could be huge to you, and that's all that matters! There are moments on my list that no one other than me would care about or be impressed by, but I have them on there because when I think about them, I feel super proud. Another cool thing to remember is that your list is ever growing and evolving, and you will be adding moments to it for the rest of your life. It's another tool you can add to your toolkit to help you to celebrate yourself. Because believe me, friend, you are marvelous, and when you find a time where you don't believe me, *that's* the time you need your Badass List the most, because you won't have to take my word for it.

You'll be able to take *your* word for it.

Every time I start to question if I'm worthy enough to do something, or I start comparing myself to someone else's highlight reel, I refer back to this list and remind myself just how badass I am.

BRENDA THE BADASS

This is going to sound like I'm exaggerating, but the Badass List even saved my client Brenda's life. You might have noticed Brenda's name on my own Badass List, which is a hint at how absolutely incredible this story is.

In May of 2020, Chris and I were all set to hold our ninth Unfair Advantage Live event in NYC. But when COVID-19 came in like a wrecking ball and the world literally shut down, we were forced to postpone our event with no real clarity on when or *if* we would ever hold it again. Along with millions of other live event companies, we had to pivot and figure out a way to replace that seven-figure payday we would've had from the live event. And, if we had any hope of our company surviving the pandemic, we had to figure it out fast. We had a full team of employees whose salaries we were responsible for, and laying them off wasn't an option. Chris and I didn't know it at the time, but being forced to pivot was one of the greatest gifts to our business, because it birthed our now-famous Be on TV Bootcamp. This is a five-day virtual challenge that has since helped thousands of business owners completely transform their businesses by learning how to target, pitch, and book television segments. Aaaand since we are secretly a personal development company that uses media and visibility as the gateway to transformation (it's our worst-kept secret, honestly), it has also helped many people totally transform their lives and create authentic, relatable brands that audiences are drawn to like magnets.

Brenda was one of those people. In fact, at the end of each five-day challenge, we pick a winner of the entire bootcamp, and she ended up being our winner in more ways than one. Brenda was a former Marine, a sexual assault survivor, and going through a divorce, and as a Black woman in America, the death of George Floyd was the straw that broke the camel's back. The day before she joined our bootcamp, Brenda was on the phone with a suicide hotline, a bottle of pills in her hand, and a sense of hopelessness in her heart.

"Brenda, I want you take *one* of those pills," said the hotline representative on the other end of the phone. "Not all of them, just one. I want you to go to sleep, and in the morning, I want you to find something to do. I don't care what it is; I just want you to do something."

So Brenda listened, and when she woke up the next morning, there was an e-mail in her inbox about our Be on TV Bootcamp. Now, Brenda didn't want to be on TV, but it was *something*, just like the person on the hotline told her, so she signed up anyway.

The way Brenda tells the story is that she showed up to boot-camp to find some crazy white girl screaming and yelling at every-one to dance. (Me. She's talking about me.) Brenda took one look and thought, *This girl is batshit crazy. I am not here for this.* But she stuck through it. She had to do *something*.

That first day was all about mindset, and I taught Brenda and the rest of the group about the Badass List. As she began to cre-ate her own, suddenly all these amazing moments from her life started flashing before her eyes, and Brenda began to reconnect to the badass woman that she is. It inspired her to go live on her Facebook page and talk about her badass moments. She was kind and inspirational to the people who were watching, and when she got off, she felt better than she had in weeks. But the real reward came when Brenda got a message from a woman who hadn't been able to get out of bed after her child committed suicide. She was in a severe depression and hadn't been there for her other kids in months. She reached out to Brenda and said, "Your Facebook Live inspired me to get out of bed and be with my kids today."

The moment stopped Brenda in her tracks because it made her realize that she could actually make a difference in people's lives by showing up, being seen, connecting to people, and sharing what she had to give. She kept going with the bootcamp and she kept sharing, and at the end of the five days, she won the grand prize.

But that was just the beginning for Brenda.

Brenda has now written a book. She makes six figures with her full coaching business, The Soulutionist, where she helps the voiceless find their voice. She hosts a podcast and livestream show and speaks onstage at live events. She is a completely transformed woman and one of our most successful clients to this day, all be-cause she was able to discover her inner badass and allow that badass to be visible.

THE SCIENCE BEHIND YOUR BADASSERY

There's a reason the Badass List works, and it comes down to something I mentioned briefly in Chapter 3: self-distancing.[1] Self-distancing means creating space between yourself and the actions that you're taking. Consider this example: Imagine you get home after a networking event, and you can't stop dwelling on that one super cringey comment you made to somebody you wanted to impress. You keep going over that moment because you don't have any distance between your perspective and the event. The truth is, the people you were talking to have almost definitely forgotten about it by now, even as you're busy obsessing over it.

Being able to remove ourselves from the equation entirely is a great way to cope with anger or stress because detaching from emotional situations minimizes the significance of whatever caused them. Reflecting on *anything* works best when we're able to take a step back and see the whole picture, after all. Forcing a sense of objectivity onto our emotions allows us to see that picture a lot more clearly instead of through the overwhelming Snapchat filter of our own biases, which heightens the contrast until the picture looks unrecognizable. But while psychologists agree that distancing is an effective way to calm our painful memories and emotions, I've found it's also an amazing way to tap into our *positive* feelings.

That's why the Badass List works. It makes you step back from all the messy emotions connected to you and your memories—like all the doubt and fear and stress that you know went into planning and running your latest event—and forces you to look at it from the outside. The attendees of your event didn't see the hours of work and the four and a half tearful breakdowns that went into it. They just saw one kickass final product and had the time of their lives making connections and learning something new. They saw you on that stage looking confident and fly as hell and completely missed the part where you were a bundle of nerves right before you got onstage.

If the first step to being seen is seeing yourself, then using your Badass List allows you to see the person others see. It allows you to look at your life and your experiences through the eyes of someone who loves and admires you, someone who keeps track of your wins and uses them to help fuel you toward the next one.

Think about it: if you were at a party where you had the opportunity to brag about someone you love—your partner, your best friend, your kid—you could probably do it all day long. With zero hesitation, you could tell everyone how fabulous they are, and about all the impressive things they've done. When you're talking about someone you really love, you want the entire world to know how proud you are of them. So why can't we talk about ourselves that way?

With the Badass List, we can!

EVERYBODY POOPS

We talked about fear and its symptoms in Chapter 2, but knowing those symptoms will be with us on our entire journey to fully being seen and actually having to *live* and continue to *thrive* with that? Those are two very different slices of pie. As you know by now, fear isn't going anywhere. If we don't get it into the passenger seat, we'll end up on a joyride from hell with fear as our sadistic chauffeur. The Badass List is another handy gadget in our Be Seen toolkit that helps us get fear away from the steering wheel, but just like everything else we've talked about, it takes consistent use. Take imposter syndrome, for example. Every smart, successful person you've ever met, no matter how much you think they have their shit together, has had imposter syndrome.

What I love to say is this universal truth: everybody poops.

We're all human beings, and none of us are inherently on a higher level than anyone else. And every one of us suffers from feelings of insecurity at times. Me and you and Jennifer Lopez and Serena Williams and Zendaya and Reese Witherspoon and Lady Gaga *all* get that feeling of *maybe I'm not good enough for this new and scary thing I'm about to do.* I know I do. I've come a long way from where I once was, but I still feel imposter syndrome almost every single day. In fact, I'll let you in on a secret: I'm having it big time while writing this book. I can't tell you how many nights I've spent tossing and turning with the thought loop of, *Am I really worthy of being the person to write this? Will anyone even want to read it?* The urge to compare myself to the people around me is so strong. But one of the things that makes the Badass List such an incredible tool is that it lets you compare yourself to *you*. Take a look at your list. Recognize that all those amazing items are things you've *already* accomplished!

While writing this book, I had the opportunity to get together with four authors whom I've admired for years. Each of us was working on a book, and we decided to plan our book launches together at Soho House in NYC. This was a huge deal for me, like dreamcometrue.com kind of stuff, but I had a hard time believing I had what it took to be included in this group of already established authors. Marie Forleo, Amy Porterfield, Kris Carr, and Gabby Bernstein are all now my good friends, but this was my first time meeting them all together, and let me tell you, my imposter syndrome was in overdrive. I remember sitting at my vanity getting ready for the day and hearing the voice of fear screaming nasty lies on repeat in my head.

What if I have no value to offer the other women?

I've never launched my own book before. What the hell do I know?

Maybe they just invited me to have an extra person in the room.

I knew in my gut that fear was just popping in to show me that this was a mega-opportunity for growth, but it sure didn't make it any easier to regain control of the wheel. I knew I needed to bring out my most powerful tool, so when I was fully dressed and ready to go, I looked in the mirror and read my Badass List out loud. An immediate sense of calm filled me from head to toe as I exhaled and looked at my reflection. I was standing a little taller. My shoulders had pulled back, and a smile was beginning to crack the corners of my mouth. My leather blazer, white tank top, and wide-leg jeans suddenly looked so much cuter than they had 15 minutes ago. I was ready, I was worthy, and while my confidence wasn't anywhere near 100 percent, I definitely believed in myself a little bit more than I didn't! Badass!

In case you were wondering, the meeting was amazing. All my fears totally disappeared amid the warmth and love in the room, and I was able to both receive and provide priceless value. As a bonus, I made powerful friendships with some kickass inspirational women whom I deeply admire. After the day ended, one of them actually texted me saying that she had massive imposter syndrome too! This absolutely blew my mind—I thought she had it all together and I was the only one feeling intimidated. But knowing that she also felt uncertainty before the meeting was just another reminder to never underestimate the power of fear. It doesn't discriminate, no matter how successful someone is. People are people are people. (And I'll say it again for the people in the back: everybody poops.)

I have a friend, Jonathan Fields, who runs a top-rated podcast called *The Good Life Project.* We had the opportunity to interview him for one of our Super Connector Mastermind events, and our attendees asked him what he thought made his podcast a hit. What Jonathan told them wasn't necessarily the sexiest answer or the answer they wanted to hear, but it's an important truth nonetheless. He reminded them that his podcast has been around for over a decade, and for the first few years, no one knew about it. He put in the work anyway, despite it feeling like a completely futile gesture without any real base of listeners. After years of consistently putting out powerful content, his hard work eventually paid off. Now, people who are just starting out look at him and think, *I'll never get my podcast to that level.* They completely forget to acknowledge that everything looked vastly different for Jonathan on day one—that he once stood where they are now.

Just like everybody poops, everybody starts with nothing but an idea and a little bit of determination. It's true that some people with ideas have a lot more resources at their disposal than others when it comes to turning them into reality, but what we all share in common is that there's a (sometimes long!) process to get from point A to point B. It's so easy for us to compare our Chapter 1 to someone else's Chapter 20, but what if we didn't? What if we gave ourselves some grace and looked at ourselves not like someone who is lacking, but like someone we love who is still on their journey and making amazing strides?

You see where I'm going with this, don't you?

After teaching this tool, I know people in my community who laminated their Badass Lists and keep them in their wallets or purses. They look at their list as a legacy, a mini memoir of their life and their greatest accomplishments that they can show their kids and grandkids. It's an ever-changing document, and when you use it regularly, it's such a beautiful way to celebrate yourself. We talked a little bit about celebration as one of the six Cs of the Confidence Continuum workout, and I just want to say it again here: celebrating your wins through your Badass List or otherwise is so, so, *so* important, because that's what's going to launch you forward into future wins as you achieve your vision for your brand, life, and business.

MIC DROP MOMENTS

- The Badass List is a powerful tool you can use to combat imposter syndrome and banish your nerves.

- Self-distancing (creating space between yourself and your actions) is the reason the Badass List is so effective. Removing yourself from the equation means removing yourself from all the sticky emotions involved with it, allowing you to see your actions from a big-picture standpoint.

- Every smart, successful person you've ever met, no matter how much you think they have their shit together, has dealt with imposter syndrome.

A QUICK WIN

- Create your Badass List!

PUT IT ON A POST-IT

- Everybody poops. 💩

PART II

....

BE CREATIVE

. . . .

CHAPTER 5

SEEING FUTURE YOU

If you don't know where you're going, then you can't get there.

Period.

Stepping into the spotlight and being seen begins with gaining clarity on how you see your future self *while* living your most fulfilling life. Many of us have spent so much time building a future that we never really wanted just because it was what someone else saw for us. When we're living in alignment with someone else's truth instead of our own, how the hell are we supposed to have the confidence to be fully seen? (Spoiler: we *can't*!) We will always have that little voice behind the scenes whispering something along the lines of "This just isn't it . . ."

Good news, though: it's definitely not too late to rewrite the story and figure out what that ultimate future looks like for *you*— not your parents, your boss, your siblings, or the Kardashians. The only one you need to keep up with is *you* and what you desire for *your* ultimate future. Now that you've been reintroduced to Real You and have the tools to get into the pocket, move through imposter syndrome, and give fear the finger, you can start to create a vision for yourself that aligns with who you were born to be, not what others want for you.

So welcome to Part II: Be Creative. Come on in, take your shoes off, grab a seat, get comfy. This is one of my favorite parts of this book, because we're creating a reality where you get to be seen as the most fulfilled, badass, successful version of yourself—someone I like to call "You 2.0." You 2.0 is who you become when Real You finds your purpose and starts living in it with laser-focused intention, enthusiasm, confidence, and ease. It's Real You, just upleveled, and maybe best of all is that You 2.0 isn't someone you need to create from scratch. You 2.0 is already in there and has been all along—just look back at your Badass List if you don't believe me. Now your job is to give yourself permission to build a future for yourself and your brand with You 2.0 as the star. It's time to step out of the wings and into the spotlight!

You already know this book is about being seen. But now, it's about being seen as that high-vibe, super confident, in-the-pocket version of yourself so you can give the world the gifts you were born to give. As we create a future that aligns with what truly fulfills you, it will be pretty difficult to stay hidden away. I'm going to share the most powerful strategies in my toolkit to help you map out a future so bright it would be impossible for the world (and of course, your ideal customers, audience, and followers) to ignore!

These techniques helped me go from a struggling, broke actress to a confident entrepreneur who's built a seven-figure business that feels even more fulfilling than seeing my name in a Broadway National Tour playbill (believe me, I never thought I'd say that!). Throughout this section of the book, you're going to learn how to find and follow the neon signs pointing you toward your ultimate potential. You will learn to bend time and see the future so you can be the director of the show instead of just a member of the audience.

And it all starts here, with a little friend who's been with you all along: your subconscious mind.

Sigmund Freud once described the mind as an iceberg.[1] Your conscious mind is the part of the ice that's visible above the water, but that really freaking massive portion of the ice below the surface is your unconscious mind (that's the term Freud used for what I've been calling the subconscious). Your conscious mind, up there in the sunshine, is the part of your brain that makes you think and speak and rationalize; it's driven by logic and your five senses. Reach up and touch your nose right now. That's a conscious action.

But your subconscious mind is a different story. That's where we do all the behind-the-scenes work—where we keep all those feelings, thoughts, urges, and dreams that drive our conscious mind through mental processes we're not even aware of. The subconscious mind is ruled by emotions and instincts, and despite the fact that it's hidden beneath the surface, it controls pretty much everything we do behind the scenes. Have you ever had one of those nights when you're driving home after a long day and, suddenly, you're safe and sound in your driveway but can't for the life of you remember the actual drive? That's your subconscious in action. But just because our subconscious is in the driver's seat doesn't mean we can't program it to take us exactly where we want it to go!

The cool thing about the subconscious mind is that it doesn't know the difference between a real memory and a fake one. So the more you can see what you desire in your mind and then feel the feelings in your body, the more the subconscious mind will believe that you already experienced that event. Wild, right? This right here—reprogramming our subconscious mind—is the key that will unlock everything you're about to learn in Part II. It will help you lay a foundation in the construction of your own power, and it's what has allowed me to achieve some of my most seemingly impossible dreams. Don't believe me? Keep reading.

SEEING LINDA

"I'm going to play that part one day," I yelled to my friend Pat over the roaring crowd as one large *Jerry Maguire* you-had-me-at-hello-style tear rolled down my cheek. My arms were covered in goose bumps as the orchestra hit its final chord. Pat rolled his eyes as he watched me applaud like my life depended on the number of times I could slam my palms together—he clearly wasn't on the same "revelation from God" train as me. I didn't care. I knew in that moment, in that Broadway theater, I was seeing my future in front of me.

At 20 years old, I had dropped out of college, quit my waitressing job at Hooters, and moved to New York City to attend the American

Musical and Dramatic Academy (AMDA). When I initially envisioned moving to New York, it looked a little more glamorous in my mind than what greeted me when I got out of the taxi. My new home was one of those tiny eight-by-eight-foot rooms in a prewar building with a bathroom sink a foot away from the bottom bunk where I slept. I cohabitated this windowless, closetless cell with a roommate, and we shared a single shower with the entire fifth floor. I was so excited to be in New York City that I didn't even care that all my clothes were stuffed in a plastic under-the-bed box and that my one towel hung to dry over the ladder that my roommate used to climb into bed each night. I was in my dream city, doing what I loved all day every day—singing, dancing, and acting with amazing teachers and super talented classmates from all over the world.

Broadway theaters do this dope deal where they sell super cheap tickets for students if you get to the box office early enough. It's called "student rush," and my friend Pat had gotten us some for a new show, *The Wedding Singer*, based on the iconic film starring Adam Sandler and Drew Barrymore.

We took our seats in the back of the theater, where the ushers hung out during the show, and anxiously waited for the overture to begin. I still get emotional thinking about the first electric guitar riff in the opening number. The energy in that theater was something I'd never experienced in my life: an aura of magic completely filled the air, and it threatened to lift me off my feet. About 15 minutes into the show, the character of Linda (played by an actress named Felicia Finley) strutted out onto the stage in her 1980s "Like a Virgin" Madonna wedding dress complete with fingerless gloves, layered studded belts, and thigh-high stripper boots. She performed a hilarious song where she sang the breakup letter she wrote to her fiancé, explaining why she was *not* showing up to their wedding that day.

> *To my dearest Robbie,*
> *I think we need some space.*
> *Please forgive my timing*
> *Dot-dot-dot, smiley face.*

I couldn't stop laughing, and as she hit her final note and disappeared into the dark, dreamlike fog that enveloped the stage, those laughs turned to tears. Suddenly, I wasn't watching Felicia anymore. I was watching *me* in that costume, singing that song and making the audience roar with laughter. I could feel those lights on my face, those studded belts around my waist. I could taste the notes and lyrics of that song on my tongue. I *had* to play this part on Broadway.

Now let's be real—there were a few obstacles in the way of this big, hairy, audacious goal of strutting across a Broadway stage in Felicia Finley's thigh-highs. One being that I was just a student with zero connections and experience. I had never been to an audition in New York City, let alone a *Broadway* audition. So to say that I fully believed I could make my dream come true would be, well, the overstatement of the century. But that magical moment in the nosebleed section of the Al Hirschfeld Theater gave me enough belief to kickstart some momentum with one tiny action step.

THE CREATION PROCESS

A few months before I moved to New York, I came across a popular book called *The Secret* by Rhonda Byrne. You've definitely heard of this book; it was—and still is—a best-selling phenomenon about how you can create anything you desire using your thoughts and energy. At that time, I was pretty skeptical about anything that could fit into the woo-woo box until one day, shortly after seeing *The Wedding Singer* on Broadway, I saw Oprah talking about how she used the "law of attraction" to manifest her dream role in the movie *The Color Purple*. I was absolutely fascinated and couldn't take my eyes off the screen. As I listened to Queen Winfrey tell this incredible tale of making her dream come true with her thoughts, energy, and intentions, my BS-o-meter started to lower a few levels.

I thought to myself, *If it worked for Oprah, maybe it could work for me?*

I shut off the TV and decided I was going to do an experiment. I was going to learn everything there was to know about the law of attraction so I could land my dream role just like Oprah did. I was going to "manifest" becoming Linda in *The Wedding Singer.*

Before we continue, I'm gonna spoil the ending for you: the experiment worked. This story ends with me living my actual dream, complete with smoke machines and bedazzled microphone. If you didn't see that coming, then, well, sorry, not sorry. I literally went from daydream to dream-come-true, and yeah, yeah, good for me, but the real point of this story is to teach you *how* I made my vision a reality so you can go off and make it rain dreams-come-true in *your* life.

When I look back at the road to Linda and the process that went into making what I saw in my mind a reality, I realize that it took much more than just gluing some photos to a vision board and thinking about playing the part. I have narrowed it down to a five-step process that's easily repeatable and really great for those of you who love tactical frameworks. I call it the Creation Process, and the steps are:

> 1. SEE IT
> 2. BELIEVE IT
> 3. DO IT
> 4. RECEIVE IT
> 5. REPEAT IT

1. See It

The first dip of my toe into my "be on Broadway" experiment was visualization. Each night before I went to sleep, I'd lie in my tiny bottom bunk, close my eyes, and envision myself singing "A Note from Linda," that first hilarious song that gave me all those magical feelings when I saw it onstage. In this movie in my mind, I could feel the scratchiness of the lace bustier on my chest and the tight buckles that kept my boots up over my knees. As I drifted deeper into the reality I created for myself, the heat of the lights warmed my skin and I could hear the audience laughing and clapping as I hit each beat. Every single night (much to my roommate's dismay) I sang myself to sleep, and the more I could see the experience in my mind's eye, the easier it was for me to believe it was possible. I started to love living this performance every night, because each time I did it, the vision would become more and more detailed.

I didn't realize it at the time, but I was implanting a memory of an experience into my subconscious mind. In his book *Becoming Supernatural*, Dr. Joe Dispenza explains how the familiar past becomes the predictable future. From the second we open our eyes in the morning, we enter into a series of routines and patterns that have been carved into place by habit and memory. Our brains tell us that doing things this way leads to predictable emotions rather than the potential chaos and negative fallout of the unknown. Don't worry, this isn't about to become a Psych 101 textbook. I tell you all of this to remind you once again that it feels easier, and safer, for us to stay in our comfort zone and let our subconscious mind run the show.

But here's the thing: Remember how I said before that our subconscious mind has no idea how to tell the difference between a real memory and a fake one? If you didn't believe me before, believe me now! Our subconscious mind is driven by memories and preconceived routines, so by practicing visualization when it comes to our goals, what we're secretly doing is implanting a fake memory in our brains, *Inception*-style. And it's way easier than you think.

We see this all the time in eyewitness testimonies.[2] When people witness a crime, they're often looked at as the be-all, end-all of reliability, but there are so many factors at play—stress, emotions, and their own memories, beliefs, biases, and experiences—that can mess with their perception of a memory they've *just* experienced. If Person A and Person B witness the same convenience-store robbery, and Person A tells the police, "The robber was wearing a red shirt," Person B automatically starts to fill a red shirt into their own memory, even if, in reality, they never noticed the robber's shirt at all. Soon, they've cemented it in their brain as the truth—"Yes, of *course* they were wearing a red shirt, officer! I saw it with my own eyes! Are you calling me a liar?"—and meanwhile, the green-shirted thief is strolling away down the street.

This happens because our memories are not cameras recording video. They're so much more subjective than that. Our memory creates stories based on our experiences and follows trains of those memories until we draw a conclusion, often drawing from the tiny cues we receive from those around us or the confidence of another supposed witness. (See the power of confidence at work here?) Our memories can be scary accurate or scary *in*accurate, but more often fall somewhere between the two. While this might be bad news bears for anyone walking down the street wearing a red shirt near a recently robbed convenience store, it's great news for us.

Our job—and this is so, so important—is to be able to see our dreams so clearly that our subconscious mind believes that they already exist as our reality. The trick is to make big neon arrows light up over the futures we want, because those lights will become breadcrumbs that lead us to *that* future instead of the one that has us always thinking "what if."

Now it's your turn!

Think about a moment in the future where You 2.0 (the version of you that you want the world to see!) is totally in the pocket and living your fullest potential. What do you see in your mind's eye?

What are you wearing?

What's your environment like?

What emotions are you experiencing?

Is anyone with you? If so, who?

Pro tip: get as detailed as possible!

2. Believe It

Seeing my vision with clarity each night brought me to the next step. You can see what you want and think about it until the cows come home, but if you don't change your beliefs about what you're capable of achieving, your dream will stay just that: a dream. Napoleon Hill, author of the famous book *Think and Grow Rich*, said it beautifully: "Whatever the mind can conceive and believe, it can achieve."

This is exactly what I've experienced, just with a twist. Our beliefs are what dictate our actions, and as we discussed earlier when we dove into the Confidence Continuum, our actions are what create our reality. Now I definitely didn't believe 100 percent that I would one day be living my Broadway fantasy, but the more I visualized it, the more achievable it began to feel.

When we trick our subconscious mind into believing that the things we want are actually our reality, what we're doing is steering the ship toward that beautiful tropical paradise. Once our subconscious mind believes that we've already experienced every amazing thing we've ever wanted, it clears our internal path so the outside world can catch up.

We do this by forcing our brains to recognize different patterns. Go outside right now and tell yourself, "Every time I see a silver car, I'm going to eat a piece of chocolate." Wanna bet you're about to spot more silver cars than you've ever seen before? (Yum!)

This isn't because everyone in your neighborhood is in on some silver-car conspiracy. The world isn't changing around you. What's changing is your perception of it. This is called the Baader-Meinhof Phenomenon, also known as blue-car syndrome or frequency illusion.[3] It refers to the cognitive bias that comes when your awareness of something increases, leading you to believe it's actually happening more often, even if that's not really the case.

It's like when you hear a song on the radio for the first time and suddenly it's all over your TikTok, or when a friend names her newborn baby something beautiful and uncommon but then in the next few months it seems like *everyone* is choosing that name for their kid. Chances are your friend didn't start a new trend all on her own—you just never had reason to notice that name until she brought it to your attention and created a cognitive bond between you and it.

What we need to do is create that same cognitive bond between us and what we want to manifest. The reason the Baader-Meinhof Phenomenon works is because our brains are overloaded with information and sensory input every day. We can't possibly absorb and retain it all, so our brains filter it, throwing away the details they think unnecessary and holding on to what their subconscious tells them to keep. Reprogramming our subconscious mind allows us to say, *No. This is important to me. Take notice and take action when it comes.* So when we start seeing all those blue cars—or those big neon arrows signaling opportunities—we've trained our brains to point them out and walk straight toward them with more certainty and less fear. This is how you can take a belief that's holding you back and turn it into one that actually moves you forward!

I can hear you now saying, "But Jen, what if I just don't believe I can do this?" I said it before, and I'll say it again: 51 percent of belief is all you need to take that first action step, which builds motivation and therefore more belief.

One simple trick I use to supercharge my affirmations is tying them to a vision that triggers me to feel the feelings of accomplishment. For me, I envisioned calling my mom and being able to tell her I'd been cast as Linda in *The Wedding Singer*. Every time I played this experience in my mind and celebrated with my mom (also in my mind), I kickstarted feelings of gratitude and excitement, which overrode many of the limiting beliefs that fear had helped me to create over the years. I'll just tell you right now that it was super cool to be able to play out that moment for real when it actually happened. Talk about déjà vu!

Your turn!

Create an affirmation that will help you build your new belief. Go a step further and tether it to an experience where you can celebrate achieving what you saw in step one.

3. Do It

You can visualize and say your "gratefuls" (that's how my grandma refers to her gratitude practice) all day long, but at the end of the day, these are just tools to help you get to the part that actually makes things happen. Step three in the Creation Process is probably the most important, and it requires taking consistent action—otherwise known as "doing the damn thing!"

So many people have these big dreams that stay big dreams because they don't ever move from the "dreaming big" phase to the "doing big" phase. I definitely wouldn't be writing about how

I was able to land my dream role in a Broadway show if I didn't take action (sometimes with a hell of a lot of fear in the passenger seat). So while I do encourage you to dream big, believe me, none of that shit even matters unless it's followed by a ton of hardcore, down-and-dirty *doing*!

I remember the moment my dreaming turned to doing like it was yesterday. I was at the newsstand on the corner of West 81st Street and Broadway, buying my weekly copy of *Backstage* magazine. In case you're not in showbiz, *Backstage* is a big publication that lists all the auditions happening in New York City each week. I flipped it open, and my belly dropped into my crotch when I saw the words:

CASTING FOR *THE WEDDING SINGER* BROADWAY NATIONAL TOUR

There it was, my shot! Please note that I had never been to an actual NYC audition yet, but because I had rehearsed this moment in my brain a bazillion times, I wasn't scared. My subconscious *and* conscious mind were ready for this.

I arrived at Chelsea Casting on the day of the audition in my most "Linda-esque" outfit, complete with fishnet tights, a tiny leather skirt, and a white ribbed tank top that I tied in a knot right above my belly button. I took the list hanging on the door and signed in as number 532, then sat down in the large dance studio that was full of girls who looked just like me.

I waited in that room full of actresses for what felt like hours, but when I went in, I was fresh as a daisy. I was so excited to show them all the work I'd put into this character. And that's exactly what I did. What happened next was a whirlwind of singing, dancing, and acting callbacks. As the hours passed, I watched the group of girls surrounding me get smaller and smaller until it was just two: me and this tall, beautiful blonde named Nika. This girl was a seasoned pro with the voice and dance moves to back up her very impressive resume. Talk about comparisonitis in overdrive—but then it hit me: even comparing myself to Nika didn't dampen my resolve. All of the seeing and believing work I'd done leading up to this point had turned what would normally have been nerves into excitement and confidence. My subconscious mind had already been through this and knocked it out of the park, so I knew once I handed the reins back over to my conscious brain, I'd kick just as much ass. That is how reprogramming your unconscious mind really works. It doesn't make anything magically come to you, but it does make the "doing" a hell of a lot easier and less scary!

Your turn!

What are three action steps you can take right now that bring your vision closer to a reality? These don't have to be huge steps; they can be as small as writing one page of the book you've been keeping in your mind or setting a date for the event you've always wanted to host. Remember that you just need one tiny action step to kickstart your momentum.

3.5. Do It Again (and Again and Again . . .)

I had to add step 3.5 because most of the time, the thing that you want doesn't come on the first try (or the second or the third). Most of the time, the road to seeing your ultimate creation IRL is a winding one with lots of red lights, heavy road construction, and U-turns. Just like when you're building confidence, when you're working through the Creation Process you will have to consistently take action, even when you feel like you just keep hitting dead ends.

My story wouldn't be very interesting if I landed my role after that first audition, now would it? I found out a few weeks after that audition that it was Nika, not me, who won the role of Linda.

This moment of rejection didn't affect me as much as it would have a few years prior. The second I found out I didn't get the part, my well-trained subconscious mind put me in my place with one simple thought that has since carried me through so much heartache:

It's not a "no," it's just a "not right now."

Getting comfy with rejection is something we're going to talk about in a lot more detail later in the book, but for now I'll tell you

I know it's not easy, but it *is* important. Cause guess what? You're gonna hear "no" a lot.

The other reason the disappointment didn't hit too hard was because those trusty neon lights appeared again, and this time they pointed me right in the direction of an audition for the show *Footloose* (yes, the Kevin Bacon movie, but as a musical!). When I looked at the casting breakdown, I noticed that the director was also going to be directing the second Broadway national tour of *The Wedding Singer.* You bet your ass *that* caught my attention, so I did what any girl making her dreams come true would do—snuck into the *Footloose* audition dressed as Linda and sang music from *The Wedding Singer* music for the director, of course!

In case you're not familiar with the entertainment industry and can't hear my sarcasm, I need you to know this was a *huge* risk. Sneaking into an audition in the Broadway world is a move that can get you canceled in the entire industry if you're not careful. But something inside of me knew I needed to start doing big if I wanted this to happen.

As I walked into the audition room, I kept my focus on a tiny crack in the wall behind the decision-makers' table. For some reason, I thought if I didn't look the casting directors in the eye, the crime I was committing wasn't as bad. I dialed in on the task and *nailed* that performance, but as I belted the final note, it was clear to everyone that I wasn't actually there to be cast in *Footloose.* Back in the waiting room, the reality of what I'd just done hit me.

Oh my god, I thought, my heart racing. *What if I just destroyed my entire career?*

Several minutes after my risky cancellation.com performance, the director appeared in the holding room and pointed right at me. "You. Come here."

Here it was. The moment of truth. I'd ruined everything, and he was going to tell me I should leave and never step foot in one of his castings again.

"Here's my card," he said, holding it out to me. "I'm not casting *The Wedding Singer* right now, but when I do, I'm going to call you."

Holy shit.

I had a golden ticket, and I made sure nobody forgot it, least of all the director. I followed up with this poor guy every single week for six months. I had nothing to say to this man, and we both knew exactly why I was e-mailing, so I made small talk. I sent him pictures of my dog, Dexter, and updates on my life. He never answered me, but I made sure he wouldn't forget me, and finally, he called me back in to audition for Linda.

I went through another rough round of callbacks until one day, I found an e-mail in my inbox with the subject line *"The Wedding Singer* National Tour Offer."

My stomach did the moonwalk and a few double pirouettes as I clicked the link.

> *Congratulations Jen,*
> *We're thrilled to offer you a role on the Broadway national*
> *tour of* The Wedding Singer . . .

My heart skipped a beat, but I didn't break out the champagne just yet, which was a good thing, because the e-mail continued,

> *. . . as a member of our ensemble/understudy for Linda.*

So close.

So. Freaking. Close.

I was thrilled, but knew I still had some "doing" to do to get to that moment I had been visualizing for a year now. So I packed up my bags and traveled to Fort Myers, Florida, to start rehearsals for my first Broadway national tour. As the understudy for Linda, I would also play a few other characters in the show, one of whom wore a fat suit and did the zombie dance from Michael Jackson's "Thriller" video. So, yep, for months, I had to stand in the wings and watch another girl play my dream role while I sweated gallons in a rubber casing. But it didn't matter because this was just a hiccup. I was on my way.

What are three obstacles you might hit along your path to success? How will you overcome them?

4. Receive It

I sat in those wings, watched that girl play Linda, and waited for my moment. She probably hated me, because she knew I was there in my fat suit studying her every move like a creeper, just waiting for my chance. I practiced every single day, because I knew that once I got my shot to take the stage, I was going to crush it.

After four months of prep and rehearsals in Florida and Pennsylvania, it was time to take the show on the big national tour. And just before we left, the director, Seth, who had dealt with months of e-mails from me and watched me work nonstop throughout rehearsals, called me aside.

"When we go on tour," he said, "I want you to be Linda."

They say luck is what happens when preparation meets the moment of opportunity. Well, I had never been more prepared for anything in my life, and just like that, my moment of opportunity was finally upon me. On my opening night, I stood there in the exact costume I'd dreamt about, singing the exact songs I'd sung to myself every night before I went to sleep. The experience was like déjà vu. I saw the same sights, heard the same sounds, and felt the same feelings I had when I was experimenting with visualization for the first time in my tiny dorm room.

It. Was. Magical.

When I got off that stage, I was walking on air. I felt so proud and so powerful because I'd made one of the most important realizations of my life: I can create anything that I want. I just have to see it, believe it, take action relentlessly, and *receive* it. When the universe gives you what you desire, please for god's sake, marinate in it. Enjoy the crap out of it, because the more grateful you are, the more you will get. I'm so glad I truly basked in the lights that I dreamt of for so long because it has become a memory I return to often when I set the SEEN to get in the pocket today. Trust me, that moment of receiving your creation with a full glass of gratitude and pride will come in handy again and again throughout your life.

Your turn!

Practice receiving! Celebrate three things you've created in the past by congratulating yourself. Go get (or make) yourself a "Congratulations" greeting card or buy yourself a small gift to fully celebrate. When you read the card or purchase the gift, really soak in the feeling of gratitude and pride you have for yourself.

5. Repeat It

The Creation Process works. It allows us to achieve the future we see for ourselves so we can be seen in all our glory as who we truly are. But there will be times when you forget how powerful the process is. You will forget that you possess the power to turn your thoughts into things, and you might even subconsciously stop yourself when it starts to get too good. I definitely did. Remember my bathroom floor breakdown in the *That Metal Show* dressing room? That happened long after *The Wedding Singer* tour, because I forgot this important step. We'll do a deeper dive into self-sabotage later on, but for now I'm going to leave you with step number five, which is to repeat it. The more you practice, the better you'll get.

Your goals might change, and that vision of your future might need adjusting now and then. But by using the Creation Process consistently, you can create the vision you see for yourself, and if it doesn't manifest exactly as you envisioned, it will most definitely show up eventually as something so much better than you could have imagined.

Your turn!

Think of a time when you took your foot off the gas after you got the results you desired. What happened next?

Now imagine what would have happened if you kept going and it kept getting better. Which of your recent wins need a boost of repeat energy to take them even further?

CHOOSE YOU (2.0)

When I decided I was going to be Linda—and then moved into actually believing that I already *was* Linda—opportunities started presenting themselves. The first audition. The second (very risky) audition. The director's business card. The ensemble role. I'd spent so much time seeing the sights and feeling the feelings as if they were real that I successfully tricked my subconscious mind into believing that starring in this show was a reality. Since this was already a part of my life's feature film, I was able to easily spot the doors I had to open to lead me there—even when some were locked or slammed back in my face.

Yes, there were points when luck came together for me, but not because the world changed around me to suit my goals. It's because I *made* it that way. I took action relentlessly and turned every no into a yes. I changed my perspective around what the world told me was possible and I kept going even when my belief in myself dipped well below 51 percent.

I know I went into this experience with a crap ton of privilege, because of where I lived and how I grew up and the color of my skin. I'm not trying to pretend that privilege doesn't exist, or that my experience means you won't face obstacles in your Creation Process that I never had to encounter. But one of the most amazing gifts we've been given as humans is the gift of choice. We get to choose what we want to create and which action steps we take to get there. And regardless of where you're starting, you have the ability to see who You 2.0 is, and to choose to start embodying that version of yourself now.

Remember that your desires come to you for a reason, and when you're looking for those neon signs to point you in the right direction, they might not lead you to the destination you have in mind. What you want to create may change, and that's okay! I would not be sitting here writing this book right now if my dream of being a Broadway star as my end-all goal came true. (I might be writing a different book, sure, but not this one!) My neon lights led me to Linda, and then they *kept* leading me places, to *That Metal Show*, JLG Fitness, Super Connector Media, and eventually to this moment, right now, here with you. When you keep your eyes, your heart, and your consistent action focused on You 2.0, your path will always take you where you're meant to go.

🎤 MIC DROP MOMENTS

- If you don't know where you're going, then you can't get there.

- Living in alignment with Real You allows you to look through the future and determine your most authentic goals—*not* the ones you think you "should" be living or the ones that other people want for you.

- Your subconscious mind runs the show when it comes to most of your daily actions, but it can't tell the difference between a real memory and a fake memory. This means it's easy for you to implant your own goals into your brain and trick them into thinking they're already a reality.

A QUICK WIN

- Discover You 2.0. Set a timer for 15 minutes and describe whom you would meet if you were introduced to the most fulfilled, successful, confident, in-the-pocket, aligned version of you. When you visualize yourself shining your brightest, what do you see?

✍️ PUT IT ON A POST-IT

- If what you want doesn't manifest exactly as you envisioned, it will show up eventually as something so much better than you could have imagined.

CHAPTER 6

HOW TO TRAVEL THROUGH TIME

Have you ever watched a movie and noticed when life seems to be going really well for the main character, but then you realize there's still an hour left to watch? And then, sure enough—*SPLAT*—they land on their face?

That's because their story isn't over yet. Good stories are entertaining and meaningful to us because they're made up of endless cycles of trying and failing, trying and failing, trying and success(!), and then failing and trying again. This book would be pretty boring if everything happened easily for me, wouldn't it? It's that Step 3.5 of the Creation Process—do it again and again and again—that creates the most personal growth.

What I'm trying to say is that my story didn't end with landing my dream role in *The Wedding Singer*. Just because I learned the steps to make this particular dream a reality doesn't mean I always followed my own advice. It's a key concept, yes, but who among us hasn't been late to work because we couldn't find our keys? In this chapter I'm going to show you how all the crap life throws your way can either get you down or lead to change, and how—when you choose the second option, at least—those "shit to shift" moments will lead you to a future where You 2.0 has the starring role.

After *The Wedding Singer* tour ended, I went back to New York City life with Hedge Fund Rob and got cast as Miss Box of Junk on *That Metal Show*. We already know what the mess looked like when shit hit *that* particular fan, so let's fast forward past Heavy Metal Jennifer on the floor of her dressing room and move on to what happened next. Rob and I split, and he began dating the woman he had been cheating on me with. If that wasn't enough of a kick in the pants, *That Metal Show* got canceled.

Just like that, I went from having a lucrative, consistent gig on TV and living in a beautiful Upper West Side high-rise with a guy I thought I was going to marry to being single, jobless, and renting a tiny room with a window that faced a brick wall, along with six other actors.

To say that moving into my new "home" was a dark day would be the understatement of the century. I had six large cardboard boxes that somehow housed the contents of my entire life, and they managed to fill my tiny new room—which was about the same size as my former bathroom—until I could barely fit inside with them.

What the hell am I going to do now? I lifted my eyes to stare out my pathetic little window at my pathetic little view. *I have nothing.* I felt like life had created an evil plan specifically to take me down.

I want to pause here and let you know that I'm currently writing this section, years later, halfway blinded by the sun beaming in through the massive floor-to-ceiling windows of my dream home. I wish I could have traveled through time in that moment and shown myself what was *really* on its way for me. If I had that superpower, I probably would have had more hope and a hell of a lot less fear. The good news for you is that you're about to learn how to seemingly manipulate time and experience the future you desire right now so you can skip what I did next.

That day, the pain and terror of not knowing if I would ever be okay completely overcame me, and the next thing I remember is icing a throbbing bump on my forehead. Apparently, I'd been banging it against the cement wall.

What are you doing? I thought, pain blossoming in my forehead. *You're a fucking idiot. You should have found a way to stay with Rob. You should go get him back. You've ruined your whole life, and for what?*

I was dreading having to start auditioning again, and I had no idea what my next steps should be. I was a hot fucking mess, and everyone who loved me could see it. Finally, after weeks of trying to get through to me, my mom had had enough and came into the city to take care of me the way only moms can.

"Get dressed, Jenny," she told me one afternoon. "I'm taking you to dinner."

I pulled on a pair of pants, scraped my brittle, bleached-blond hair into a ponytail, and met my mom at a cute little Italian place on Columbus Avenue, where my mom pulled out a book, *You Can Heal Your Life*, by Louise Hay.

"This book helped me out of some tight spots," she said with a smile, sliding it across the table like a shady business deal. "I hope it can do the same for you."

I looked at the book and then back at the woman who gave me life and loved me so unconditionally, and suddenly, Real Jen peeked her head out of her dark cave and surrendered, allowing herself to be seen for the first time in a while. My mom held me tight at the corner table of that Italian restaurant just like she'd held me as a baby. And in that moment, I caught a glimpse of the magical power of gratitude. For a few seconds, the realization of just how lucky I was to have a mom who cared so much overcame my helplessness, fear, and anxiety. I realized that when you allow yourself to be seen in the rawest, realest, and sometimes darkest of times, you give yourself permission to heal.

When I got home that night to my crappy little bedroom, I noticed that inside the cover, she'd left a photocopy of one of the affirmations from the book, clearly knowing I wasn't going to read the whole thing:

> *In the infinity of life where I am, all is perfect, whole, and complete. I no longer choose to believe in old limitations and lack. I now choose to begin to see myself as the Universe sees me—perfect, whole, and complete. The*

truth of my Being is that I was created perfect, whole, and complete. I will always be perfect, whole, and complete. I now choose to live my life from this understanding. I am in the right place at the right time, doing the right thing. All is well in my world.

I took out some tape and stuck the affirmation to the refrigerator. Even though I was definitely skeptical about all of my mom's woo-woo stuff, I told myself, *Just read it once every day. Even if I don't believe it, I'm going to read it every day.*

Affirmations work because they give us a sense of self-efficacy, which basically boils down to a belief in our own abilities. By constantly telling ourselves something positive, even when we don't believe it all the way, we're giving a quick nod to what we learned in Chapter 5 by tricking our subconscious mind into believing it's true. Affirmations alone won't solve all your problems, but they are a great tool to get you to that magical number of 51 percent when it comes to your confidence, self-belief, and allowing yourself to be seen.

At the time, the affirmation from my mom didn't seem life-changing at all, but it did get me out the door in the morning and created that momentum for me to go outside and see the world (and myself) a little bit differently. It did get me looking at jobs and auditions again, and kickstarted my desire to immerse myself in words and books and stories from people who changed their perspective. Soon, I was back to being a functioning human doing human things again. Even if those things didn't feel quite right, I had a tiny bit of momentum, and sometimes that's all you need for the universe to step in and help you see the signs that are secretly pointing you in the direction of the future you desire. And that's exactly what happened.

ONE DAY I'LL KNOW WHY THIS HAPPENED

One morning that was 10 degrees below zero, I was lugging my suitcase full of audition dresses through Midtown, going from casting call to casting call, when I saw a quote written in chalk on the sidewalk:

> If you don't like the road you're walking, start paving
> a new one.
>   — Dolly Parton

I knew right then and there that if I didn't change, nothing would change. (Thanks, Dolly!) So out of desperation—and with no other choice, really (seriously, it was *freezing*)—I rolled that old suitcase into a Barnes & Noble and parked myself on the floor of the personal development section, where I began pulling every book off the shelf, one by one. From that day forward, motivational authors like Wallace D. Wattles, Gabby Bernstein, Louise Hay (thanks, Mom!), Oprah Winfrey, Brené Brown, and Tony Robbins became my mentors, and I began spending hours with them each day.

What I soon noticed was that every single one of the successful people I read about had been through some kind of breakdown, which had then led to a massive break*through*. The bad stuff always led them to the opportunity that changed their lives forever. In other words: *shit* had to happen before *shift* could happen.

So every morning I pulled out my journal and repeatedly scribbled the only sentence that gave me any hope: "One day I'll know why this happened."

I wrote it over and over for months, sometimes cursing myself for blowing up my perfect-on-paper life. I had moments of desperation when I considered going back to Rob and turning the other cheek to his cheating, but something wouldn't let me. I realized it was the people I'd begun calling my "friends in my head." Just like affirmations will slowly make you change your beliefs, surrounding yourself with the positive lessons of people who have done what you want to do before you, or who have pushed through their own rock bottom moments of discomfort and gotten through it can really shift your own belief and perspective about what can happen for you. My shiny new personal-development addiction had led me to find even more affirming voices—Lori Harder, Jonathan Fields, Lewis Howes—through pod-casts. Unlike my IRL friends, most of whom had ditched me when Rob and I broke up, these ones wanted what was best for me. They helped me realize that even though I felt like I had nothing, I still had a *lot* to be grateful for! With their help, I started seeing hints of that "one day" I kept writing about in my journal.

If you're reading this book right now, you're already light-years ahead of where I was because you understand that you need to fill your brain with lessons from people who can constantly remind you of what's possible. I'm so grateful to be in a position where I'm creating content, producing a podcast, and speaking on stages to help people to build the confidence to be seen, because the people who did this for me changed my life. It's a cycle, and by reading this book I'm inviting you into it so in six months, or five years, you too can be seen by people who are at their low point, just like you were, and need your help.

When I was in the thick of my depression, I couldn't see the purpose of what I was going through. But now I can recognize the ways that it was all secretly happening for an important reason, and just like I affirmed day after day, one day, I finally knew why it happened. Because day after day, as I began to journal about the things I *did* have rather than the ones I didn't, I began to experience a mindset shift that remains with me today.

SHIFT HAPPENS

Has anyone ever called you a Debbie Downer? Have you ever stopped in your tracks and wondered why it always seems like your glass is half empty? I ask because believe it or not, I used to be a very negative person. Really, it got so bad at one point that my castmates in *The Wedding Singer* didn't even want to share a dressing room with me. Ugh. I'm not like that anymore (thank goodness!), and now I'm a living, breathing example that with a hell of a lot of intentionality, you can change the way you choose to perceive your circumstances. Our perspective is what creates our beliefs, and our beliefs are what dictate our actions. One of the reasons I got so stuck is because I chose to focus on what I didn't have and what sucked rather than what I could be grateful for.

After the breakup, I was alone for the first time, and I had a choice to make. I could either ruminate on how badly life sucked and continue to worry about how much worse it could get, or I could choose to look at it as an amazing opportunity to rebuild my life from scratch and finally start to be seen as Real Jen. As much as I would love to tell you that I chose to dramatically rise from the ashes like a phoenix to change my life, my first thought was really more like, *This sucks and I can't do this.*

If that's where you're at right now, and you can't see yourself with a better future, you're in the right place, because as Gabby Bernstein teaches in her book *Super Attractor*, you get to choose again! I love Gabby's Choose Again method because it reminds us that it's natural to have negative thoughts. What matters is what we do next, and whether we follow three important steps:

1. Notice the thought

2. Forgive the thought

3. Choose again

Choosing to *change* my negative thoughts was something I didn't even know was possible, but with the help of Gabby and my other "friends in my head," I started taking baby steps to adjust my own mindset, and it threw me off track in the best way. I started waving the white flag. *I surrender! Teach me all the things,* I begged, and the friends in my head took me by the hand (or the earbud) and showed me the way.

Before long, I started smiling when I stepped outside into the sunshine, rather than worrying about the clouds on the horizon. I recognized good things when they happened and was able to let the bad ones roll off my shoulders without tripping me up. Instead of looking at my life with dread for all I'd need to rebuild, I began thinking, *I'm so grateful Rob left me. I would never have the opportunity to live my life on my own terms otherwise. This was the greatest thing that has ever happened to me.*

I was beginning to learn what psychologists (and let's be real, the entire personal development world) have known for some time: gratitude is a natural antidepressant.[1] Feeling gratitude, *really* feeling it, releases chemicals in our brains—dopamine and serotonin, to be precise, also widely known as our body's natural "feel good" chemicals. When we retrain our subconscious mind to feel gratitude, we're telling it, "Hey, it's time to stop and smell the roses!" Just like when we're visualizing our future, gratitude flips the on switch for some more of those bright neon lights. But instead of pointing us to our next step, they're highlighting the best parts of what we're experiencing, which in turn conditions our subconscious mind to *keep* noticing the good stuff, because come on, who doesn't like to feel good?

Soon, I was walking with a spring in my step. I went for walks listening to podcasts and audio books for hours, and they helped me realize I needed to think about what I wanted for me, and for Jen 2.0. One day, on one of our walks, I knew I had the answer I needed.

FUTURE GRATITUDE

When you think of your dream future, what do you see? What kind of kickass life is You 2.0 living? Got the vision in your mind? Okay, now I want you to think about sharing that dream with someone close to you. Does that make you feel scared? Excited? Embarrassed? If the thought of sharing that dream with anyone terrifies you, and that fear is keeping you stuck, it might be time to start surrounding yourself with people who get it (but more on that in Part 3!). I don't know about you, but one of the ways I used to hide was by not telling anyone in my life what I truly wanted because I was secretly afraid they would judge me. As a result, I buried those hopes for my future so far down that eventually, I couldn't even find them myself.

Think deep about those dreams, the ones you're afraid to say out loud. Write your dream down, or whisper it into an empty room. I promise, I'll never judge you for it. You already know what you want You 2.0 to be like, so wouldn't it be great if you could peek into your future and know without a doubt it's where you're headed? Well, that's exactly what I'm going to ask you to do.

When Rob and I were together, I had this secret dream of becoming a personal trainer. I never thought I could tell him, because it would mean I would have a job other than being his full-time arm candy and party partner. Just as I suspected, it didn't go well when I admitted I dreamt of starting a personal training business.

"Why?" he'd asked, completely flabbergasted.

I looked at him like the answer should be obvious, because, duh, it was! "I love working out," I told him. "I'm like an expert at it, and I love helping people." My mind was running wild. I could make my own schedule and develop my growing love for teaching—it felt like such a win-win!

"What about auditions?" Rob had a sour look on his face that I recognized instantly, and it struck disappointment deep into the pit of my stomach. "What about our future?"

I knew the future he was talking about. I was on the wifey track, set to become a pampered housewife to a rich Wall Street guy. Rob offered me everything I could possibly want when it came to money and material possessions, to the point where, looking back, it felt like I was being held hostage. It was clear the idea of me owning my own business and gaining that much control over my own life scared him. Sure, he tolerated my dreams of being onstage, but Rob and I both knew what my future held: nannies, personal drivers, glamorous charity events, and carte blanche on his Amex—aka everything I was supposed to want in a marriage. That was, as long as I continued to overlook his rampant cheating, cocaine habit, and late-night partying. Oof, when I peeked into that future, Real Jen had quite a few things to say, but at the time, Real Jen was buried under a mountain of self-doubt, fake friendships, and Louis Vuitton purses, so she wasn't exactly coming to the phone right now.

Now that I was out of that relationship, there was nothing standing in the way of me and my fitness business dreams. One of the "choose again" thoughts I created was that I was excited to finally get to pursue my dream of becoming a trainer now that Rob was out of the picture, so one day after a long walk with one of my favorite podcasts playing in my ear, I took out my AirPods and marched up the steps to the Reebok Sports Club, one of the fanciest gyms in New York City. I'm gonna get geeky here for a sec, because let me tell you, I *loved* this gym. It was six floors of fitness heaven, complete with every piece of top-of-the-line fitness equipment you can imagine, a full-size basketball court, a locker room straight out of Canyon Ranch, and mini fridges with cool eucalyptus-scented towels next to every ultra-filtered water fountain. If that wasn't enough to make you want to empty your bank account to join, get this: the likelihood that you would find yourself doing squats next to Madonna while watching Adam Sandler shoot hoops was super high—like, almost guaranteed!

It was the gym for NYC's rich and famous and, thanks to Rob footing the bill, I was a member. After we broke up, I still had a month left at Reebok, but I was going to do whatever I could to stay in that building as long as possible. Because I decided I wasn't going to be *just* a trainer at *just* any gym, after all. I was going to train *here*. This was the future I wanted. So I scraped and scrounged and begged money off my grandma to keep my membership going ($300 a month wasn't just painful for my bank account, it was a death blow), and I started making it a point to meet everyone there. The members, the trainers, the managers—I schmoozed and made friends, asking them how they got where they were, all while occasionally running into my cheating ex-boyfriend, always with a shocked expression on his face.

The trainers at Reebok all wore these super tight black V-neck shirts that said TRAINER in big white letters on the back. You could tell they were strategically designed to make you look superhero-level buff because of the stretchy fabric, short cap sleeves, and tapered waistline. I wanted one of those damn shirts so bad. I mean, how cute and authoritative would I look walking around Reebok in my Lululemon leggings, black trainer shirt, and sleek magnet name tag? I set my sights on that shirt as I learned about all the certifications and training hours I'd need. I was going to wear it one day. I was going to train here; I just knew it.

I had a goal again, and just like I'd done with Linda, I started working the Creation Process. Only this time instead of thigh-high boots and standing ovations, I had my sights set on a TRAINER shirt and a biweekly paycheck from Reebok Sports Club. That's right, ya girl was studying her ass off for her certifications, and this time I had a secret weapon, courtesy of my new gratitude practice.

The gateway to manifesting my role of Linda was feeling the experience as if I'd already done it. I remember feeling so grateful for that costume, those lights, and that audience before I'd ever stepped foot on that stage. So now, with a new goal in mind, I visualized myself in that TRAINER shirt, and the first emotion that came to me was, once again, gratitude. Whereas last time I was making it all up as I went along, this time I had the blueprints in front of me, and it struck me like lightning: the fastest way to tap into the feelings of already having what I want was to be grateful for it!

If I could find a way to be grateful for all the shitty things that had happened in my past, what was stopping me from extending that gratitude to all the incredible things I had coming in my future?

"I'm so grateful that today was amazing," I wrote in my journal every morning, when I'd barely had a chance to get out of bed and start my day yet. "I'm so grateful I'm a personal trainer at Reebok. I'm so grateful for my trainer shirt. I'm grateful that I get to help people feel better about themselves every day. I'm grateful I feel so fulfilled doing this work and absolutely love my job."

Think about those goals we talked about in Chapter 5, the You 2.0 I know you're gearing up to be. Just like we did in the Creation Process, I want you to envision being that person. What will it feel like when you achieve that goal? What will you be most grateful for?

Why not travel through time and start being grateful for it now?

Right here, right now, I want you to write down three things you're grateful for that haven't happened yet. They can be big or small, looking forward to this afternoon or next year.

I'm grateful that I was featured in Forbes.

I'm grateful that I landed the new client.

I'm grateful that I launched my new course and it was a huge success.

Practicing future gratitude unlocked something in me, like a secret door inside the door of gratitude inside the door of retraining my subconscious mind. My confidence bank overflowed and an amazing, unstoppable feeling filled me from head to toe, which helped me take the action steps I needed to get to where my sub-conscious mind could already taste.

Once again, I'm gonna spoil the ending for you: I got the shirt—and the job along with it.

There was a catch, of course. I had to work my ass off. Since I had zero experience as a personal trainer, Reebok made me pay my dues first in the form of "floor hours," which meant I was basically a glorified janitor, cleaning the gym, wiping equipment, and rack-ing weights. The other part of the deal was that I had to shadow one of the head trainers for their sessions on the days I wasn't working the floor. To put it lightly, I was doing physical labor from 6 A.M. to 8 P.M. every day for minimum wage, but since I could lit-erally taste the amazing feeling of freedom and fulfillment I would have when I reached the end goal, I was able to move through the temporary discomfort each day with a positive perspective. It was during this time that I truly started to understand the free-dom and fulfillment that comes as a result of discipline. I'm pretty sure I was the cheeriest gym cleaning queen anyone had encoun-tered! After months of earning my stripes, I finally began training my own clients and helping them achieve their fitness goals, and it wasn't long before my future gratitude eventually became my present. I had a job I absolutely loved, and the trainer shirt just ended up being a bonus!

JLG FITNESS

In Chapter 3, you learned all about the power of momentum in the Confidence Continuum. The super cool thing about it is that it keeps building on itself—getting one win makes that next win feel so much easier, and the next one even easier than that, because by the time you've got a few wins under your belt, you've already locked in the steps of the Creation Process as a habit or routine, like a program that your subconscious mind runs on autopilot. That's the real power of everything I'm teaching you here—not only will you be working toward a win, you'll be building your *own* system that makes racking up more and more of those Ws even easier.

The momentum I initiated put my life into a serious upswing, and it wasn't long before I was able to move out of my tiny room and into a high-rise apartment (also tiny, but with only *one* roommate instead of six!). I cheerfully said good-bye to my terrible little window and my closetless little bedroom, and strode purposefully into the next phase of my life. I loved being a personal trainer, but working overtime for $30 an hour was starting to run me ragged. My clients were paying five times that for me to train them, and I couldn't believe Reebok took such a huge cut. There was a pretty nice gym in my new apartment building, and one day, on my way home from work, a thought struck me. *I could keep getting paid $30 per hour to train people at Reebok, or I could start bringing them here, make $150 an hour, and keep all of it.*

With that one idea, JLG Fitness was officially born. With my creative, entrepreneurial mind in overdrive, I started taking clients from Reebok and bringing them to the gym in my building, which quickly turned into bringing Reebok clients to private gyms all over the Upper West Side. Within months, I was making more money from my side hustle than I was at my real job. *Holy shit,* I thought. *It couldn't possibly be this easy.*

It wasn't.

Reebok found out I was training clients on the side and fired me, banning me from their gym for life. Just like that, my biggest lead generator was gone. After the mini meltdown and minor panic attack this caused, I forced myself to look for reasons this was happening *for* me instead of *to* me. One being, without that push, I wouldn't have had the courage to leap into running my own business full time. When I look back, this was one of the best "bad" things that ever happened to me.

After a year of pounding the pavement and working my ass off to build a consistent loyal client base in private gyms all over Manhattan, I built JLG Fitness into something that grew bigger than I could handle on my own. I started hiring trainers to work under me and writing workout programs for some of the most successful celebrities, billionaires, and CEOs in New York City. I was #girlbossing my little butt off all over the city and starting to feel like a real business owner, beyond proud that I'd begun making six figures for the first time. I published an e-book, built an online coaching program, and above all, with the help of my client-turned-BFF Amanda, who worked in PR, I successfully re-branded myself. Good-bye, Heavy Metal Jennifer. I was now Jen 2.0. I took control of my own narrative and became the person I was meant to be.

The *shift* was hitting the fan, and it smelled great.

HOW TO TRAVEL THROUGH TIME

Even with all the growth and transformation in my life, the resur-gence of Real Jen—and the advent of Jen 2.0—didn't completely come together until one magical weekend when I dove headfirst into a time machine for real.

Lewis Howes, best-selling author, was one of my favorite pod-cast hosts. I listened to his show *The School of Greatness* on repeat and often felt like he was talking just to *me*. One day while I listened on a Wonder Walk through Greenwich Village, he an-nounced he was hosting a live event in Ohio called the Summit of Greatness, where like-minded people could connect in person and experience an incredible lineup of motivational speakers.

First, I felt excited! This would be my chance to start to connect with other entrepreneurs! But then utter dread chased away my excitement. Every symptom of fear flooded my system and, like clockwork, the lies lined up in the form of highly realistic excuses as to why I shouldn't go.

You aren't ready to go to an event like that.

Do you really have the money to travel right now?

What will your friends think if you go to some event you heard about on a podcast?

I knew this was fear BS'ing me, so I put its ass in the passenger seat and told it to strap in, because we were *both* going to Ohio. I even invited my bestie Amanda to come along with me. Before I knew it, we were stuffing more dresses than we could ever have needed into our suitcases and hopping on a plane.

The second I stepped foot into the theater where the event was held, I knew I was in personal development heaven. The speakers were incredible, and the people I got to connect with were, dare I say, just like me! Everyone was focused on becoming the best version of themselves. They were all stepping slightly outside of their comfort zones and opening their lives up to opportunity and growth. It was both exhilarating and overwhelming to be around so many positive humans all at once. But one specific moment from that magical weekend will forever stand out to me.

"Close your eyes," said one of the speakers. "And envision what your perfect day would look like if a little fairy came and tapped you on the head and told you that you could have absolutely anything you wanted. What would your life look like?"

They turned on some meditative music as we closed our eyes, held each other's hands, and hopped into a time machine that transported us where we were able to see ourselves living the life of our dreams. I was familiar with the power of visualization from back when I practiced manifesting my dream role as Linda in *The Wedding Singer*, so I was ready to let go and trust the process. As the music crescendoed, I floated away to a place where other people's opinions didn't exist and my deepest desires projected onto the big screen in my mind. It was magic.

"Okay, now turn to the person next to you and tell them what you saw," the speaker instructed as the music faded.

I turned to Amanda and told her, a huge smile on my face, "I saw love."

That's what it was for me. A vision of love in more ways than one. Here's the detailed version: I was as one-half of a power couple, like Jay-Z and Beyoncé. We were madly in love and had built a successful empire together. We traveled all over the world speaking on stages and helping people, just like the speakers at that event. But, of course, in my vision, I did it *my* way, like Tony Robbins meets Britney Spears circa 2003 (because let's be real, it always comes back to Britney for me!), so I could dance in beautiful outfits onstage while motivating people to step into their best selves.

This was the first time I realized that while I had always thought my purpose was to be a performer in the traditional sense, I was

really meant to use my gifts in a different way, more than reading lines from a script someone else wrote. A way where *I* got to
choose the words I said, and those words could inspire people to
see their full potential.

I had never gotten the memo so clearly in my life. For the first
time, I knew with complete certainty that I'd fallen into a worm-
hole and caught a glimpse of my future. The Jen 2.0 in that vision
was exactly who I wanted to be, and now that I had her in my
sights, I wasn't going to let go. And here's the best part: I envisioned the life I'm living right now. No, seriously, I am not fucking
around!

If you guessed that this is the part where I ask you to join me in
seeing your deepest desires in your mind's eye, you're right! Let's
travel through time and catch a glimpse (even if it's just for a moment) of what You 2.0 looks and feels like in action.

Get comfortable, in a quiet place where you won't be disturbed.
Now, I want you to close your eyes. Breathe in, then breathe out.

And travel through time with me.

It's five years from now, and you're opening up this book again.
You're a different person than you were because you accomplished
That Thing. You created it, and you brought it into reality. What
thing? Oh, come on, don't play coy. You know what That Thing is.
It's that big, hairy, audacious goal that you think about every single
day. Or maybe you don't consciously think about it, but you know
in your subconscious mind that's The Thing you were born to do.

And now you've done it.

How do you sit? How do you feel? What are you grateful for?
Look around and see all of your friends here with us. They are all
applauding you because *you did it*. You said you were gonna do it
and you did. You feel a new confidence, a new swagger, because
everything you need to create what you want is inside of you. How
do you know this? Because you've lived it. You took one year, or
three, or five, and you did the damn thing.

What does that feel like? Sit in that. Take a deep breath and
open your eyes. What did you create? Take a moment to write out
what you just saw.

Feels fucking amazing, doesn't it?
Why not do that now?
Why wait?

🎤 MIC DROP MOMENTS

- Your rock-bottom moments—even the cement walls and tiny closet-sized bedrooms—are there to teach you something. Even if it might be hard, find the gratitude in them. One day you'll know why this happened.

- When you allow yourself to be seen in the rawest, realest, and sometimes darkest of times, you give yourself permission to begin healing.

- Gratitude is a natural antidepressant.

- Being grateful for things that haven't happened (yet!) is a great way to trick your subconscious mind into leading you down the path to get there.

👏 A QUICK WIN

- Write out a "future gratitude list." Add a minimum of three things that haven't happened yet and write them out as if they've happened!

✍️ PUT IT ON A POST-IT

- Gratitude conquers all.

....

CHAPTER 7

HARNESSING THE LAW OF ACTION

When was the last time you started something new that put you slightly outside of your comfort zone? Maybe you started posting on social media about your new business, began a meditation practice, or started taking a new exercise class. Remember how great it felt when you started gaining momentum?

Do you also remember that moment you got that wacky thought in your head: *This can't last.* It's the kind of thought that stops you in your tracks, isn't it? Every time you start to tinker with *great*, you feel precarious. Our good ol' frenemy fear comes in and tells you if things are *great*, you could lose it all in a heartbeat. The whole Jenga tower will come crashing down. So you rein yourself back into what feels more comfortable. You stop posting on social media, you stop going to events to connect with new people, you ignore the opportunities in your inbox. You stop taking action and start to slow your momentum. But here's the thing—we are the only ones who can initiate our own stuckness, and we are also the only ones who can get us out of it. There is no magic You-Tube video, podcast, or course to get unstuck. Journaling, whiteboarding, and thinking "big" about it won't fix it either. There is really only one thing that can reengage your momentum when you've stopped it—and that's what this chapter is all about.

My personal training business was earning multiple six figures, I was building an actual brand by being regularly featured in the media, and I finally had a community of new friends who were super supportive and held me accountable to my goals (like Tory the Badass, whom I met at that event!).

There was just one problem. Now that I'd rebuilt my life and was completely independent, I was terrified one false move would jinx it and I would lose it all. I was like a scientist mixing danger-ous chemicals, knowing that even the slightest mismeasurement could blow up the whole damn lab. Taking risks was out of the question. I couldn't shake the feeling that if things got *too* good, something bad was bound to happen. I was petrified of losing everything I'd built, so I stopped reaching and became obsessed with structure and control. I ate the same grilled tilapia with burnt vegetables for dinner every night and strategically filled my work schedule to the brim so I wouldn't have time to do anything other than train clients, eat, walk my dog, Dexter, and sleep. Oh, and forget about dating! While I was definitely wishing for my "Jay-Z" to appear, I made sure I was too busy to notice even if he was standing right in front of me. I was wishing and praying for some-thing amazing to happen to me, but my actions were making sure there was no chance of that.

As a result, I was permanently at "level good." Nothing ever got bad, but nothing ever got great either. It was always just "eh." And "eh" started to get really, really lonely. I had hit what I now know (thanks to Gay Hendricks's book *The Big Leap*) as my Upper Limit: the point where we stop moving forward because the fear of failure becomes greater than our belief in what's possible. I was working against myself. If this sounds familiar, keep reading, my friend, because I'm about to give you some tools I wish someone gave me.

For years, I've had a hot-pink sticky note on my computer with two words that have helped me avoid self-sabotage before it hap-pens. This one little statement has landed me massive speaking engagements, made me millions of dollars, played a big part in getting this book published, and gotten me back on my feet after some epic failures. It's like kryptonite for stuckness. Ready for it?

DO SOMETHING!

I'll pause while you grab a sticky note (any color will do!) and stick this magical sentence on something you look at every day.

Now, let's go a bit deeper down this rabbit hole, because what I'm about to teach you is crucial to being seen instead of being stuck. As we discussed in Part I, the thing that initiates momentum is *action*. A lot of people think their actions need to be huge and profound, but it's quite the opposite! Any type of action step in the direction of a goal, whether it's texting a friend, creating one piece of content, drafting one e-mail, or purchasing a new journal, can all produce a tiny win that will give you that little bit of dopamine you need to kickstart some momentum.

THE LAW OF ACTION

The Law of Attraction (LOA) tells us that like attracts like. It's a shortcut to what we talked about in Chapters 5 and 6 about creating your own reality so you can be seen as the best version of you. If you couldn't tell by now, I am the biggest LOA believer of all time. I have (and continue to create) endless examples of how I used this law to build a life that far exceeds what I ever imagined when I was staring out a tiny window at a brick wall.

However, many books that teach this universal law are missing one critical component. Without this second piece of the puzzle, you will just become a fabulous daydreamer. And while I love getting lost in a good fantasy, I know you didn't pick up this book to learn how to hope for your desires to magically appear. You can visualize and vision board and be grateful until the cows come home, but if you're not doing anything about the opportunities that come as a result of the seeing and believing, all you've got at the end of the day is a cute collage and absolutely zero results.

You can't have the Law of Attraction without the Law of *Action*.

We've talked about this a few times before, so it should really be sinking in by now. Building confidence requires action. The Creation Process requires action (step 3!). Future gratitude is just daydreaming without action. Getting from You to You 2.0 requires—any guesses?—*action*. So now we're going to double down on how you can consistently take action so the future you desire turns into your reality.

If you ever need a reminder of this, just take a look at that sticky note, and *do something.*

Here's a great example of how taking action can work. One morning I opened my Instagram to find a DM from Dina, a Mastermind member who had been crushing it in her life coaching business. I definitely thought I was going to open the message and find another GIF of a dancing monkey in celebration of a big win, but I was wrong.

Hi Jen, I need some of your Chief Mindset Officer wisdom because I'm definitely sabotaging myself. Please help!

This was totally out of left field. Just two weeks prior, Dina and I had been doing the happy dance together over her first feature on national TV, a major goal of hers. A few seconds after this DM, I got a voice memo from her in tears explaining that the win put her on a huge high for about a week until she began to self-sabotage. After the TV segment aired, she received message after message from potential clients who wanted to hire her, but she didn't respond to any of the leads that came in because she was scared it would be "too much to handle" if they all signed on. She also feared that once she got on calls with them, they would realize she wasn't as good as they thought when they saw her on TV. A classic case of imposter syndrome! We hopped on a call, read her Badass List out loud, and then, instead of a pep talk, I gave her a simple homework assignment: I told her to respond to *one* of the leads. Not all of them, just one. "Do it with your fear and doubt in the passenger seat of the car," I said.

You see, Dina didn't need me to give her a TED Talk to get unstuck, she just needed to take action on *something* that would give her a tiny win. That win would be enough to regain some trust that she was, in fact, the badass from the list. It worked! She e-mailed a response to one of her new leads, got on the call, and closed the sale. *Now* the moment called for that monkey GIF!

Completing one small action gave Dina the confidence to take on the next step. She went from success to self-sabotage to stuck and back to success again by simply implementing the Law of Action. And within a week, she had six new customers and a hell of a lot more confidence in the bank!

THE YEAR OF CONNECTION

When it came to my own stuckness, I know you're wondering how I got out of that rut and found my way back to action. Well, I ran there.

I'm happy as a clam lifting heavy weights, but if you ask me to run a mile, I'll probably pretend I didn't hear you. So why did I agree to spend New Year's Eve doing the Midnight Run in Central Park with my friend Amanda? Because I knew if I continued to do what I'd always done, I would continue to get what I'd always gotten. And what I was doing at that time with my strict "never change it up ever" schedule clearly wasn't getting me the life I really wanted. I knew if I wanted to create the perfect day I had visualized so clearly at that event, I needed to start walking—or running—in a different direction. So I bundled into six layers of Lululemon at 11:30 P.M. and dragged my ass on a three-mile run around Central Park with hundreds of other determined New Yorkers.

Crossing the finish line that night was exhilarating! I stepped outside of my comfort zone, did *something* challenging, and sent new momentum pumping through my veins. Waking up New Year's Day felt different. I had dropped a shiny new coin in my confidence bank, and I was ready to kickstart my new year with a personal development strategy I heard about on one of my favorite podcasts: choosing a word of the year to drive my decisions, intentions, and actions for the next 365 days.

That January first, with sore legs and a heart full of hope, I pulled out my journal. What was a word that would challenge me to do things differently? I looked at my surroundings, and what

I saw was me, myself, and I—alone (if you didn't count my dog, Dexter, which for the purposes of this story, I won't). I'd been single for a few years and, combined with my 33-year-old workaholic grandma lifestyle, I was starting to feel the void where a meaningful relationship should be. Good-not-great wasn't the kind of life that would lead to my power-couple dreams.

Instantly the word *connection* flew through my brain, into my fingertips, through the pen, and onto the page. If I wanted to meet my person, I had to get out there and start actually connecting with other humans.

Not gonna lie, the word *connection* made me want to throw up a little (we'll talk soon about why that was a good thing). Really connecting would mean opening myself up to potential rejection, failure, and, even worse, success that could lead to losing myself again, like I had in middle school, with *That Metal Show,* and with Rob. I could feel myself being shoved against my Upper Limit, but for the first time in a long time, I wanted to shatter that barrier and keep rising. I was gonna run right through that finish line just as I had the night before, because becoming Jen 2.0, I realized, meant allowing others (specifically my future soulmate) to see me. Really see me.

SEEING LOVE

I'm a little bummed to tell you that my Year of Connection didn't get off to a great start. I was anxious all the time and felt kinda desperate. I feel gross admitting that to you, but I was clearly displaying what my teenage stepdaughter calls "pick me energy." Though it was clear none of the guys I met fit my dream scenario, I transformed myself into their perfect girl, even if it was the opposite of who Real Jen truly was. I found myself on dates with these Hamptons-obsessed, party animal, keeping-up-with-the-Joneses narcissists, telling them that of course I loved all that stuff too!

Despite these efforts, all I got were a lot of guys who would ghost me a few days after our date. Let's be real, people can smell desperation from a mile away, and being a "pick me" was a surefire way to deflect any form of connection.

After my fourth shitty date of the month with a douchebag who spent the whole evening staring at my boobs and talking about all the clubs he could get into, I came home frustrated as all hell. I slammed the door behind me, knocking my most prized possession, a framed *Wedding Singer* poster signed by my entire cast, from the wall in my entryway. I dropped to my knees to check the glass—still intact, whew!—and was struck by the realization, OMG, the Creation Process! Seeing the photo of me living out my dream on that poster was the exact reminder I needed. I realized I couldn't just achieve a goal and leave the rest to chance, so this is when I added the fifth step, Repeat It, to the Creation Process. I had to keep working to create my reality. The good news was I'd done it before—twice!—and I could do it again. I was going to use the same steps I used to become Linda and get my trainer shirt to connect with my soul mate. And as you already know, it worked!

If you're single and part of your Be Seen journey is to be seen by your future life partner, you're going to want to pull out your highlighter, because here is how my Year of Connection resulted in meeting and falling in love with Chris "the Super Connector" Winfield. Just like I did with *The Wedding Singer*, I started to visualize what it would be like to be madly in love with *my* guy. I watched a movie in my mind and saw myself with him in real time, then I wrote out what I saw. Here's the list I created:

1. Six feet tall

2. An entrepreneur

3. Into personal development / has a growth mindset

4. Lives on the Upper West Side

5. Doesn't drink alcohol

6. Works out at Equinox

7. Has tattoos

8. Healthy but not obsessed with fitness

9. Funny, good sense of humor

The man I mapped out couldn't have been more different from the guy I always thought I should want. I had spent years trying to make the "NYC finance dude" work for me because that's the box I thought I should check to impress all the people I was supposed to please. Giving myself permission to see the type of person *I* really wanted was freeing AF. I wish someone had given me this tip back then, so I'm giving it to you now: don't ever "should" on yourself, because it will only leave you with a big mess.

I got so excited about the guy on my list that I decided to search for a photo to make him even more real. I found an old travel magazine in the back of my drawer and feverishly flipped through it until I found a tall, buff guy looking over a tropical paradise from a balcony, holding a baby. I liked the image because you couldn't see the guy's face. He could be a representation of anyone I wanted him to be! I fell deep into the photo, picturing myself on the crisp white bed in the suite we had booked for our two-week Hawaiian vacation. Hair still wet from a morning dip in the ocean, lovingly watching him have a moment with our baby while I called room service, about to ask him what he wanted for breakfast. I held the image close to my heart, feeling a massive flush of future gratitude surge through me. Slowly, I drifted back to my little New York apartment, every part of me still buzzing with joy.

Every morning, I accessed this feeling. I even went a step further with my future gratitude practice and talked to my vision board guy, telling him how much I loved him and couldn't wait for us to find each other. And this was actually working. I was no longer being a "pick me" on dates because I was so familiar with *my* man (we "spoke" every day!). If a date didn't feel right, now I could leave without a second thought rather than pretend to be who they wanted. I wasn't anxious anymore because I knew my soulmate was out there—we just needed to cross paths.

One of my favorite things in the entire world is to walk miles around the city on Wonder Walks, like the ones we talked about while setting the SEEN in Chapter 1. That summer when I was deep in Project Soulmate, I'd take the subway to 14th Street on Saturdays, pop in my AirPods, and walk all the way back to the Upper West Side with Vision Board Guy. I would walk up Broadway and watch the city change neighborhood by neighborhood, blasting songs from my "get in the pocket" playlist and envisioning us hand in hand, headed back from a date night. With each step I milked my feelings of gratitude, joy, and love for this imaginary human. I must have gone on hundreds of Wonder Walks before my eventual second date with Chris, which ended up being a long walk uptown just like the walks I'd taken so many times on my own. Déjà vu on steroids!

DARE OF THE DAY

Clearly by this time I'd become a professional daydreamer. As we discussed in the beginning of this chapter, you can dream big all you want, but if you don't start *doing* big, you won't see your desires anywhere but in your head. James Altucher, author of *Reinvent Yourself* and host of the award-winning podcast *The James Altucher Show*, was only a "friend in my head" at the time, but during one of my walks with him in my ears, he introduced me to a life-changing exercise called Dare of the Day. It's intended to help introverts work their confidence muscles by putting in daily discomfort reps. You simply dare yourself to do one thing that scares you every single day.

Your subconscious mind, rather than your conscious thoughts, is usually the delivery vehicle for your Dare of the Day, and sometimes it creates your Dare of the Day because it knows what you need, even if you don't feel ready for it. Dare of the Day will look different for everyone who does it, but each dare *has* to be something that makes you think, *Oh god, I can't do that! There's no way I'm doing that.* But Dare of the Day is a pact you make with yourself, so once you receive your Dare of the Day, that's it. You're locked in.

James talked in his podcast about doing Dares of the Day in coffee shops and asking for a 10 percent discount for no reason. Even though he admitted (into my earbuds) that he was super nervous, he said each time made him feel a little more confident.

That's cool, I thought. *I can start implementing that.*

I added it to my journaling practice. Every morning, along with my gratitude list and letters to Vision Board Guy, I added a Dare of the Day.

I dare myself to do a Facebook Live.

I dare myself to talk to three new people.

What I found through this exercise became a daily practice for me, and eventually even inspired my podcast, *I Dare You,* where I end each episode with a dare for my audience, because by now you know as well as I do that if you don't *do something,* then nothing happens—and Dares of the Day? They make shit happen.

Try it right now (I dare you!). Over the next few days, keep your mind open to the inner voice that dares you to step outside of your comfort zone.

When you enter a new environment, what does it tell you to do? Does it challenge you to speak up during an important meeting or create that social media content you've been toying with? Is your inner voice pumping its fist and chanting, "Do it, do it, do it!" while you debate buying a ticket to that event you've been scared to attend by yourself?

That's how you know it's your Dare of the Day.

Important note: this does *not* mean you should ever use Dare of the Day as an excuse to do something dangerous or reckless. This is an exercise meant for those moments when you argue wistfully with your subconscious mind—*I wish I was brave enough to join that networking group that meets here every week,* not *I dare you to stand naked in the middle of the highway during rush hour.*

One of the biggest differentiators between a really successful person and an average person comes down to how often they stop themselves. Successful people hit the gas on their Dares of the Day because—say it with me—taking action is the only path to make your dreams become reality.

Worrying, on the other hand, is like praying for things you don't want. When you hit your Upper Limit, you make yourself stop at red lights that are only in your mind. So let me give you your first Dare of the Day. The next time you get that "when's the shoe gonna drop" feeling, instead of asking yourself how much you have to lose, try asking yourself this simple question:

How much better can it get?

What's the best thing that could happen if you finally click Purchase when browsing flights for that trip you've been putting off?

How much better could it get if you pitch a story to a network and they say yes?

Be daring!

As part of my commitment to my word of the year and Project Soulmate, I tried daring myself to actually go up and talk to cute guys who smiled at me instead of awkwardly looking down at my phone or walking away, secretly hoping they would follow me. (No wonder I was single for so long!) Each time I spoke to them, my belly did that little backflip that told me it was the right dare for my day. With each dare, and each date (good or bad), I became more and more confident that Vision Board Guy was out there. I just had to find him. And eventually, you know what?

Dare of the Day led me right to him.

WHO'S LUCKIER THAN US?

"Jen, you need to go back to that gym. There's someone there you need to meet."

A neon sign blinked on in my brain, blinding me as I walked by the building that used to be known as Reebok Sports Club. You remember—*the* Reebok Sports Club that fired me and banned me from ever coming back? It was that same building, but the signage above the door was different. In place of the Reebok logo, the word *Equinox* radiated in huge white halo-esque letters.

I did a quick Google search and discovered that Equinox had acquired Reebok, which meant it was no longer under the same management! I recognized that belly flip immediately. *There's my Dare of the Day.*

Since I'd made it my dare to walk back into that gym, I couldn't say no! Moments later, I found myself in the membership office, handing over my credit card. I was an Equinox member already, but since this was the Taj Mahal of Equinox gyms, working out here required a different membership tier. Not gonna lie, going back into that building and being able to easily afford my own membership felt pretty damn awesome (Did you spot that moment on my Badass List in Chapter 4?). What felt even better was bumping into one of the trainers I used to date when I worked there. You better believe I was excited to tell my ex-fling Jose all about how my business was thriving since leaving Reebok.

"You know," said Jose as he put the dumbbell he was holding back on the rack. "You should really meet this guy who works out here. He is an entrepreneur too, and I think he can help you." Before I could ask another question, Jose had already texted me a link to Chris "the Super Connector" Winfield's Facebook profile.

The big neon arrow flickered on again, casting bright light onto the word *Connector* under his photo—I mean, my word of the year was *connection*! I had to meet him. Networking with Chris could be good for my career and my business. Maybe he could "super connect" me to my Jay-Z. My Dare of the Day to join Equinox was already paying off. What I didn't realize was that with one tap of a finger, I was making one of the most important connections of my life.

After a few awkward private messages (Chris didn't have much DM game), we agreed to meet for a walk in Central Park. Not thinking this "meeting" was a date, I wore no makeup, black leggings, and a long-sleeved zip-up with thumbholes. As I waited for him on a park bench, I basked in the gorgeous sunshine of a rare 65-degree November afternoon in New York City. It was like a whole Upper West Side *You've Got Mail* situation. If you haven't seen the classic Tom Hanks and Meg Ryan rom-com, give yourself that gift and thank me later.

Chris, running late, strolled right up to that bench in his "too cool for school" aviator sunnies, and the first thing he ever said to me as he gestured to the amazing weather was, "Who's luckier than us?" I don't think he knew just how right he was.

That walk ended up being five hours long, and that neon arrow never turned off. Eventually, I and my six-foot-tall, hilarious, driven, law-of-attraction-personified entrepreneur with tattoos from the Upper West Side moved in together. Our new home was a sun-drenched three-bedroom apartment with floor-to-ceiling windows on the Upper West Side, and the view couldn't have been more different from the tiny little brick-wall view where I'd started. The coolest part about moving into our dream home together was the fact that I was easily able to pay half of the rent. On the day we moved in, Chris picked up my dog, Dexter, and looked out the window at the view I'd dreamed about for years, and another neon arrow buzzed on over his head, telling me, "Look over here! Quick, Jen! Come see!"

I couldn't understand why the scene felt so familiar, but I snapped a photo of the moment on my phone. Then it hit me: it was the picture from my vision board, only a thousand times better. Instead of a baby, he was holding my dog, and instead of Hawaii, he was looking out over my favorite city in the world. And instead of a nameless, faceless model, he was Chris. My Vision Board Guy. My Jay-Z. My dream turned reality. To see the actual photo, head on over to beseenbook.com/goodies!

FROM YEAR OF CONNECTION TO SUPER CONNECTION

When we first met, Chris's business was built around Unfair Advantage Live, the same event where I turned my epic fail into a dance party. Before I became part of it, Chris didn't rent out hotels and Times Square billboards or have famous speakers join him. All that came later. Back then, he ran the event from a little room with a screen and himself onstage. It was only one day, and he had nothing to sell the attendees at the end. One morning, about a week before UAL, I woke up to Chris typing frantically on his laptop. "I know exactly what I'm going to sell at the event," he said, homing in on the screen with a sly grin that I knew meant the game was on.

In an hour, he developed a program on a Google Doc that would have taken most people months to come up with. It was a "done with you" publicity program for business owners who wanted to get featured in the media. It was amazing, and sure enough, Chris Winfield Inc, soon to become Super Connector Media, took off.

By now, JLG Fitness had grown into a full-on personal transformation coaching business. I had expanded beyond fitness and was helping CEOs, celebrities, and high-performing entrepreneurs master their mindsets so they could build the body *and* the life of their dreams. I was earning multiple six figures and the company was entirely remote, so I had the freedom to work from anywhere. This meant I could hit the road with Chris to support him at events all over the country. I was having a ball and felt proud of what I'd created, but part of me wondered if I was still directly heading toward my Beyoncé/Tony Robbins vision or just sort of, you know, coming up alongside it.

The truth is, I was doing all the things I loved while supporting the man of my dreams, but something was still missing. I wasn't totally in the pocket, and deep down, I knew why. Watching Chris speak in front of thousands of people made me so proud, but when you're a performer, the desire to be onstage is something that's embedded in you. Every time I was in the front row watching, I was secretly wishing I was up there too.

"Jen," Chris said while jogging up a hill in San Diego. (Yes, this run was another Dare of the Day!) "What would it take for you to drop your company and become my partner in this business?"

And just like every other life-shifting moment on my path, I saw that neon sign, felt the flip in my belly, and took action on another dare. I shoved fear into the passenger seat of my car, sunsetted JLG Fitness for good, and stepped into my role as co-founder and chief mindset officer at Super Connector Media.

I've since achieved everything I saw in my perfect-day vision. I work alongside and come home to my Vision Board Guy every single day. I get to speak onstage and help people grow and develop their own businesses, brands, and mindsets, and I get to glam up and wear some hella cute outfits while I'm doing it! We created an amazing culture at our company where everyone feels supported and loved, and it's grown into an award-winning, multimillion–dollar business that has changed the lives of so many of our amazing clients.

THIS OR SOMETHING BETTER

Transitioning to teaching people how to be seen was a step I never saw myself taking back when I was daydreaming about being an actress, but that's the super amazing thing about creating You 2.0. The future you're building is constantly growing and changing. Sometimes, your goals are just stepping-stones toward a bigger and brighter future you never dared to dream of in the first place. Sometimes, what you think you want is a guy and a baby on a balcony of a chic hotel room in Hawaii, and what shows up is your soulmate holding a Maltese in your dream apartment in New York City—slightly different, but an outcome even better and perfectly suited to who you're becoming.

Here's the thing: you will never experience that future if you stay in visualizing mode. And you definitely won't if you continue stopping yourself when you've hit your Upper Limit. You have to take action. So, my friend, do something today that will move you one step closer to the vision you see. I dare you.

🎤 MIC DROP MOMENTS

- Beware the Upper Limit: the point where we stop moving forward because the fear of failure becomes greater than our belief in what's possible.

- The Law of Attraction tells us that like attracts like, but you can't spell "attraction" without ACTION.

- There is only ONE way to get unstuck when you've hit your Upper Limit, and that way is to *do something* that produces a tiny win.

- Instead of waiting for the other shoe to drop, ask yourself, "How much better can it get?"

- *This or something better:* Know when to transition to a new chapter in your life.

👏 A QUICK WIN

- Step out of your comfort zone by challenging yourself to a Dare of the Day.

PUT IT ON A POST-IT

- "Do Something!"

PART III

BE CONNECTED

. . . .

CHAPTER 8

YOU CAN'T SPELL "COMMUNITY" WITHOUT N-O

While I was writing this book, my dog, Dexter, went to heaven. He was my best friend for 14 years, through some of the toughest challenges of my life (many of which you've already read about). If you have any pets of your own, I know you understand that having to say good-bye to Dexter was one of the hardest things I've ever had to do.

The morning after he went to heaven, I was scheduled to do my daily Get Ready With Me Q&A Instagram Live at 9 A.M. Putting my makeup LIVE while answering questions every morning is one of the commitments I made to myself and my community. I started doing it as a dare of the day to get outside my comfort zone and form a deeper connection with my audience and it worked. To my surprise, it became one of my favorite rituals. I usually looked forward to doing it, but when I looked at myself in the mirror, it became clear that I was anything but camera ready. My face was puffy from crying, I had a massive zit on my chin, and I did *not* want to be seen.

It would have been so easy to bail, but I'd made a commitment to myself, and you know how serious I am about sticking to my commitments. So I splashed some cold water on my face, set up my phone, and turned on my camera. As I started my makeup routine, of course I started talking about Dexter. I was honest with my audience, admitting I was having a difficult time being there that day. My energy was much lower than usual until one of my dear friends, Amy Porterfield, hopped into the comments to tell me how much she loved me and how happy she was to see me still making content and keeping it real.

The cloud of sadness that had been raining on me since Dexter died began to clear a little. And it showed in my video—I perked up, and, with Amy behind me, sharing how I was feeling with thousands of people felt that much easier. Suddenly I wasn't just talking to a bunch of strangers; one of my closest friends was there. Soon I was smiling and telling my audience about Amy's book and all the incredible ways she's helped entrepreneurs.

I ended that morning feeling so much better than before I went live. I also received a long, heartfelt text from Amy about Dexter, where she shared her own journey with grief after losing a pet. I felt supported and loved, and my video was powerful because of my meaningful connection with someone who was in my corner.

This is what I want for you—to be surrounded by people who get it. It's no coincidence that my life changed so drastically during my Year of Connection, after all. Even once you've connected with Real You and traveled through time to find You 2.0, you'll never truly be seen without the right community behind you. When the people in your life don't support who you really are, it's easy to be scared of what they'll think when you start a business or make changes that promote your values. And with "friends" like that, it's no wonder you're afraid to be seen as Real You!

Genuine, heartfelt connection to other people is truly the unfair advantage that kicks your growth into hyperdrive, whether we're talking about business, relationships, or life goals, but it takes respect and boundaries on both sides to make sure you're building those relationships in a healthy, sustainable way. So in Part III, we're going to take the huge leaps you've been making internally in Parts I and II into the external world! We'll be learning tactical strategies to help you curate a community based on authentic connection that will make old-school, business card–style networking look as outdated as skinny jeans and side parts. Using strategies that have brought unexpected success to hundreds of my clients, I'll show you how to draw the right people into your vortex of Realness—and in doing so, turn them into your biggest cheerleaders, referral partners, accountability buddies, clients, and mentors.

And it all starts with one important word.

MEET YOUR NEW BEST FRIEND

The first member of your new "Be Seen" squad is someone you've definitely met before, though you might not like them much. But hear me out, because this frenemy is going to become one of the most empowering members of your team.

Allow me to (re)introduce you to the word *NO*.

NO is the word that's going to free you from what's holding you back. NO is going to launch you into your future, and I'll tell you exactly why.

The more I reconnected with Real Jen and what she really wanted, the more I began to notice that my friend group was holding me back. (That's putting it lightly!) If I'd made a live video about my dog dying while doing my makeup with a throbbing zit on my chin during my Miss Box of Junk days, the friends I had back then wouldn't have sent me love—they would have been weirded out. If I'd shown excitement about an achievement like being on the cover of *Strong* magazine, those friends would have probably tried to downplay it. I remember one instance from back then when I showed a friend that I was featured on the landing page of a major blog, and she immediately took all the steam from my excitement engine by bashing the writer, making me question if it was a good idea to have been featured by him. The next day I found out she had contacted him and pitched herself to be featured the following month.

Let me get really, really self-reflective with you for a second—I'm definitely not innocent in this situation. I attracted friends like this because that was my mindset too. Like attracts like, remember? I said yes to that group, again and again. During that season of my life, those friends and I would connect through complaining, being a victim to our circumstances and—let's be honest—talking shit about each other. We were all scared that if one of us became successful, it took away opportunities from the rest of us, so our "girls' lunches" were the opposite of supportive. In fact, they started to feel like a combination of a *Real Housewives* reunion episode and *Survivor*.

We connected through gossiping about other people, boo-hoo-ing about all the bad things that were happening or that could happen, and sneakily forming alliances so we could vote someone who threatened us off the island. Now that I look back, I know this was just a subconscious way for us to all feel a little better about our own insecurities. But in the moment, I thought it was friendship. I didn't even know that there was another way to connect with women.

When I learned about having an abundant mindset, and dipped my toe into personal growth, my friend group's way of communicating started to feel pretty gross to me. And when I tried to introduce a different way of thinking to them, it didn't go over well. Their lack of support and complete disinterest in my quest to build a business, strengthen my brand, and manifest a new life made me feel like I was doing something wrong. So I dimmed that part of myself. I'm ashamed to admit I totally hid in the wings, afraid to be seen, because I didn't think the people I was closest to would be in the audience cheering for me if I stepped out on that stage!

If you're reading this right now and nodding your head because it all sounds too familiar, I see you. I'm not just in your audience, I'm in your front row, and I'm giving you a standing ovation! But I'm also here with the tough love I wish someone had given me a lot sooner: it might be time to let go of those friends.

Real friends build you up, not tear you down.

Real friends celebrate your wins, not try to manipulate them for their own benefit.

Real friends cheer for you to succeed, not say "I told you so" when you fail.

Real friends want you to be seen for who you really are.

If your friends don't fit those descriptions, it's time to change the people you're connected to. Now I know that when you've been friends with someone for years, it feels borderline impossible and super scary to try to sunset the friendship.

It's so easy to feel like you owe something to your old friends, especially if you've been friends for a long time. There's even a psychological reason for this: You know when you sink a couple hundred dollars into fixing your car, only for one more problem to pop up? So you sink another couple hundred bucks into *that* issue, and a week after you get it home, you start to hear a strange noise when you turn on the A/C?

I should sell my car, you think, but immediately correct yourself. *No, I can't. I just spent so much money on it!*

This is called the sunk cost fallacy, which tricks us into sticking with our past investments because we've spent whatever amount of money, time, or resources on them—even when those investments stop serving our best interests.[1] But when it comes to our community and relationships, we need to be focused on the future, not the past. Sometimes that means saying no when the mechanic tells you that you need a new exhaust system and yes to the junkyard that offers to take that old clunker off your hands. When a relationship stops being good for you and any attempts to fix it just lead to more problems, it's time to gracefully retire that connection and just say NO.

And here's the secret about your new bestie NO: It's actually wearing a disguise, and underneath that NO is a hidden YES. Learning how to say no to a friendship that you've outgrown means you're rejecting your investment in the relationship of your past so you can invest that energy in your future instead. By distancing yourself from unhealthy relationships and setting emotional boundaries for yourself, you're actually creating space for something new.

That YES has been your *real* BFF all along.

When you say no to hanging out with your old crew who triggers you and puts you down, you're saying yes to going for a walk with a new friend who is so excited to hear about your big ideas.

When you say no to your ex's wedding invitation, you're saying yes to an evening spent building your brand or going on a date with a potential new partner.

When you say no to someone who was your friend for the past 30 years of your life, you're saying yes to someone who will be your friend and grow with you for the next 30 years.

When you say no to something that doesn't serve you, you're saying yes to growth, and development, and above all, yourself.

When I gave myself permission to create boundaries in my old friendships, I suddenly found myself with so much more time and energy, which I then devoted to what really mattered. It didn't happen overnight, but it helped me slowly shift my priorities to myself and my new community of friends who shared my mindset.

GETTING COZY WITH REJECTION

While you're learning to say no, there's another hard lesson I'm going to need you to learn, because remember, if it's healthy for you to say no, then it's healthy for other people to say it as well. And that, my friend, means you need to get comfy with *hearing* no.

I wish I could tell you the road to being seen as You 2.0 will be smooth, but that's not how life works. Life is all about rejection, and it comes in all different shapes and forms. I felt rejected when my parents divorced, when I didn't get my dream role (and the hundreds of other roles I didn't book), when Hedge Fund Rob cheated on me, and when Dexter died. Life took a look at me and said, "Nope. I'm taking something from you. I know you wanted this, but you're not getting it," and it hurt! There are pages and pages of journal entries from my days as an actress commiserating about what it felt like not to get what I wanted.

I can't get rejected again. I just can't, I wrote, depressed after a long day of going from casting room to casting room and hearing, "No, thank you" over and over again. I didn't want to do it anymore. I was so sick of a life that felt like rejection after rejection. Now I can actually look back at that time and smile, because if I didn't have years of practice with rejection, I wouldn't be able to teach you what I wish I knew back then when it comes to the truth about the word *NO*.

The sad truth is that fear of rejection stops so many of us from putting ourselves out there and being seen as our Real Selves. Read that again, because I said "fear of rejection," not "fear of failure." We don't fear failure. We fear other people seeing us fail and possibly being rejected as a result. If we could fail without anyone ever knowing about it, we'd have no problem trying new things, but instead, we avoid making ourselves vulnerable to anyone who could potentially see us and say, "You're not good enough."

Ready for your superpower origin story?

We all put so much effort into achieving our dreams and realizing that You 2.0 vision, and hearing no when we put ourselves out there is really freaking awful. After all, what if you take a risk and hit Publish on that post and then end up with haters in the comments? What if you finally reach out to the person who could connect you with an influencer you're dying to have promote your new product, and they say, "No, sorry, I can't put you in touch" or "No, sorry, that influencer isn't interested and never will be."

It's worst-case scenario stuff, right?

Wrong!

What if you could start to embrace the word *no* because every time you hear it, you already have a plan in place to turn it around to your benefit and bounce back stronger and better than ever?

With these five steps, you can. Because if you can learn how to love the shit out of rejection, there is nothing in the world that can stop you.

1. Diagnose the Situation

So you've put yourself out there, and you've heard the no. Now it's time to slap on a smile, avoid feeling your feelings, and immediately move on as if it never happened!

Aha! Gotcha. That was a test.

Diagnosis is a three-part process. First, what you're *really* going to do when you hear no is take stock of the circumstances. Ask yourself: What just happened? Why did they say no?

Really give yourself the space to think about it. Get a piece of paper or your journal and write it all down. Call someone from your community and talk about it. It's so easy to feel ashamed when you're rejected, but the easiest way to free yourself from that shame is actually to talk to someone. It's such a huge exhale for me to call my friend Lori or talk to Chris after I've been rejected. Saying it out loud feels like I'm releasing the power that rejection has over me.

Acknowledging your rejection leads you to the second part, which is taking responsibility. Ask yourself, "What did I do wrong here?" Don't allow yourself to slip into that victim mentality where the rejection was completely out of your control. Remember, if you're completely out of control, there's nothing you can do to fix it. And wouldn't you rather fix it for next time? Maybe you didn't research your audience enough. Maybe you sent your pitch or hit Post at the wrong time. Maybe you sent it to the wrong person. And maybe it has absolutely nothing to do with anything you did, and it's super important to acknowledge that.

The point is, you get to choose how you show up here. Are you a leader who takes charge and accepts responsibility for your actions, or are you someone who is constantly blaming other people for your failures?

When you've had a moment to sit with this, it's time to think about Part III: Ask yourself, "What did I learn from this?"

Every single failure, every single mishap, is there to teach you something. So write it out, talk it out, diagnose it, and go deep. I promise you, the more you do this, the more comfortable you'll start to feel.

2. Deal with the Feelings

And speaking of feelings, that brings us to step two. When you don't allow yourself to feel your feelings after rejection, those feelings aren't just gonna disappear. Nope, if you shut them down and don't allow yourself to experience them, they're most likely going to manifest themselves in a whole lotta other ways, like in your relationships, or your work, or your health. I used to try to personal development myself right out of feeling anything bad. Two crappy things would happen as a result of this: one, I wouldn't ever learn the real lesson from the rejection because I wouldn't allow myself to fully experience it; and two, those emotions I didn't allow myself to feel would always seep out into other areas of my life. I would often feel resentful, depressed, and disconnected and not know why months or even years later. Bottom line, I needed to deal with my feelings, or they were going to remain unresolved and eventually deal with me.

Now, when I experience my emotions after a rejection, I give myself a feelings container. In other words, I let myself feel bad within the time limits I set.

"Okay, Jen," I'll tell myself after hearing no from an event organizer. "For the rest of the day, we can embrace the suck. Let's go home, put on our sweatpants, park ourselves in front of the TV, and watch *Bake-Off*. If we happen to cry during that binge watch, that's okay, because we're gonna embracet the shitty feelings tonight."

Maybe you're thinking this seems counterintuitive, so let me explain. Just like practicing taking responsibility makes it easier to take responsibility in the future, practicing feeling like a dumpster fire helps that fear of experiencing the fire get a little smaller the next time. Every time I plop myself on that couch and give myself a moment where I don't have to force myself to bounce right back, I know that tomorrow will be better. I know that there's a light at the end of my tunnel of doom. When we can establish trust in ourselves to get through any painful situation and come out the other side ready for what's next, we're teaching ourselves that negative emotions are temporary. And more importantly, what is permanent is our resilience and our ability to strap those negative, fear-driven emotions into the passenger seat and try again.

3. Discover the Hidden Yes

Every single crappy thing that has ever happened to me in my life has led me to becoming the person I am today. Even when I thought it was the worst thing in the world, it happened for a reason. Allllllllll those nos brought me to countless yeses that were a million times better, but I can only connect those dots when I look backward with hindsight.

Remember all that gratitude work you did in Part II? Bring it all back, 'cause here is where it's going to come in handy. After you've diagnosed the situation and dealt with your feelings, it's time to make a list. (I think it's pretty clear by now how much I love lists!)

Right now, on a piece of paper or in your notes app or on a napkin, I want you to list every rejection or failure that turned into something great. Which of your best friends would you never have met if you'd gotten that job on the other side of the country? What offer would you have had to decline if that network had accepted your pitch? (If you're having trouble thinking of these, consult your Badass List, because I guarantee you had to deal with some rejections to get to each of those incredible, badass moments.)

Start training yourself to look for the hidden yeses in all of your nos. Get yourself into gratitude mode and start viewing all that rejection through a lens of extreme thankfulness. There is always something to be grateful for, even in the worst situations. The moment you can teach yourself to operate from a position of gratitude is the moment you learn that you can't be anxious and angry and sad and grateful at the same time, because gratitude rules it all.

Got your list? Now that you have something to be grateful for, you have something to celebrate. That's right, I'm asking you to celebrate yourself for being rejected. Hell yes! You took action. You did the damn thing, even though you were scared! And every time you take more action and toe the line of your comfort zone, you're building up that confidence bank. In fact, I'd go so far as to say you're on your way to yet another amazing entry on your Badass List. So go ahead and celebrate the shit out of yourself for getting that no, because it means you took a risk. Here's a fun secret: I do not know of a single successful person on this planet who got there without taking at least one risk. You're on your way, and *that* is something to be grateful for.

4. Develop a Plan

Look at the list you made in step one, where you list out everything you learned from this experience. Now that you're in the right mindset about it all, it's time to figure out what the heck to do next.

What do you want your new outcome to be?

Say you didn't get a media segment that you pitched. Yes, that sucks. Knowing what you know now, and having completed steps one through four, what new outcome would you like? Do you want to pitch that segment to a different station? Or redevelop your segment for the same station?

Whatever you decide, now it's time to figure out how to make that new outcome a reality.

List out three steps to get you there. Not 5 steps, not 17, not 10. *Three steps*, because I want this to be simple and actionable, and you shouldn't need more than three steps to kickstart your momentum. Much of the rest of this book is going to contain some amazing tactics to keep in your toolkit for exactly this type of situation, so stay tuned!

5. Do Something

Remember that pink sticky note on my computer? *DO SOME-THING*. By now, you know why the Law of Action is so important, and through this five-step process, you've developed your own next steps. So now it's time to put it all together and take your own advice. Take that first step toward your new outcome.

This doesn't need to be right away—remember, it's important to deal with your feelings, and sometimes that means taking a shower, going for a walk, or shutting down your computer and putting your phone on Do Not Disturb. Taking action in this way, by letting yourself marinate on your plan and revisit it tomorrow, is a great way to gain some distance from that original rejection. The important thing is that you do take action and move forward. Turn that no into a yes.

You've got this.

THE REAL UNFAIR ADVANTAGE

"Jen, how do you book speaking engagements? How do you make sales? How do you market yourself?" These are the most commonly asked questions on my daily Get Ready With Me Q&A Instagram Live.

The key, I tell them again and again, is building and maintaining strong, meaningful relationships. Those relationships—our community—aren't a want, they're a *need*. We're not meant to live life alone. In ancient Greece, exile was a punishment reserved for murderers, and in ancient Rome, it was considered an alternative to the death penalty.[2] In medieval Europe, excommunication from the church (the most important bond in a community) was the heaviest punishment you could possibly inflict on someone. People who were excommunicated couldn't eat or drink with anyone or buy and sell goods to anyone in the community. Once they died, they weren't even allowed to be buried on consecrated ground and were considered damned by the church, so they would never even be able to join their community of loved ones in the afterlife!

In a 75-year study done by Harvard University known as the Grant Study, researchers asked the question, "What makes a good life?"[3] They found that relationships are the single most important predictor of success in life. According to the study, people who have more deep and positive relationships are not only happier but more financially successful than those who have fewer good relationships. Solid relationships also correlated strongly with lower rates of anxiety, more overall happiness, and greater life satisfaction by the age of 75.

Need more proof? Anthropologist Robin Dunbar made a surprising discovery about community that culminated in a theory we now know as Dunbar's Number. He claimed that humans thrive best when they have a community of about 150 people. This theory is backed up by history: military fighting units have traditionally been most successful when under 200 people, and historical villages were once known for breaking into two whenever the population exceeded 150.[4]

The world has changed a lot since then, and with the rise of social media, Dunbar has elaborated on his theory by introducing layers of our communities. Humans, he argues, have social groups that contain:

- 1–2 special friends
- 5 intimate friends
- 15 best friends

- 50 good friends

- 150 "just friends"

- 500 acquaintances

Our brains, Dunbar claims, only have the capacity to handle a finite number of relationships at once in our lives. There are only so many hours in a day, after all, and we only have so much energy. With that in mind, it's more important than ever to say no to the people who don't fit in with the community we want so we can say yes to the relationships that will bring us closer to our goals![5]

Weeding Your Garden

There are some people you might not be able to weed from your life completely, like family members, or your boss, or your nosy next-door neighbor. Negative influences are always going to be there, 'cause hey, haters gonna hate—it's part of life! But even if you can't yank them off your stage entirely, what you can do is dim their spotlights and flood the stage with other people who make you feel good. Soon, you'll be surrounded with people who love you and see your vision for your future. The music of their support will be so loud, you'll play those negative people right off the stage like their speech has run too long at the Oscars.

But what about those people you love who don't "get it," but you *really* want them to? You're growing and changing, and you want them to get healthy with you, or start practicing self-care with you, or join you on your new business venture. How do you convince them to change with you?

The hard truth is that you can't. You know that old saying, "You can lead a horse to water, but you can't make him drink?" The same goes for the people in your life.

The only way you can tempt the people you care about toward change is to lead them to that "water" and hope they're as thirsty as you are. They'll most likely only resent you if you force it down their throats. You need to be the priority when it comes to personal growth, and when you lead by example, it's easier for others to come along for the ride if it feels right to them. If not, they'll go another way. It might hurt, but that's their choice, and ultimately, it's in both your best interests.

Leading by example is the best way to weed out the people who don't support your new mindset, and to say no to what doesn't serve you anymore, which brings us right back to no and its tricksy disguise. Building a new community is less about rejecting your old life, and more about being intentional about what you say yes to. It's about keeping your eyes on You 2.0 and saying yes to those opportunities that light up with neon lights. Remember, you're not rejecting other people; you're accepting yourself.

Believe me, the people from your old life who are worthy of your new life are going to take notice. And when they see all the incredible results you're getting, those horses are going to get thirsty.

From here on out, we are expanding from personal growth and personal relationships to being able to be seen by your community, your professional network, and your audience. A powerful community of people will hold you accountable and empower you to magnify your business, which will help you be seen in a big way, but those magical, fulfilling relationships don't happen overnight, and you do have to be intentional and strategic about building them. At the end of the day, your network is your net worth, and these next few chapters are where you'll start to truly build it.

Tuning out the noise of people who don't matter is the only way to find the ones who do matter. You have to create opportunities for yourself to meet and connect with them, being diligent about turning casual acquaintances into real connections who can see and celebrate Real You—and that means knowing how to say no, hear no, and understand the powerful opportunities that lie in disguise behind each.

🎤 MIC DROP MOMENTS

- Your network has the power to turn your day around, for good or for bad. A good, supportive community will not only allow you to be seen as Real You, but they will empower you to make yourself be seen on an even larger scale.

- Genuine, heartfelt connection to other people is truly the unfair advantage that kicks your growth into hyperdrive, whether we're talking about business, relationships, or life goals.

- Community isn't just a want, it's a *need*. Humans need other humans.

- Countless studies like the Harvard Grant Study show us that we thrive best when we're around other people, and other scientists like Dunbar have shown that we can handle a finite number of close relationships in our lives, so it's extra important to be mindful of the people you let into your circle.

- "No" is your new best friend (because it's secretly a yes in disguise).

    ○ Hearing no is hard, but remember: it's a no for right now, not a no forever.

    ○ Saying no is also difficult due to the sunk cost fallacy, but saying no to relationships and opportunities that no longer serve you will allow you to say yes to new ones in the future that do.

👏 **A QUICK WIN**

- Pick one time you were rejected and work the 5 steps:

  - Diagnose the situation.

  - Deal with your feelings.

  - Declare that it's for you.

  - Develop a plan.

  - DO SOMETHING.

✍️ **PUT IT ON A POST-IT**

- Every no is secretly a yes to something else.

CHAPTER 9

HOW TO FALL IN LOVE WITH ASKING FOR HELP

This might not be a huge surprise to you, but I love getting my photo taken. Something about being in front of the camera brings out that little girl rocking out to "Thriller" in my parents' basement. In fact, if you were one of my friends during elementary school, there is a very high chance I made you play "photoshoot" with me, which entailed putting on all of my mom's makeup and posing for pictures in every old dance recital costume I had. I still feel the most in the pocket during photoshoots, so what I'm about to tell you might sound a little weird or even shocking.

I H-A-T-E *hated* asking people to take my picture. To be clear, I was totally cool with paying people to take my photo because I felt like there was a fair value exchange, but I could be on vacation with a friend I hadn't seen in years, standing in front of a famous landmark, and looking cute AF, but the second my friend said, "Maybe we should ask someone to take a picture of us," I locked up tighter than the leather pants I used to wear on *That Metal Show.*

Nope.

No thank you.

Couldn't do it.

I absolutely couldn't fathom asking someone to interrupt whatever they were doing to point a camera at me while I posed. It just felt gross. I always felt like it was such an inconvenience, and I had a hard time getting past the idea that I was putting someone out by asking them to do something for me. For a long time, I never made the connection that this was more than just a specific aversion to asking about photos, until one day, I experienced something that completely shifted my mindset.

A few years ago, Chris and I were at the Santa Monica Pier in California, having the most magical day ever. It was straight from a movie montage with an upbeat pop song playing in the background. We rode the Ferris wheel, ate some junk food, and played games—I even won us a stuffed tiger. I felt like we were a couple in a story, falling in love and having the time of our lives on that pier. I wished I could make the moment last forever, but eventually the sun started to sink over the Pacific Ocean, and we headed back to our hotel. I turned around for one last look at the site of my perfect day, and the pier was gorgeous, the rides all lit up with the sunset in the background.

"We need to take a picture," I said to Chris, my eyes roving over the scene. I could already see the post I'd share online—the whole day was so Instagrammable—but when I tried to get a selfie, I realized I couldn't get everything in the background.

"Just ask someone to take it," Chris suggested, when it became pretty clear neither of us had arms long enough to get the shot.

I glanced at the people around us, all in the middle of their *own* perfect days, and felt my belly flip. "Absolutely not!"

"Oh, come on," he said. "There's nothing wrong with asking for help!"

"That's not what this is about," I argued.

"Isn't it?"

I was speechless—I knew how to ask for help, didn't I? But before I even had a chance to consider it further, Chris got a little grin on his face that I knew meant trouble. He said, "Come on. I dare you."

He'd caught me, and he knew it. I couldn't say no to a Dare of the Day! It was my weakness! I narrowed my eyes, throwing him a teasing glare, then scanned the crowd for someone to ask until I settled on a woman walking past us.

"Hi," I said, approaching her. "I'm so sorry to stop you. Please feel free to say no, but would you take a picture of my boyfriend and me in front of the pier? I'm so sorry." I was physically cringing from mortification. What if she was in a hurry? What if she felt obligated?

But she smiled and said, "Sure."

The woman positioned us in front of the Ferris wheel and proceeded to direct Chris and me in a full-on, 10-minute photoshoot that I swear to you was more thorough than the last time I was featured in a magazine, snapping shots of us from every angle, posing us, zooming in and out.

"Right there," she said, after asking us to step to the right and then just a little bit back to the left. "Chris, put your arm around her. Okay, now look at each other and smile. Now give us a kiss! Yes, just like that! You two are adorable!"

I looked at Chris with laughter in my eyes. This woman was having the time of her life! She finally handed my phone back to me, and I was shocked to see that she was practically in tears. Then, surprising me even more, before I could thank her, she was thanking *me*!

"Thank you so much," she said. "You know, I used to be a photographer at Disney World, and it was the best job I ever had. It was the joy of my life to take other people's photos, and I don't do it anymore. I almost forgot how great it made me feel, and taking these for you made my entire day. So thank you for asking me to help out."

We parted ways with a smile, and I learned a lesson that day I will never forget. I *had* been afraid to ask for her help, but now I could barely remember why in the face of her reaction. Asking for help, I learned, *helps* others.

THE GIFT OF THE ASK

Think back to the last time someone you love—a family member, or a friend, or your favorite co-worker—asked you for help. How did it make you feel?

I bet it made you feel important because you were able to provide that person with something they couldn't do or get for themselves.

I bet it made you feel seen.

Hands down, one of the fastest ways to feel great about yourself is to help someone else. So by extension, when you ask someone else for help, you're giving that other person the opportunity to feel phenomenal by helping you. (How's that for logic?) If I hadn't asked that woman on the pier for help, I would have been depriving her of a moment that changed her entire day. She got to provide value for us along with feeling great about doing what she loved! But this applies to so much more than a magical day at an amusement park. How many times have you stopped yourself from asking for help with a pitch or for an introduction to someone who can help you achieve your business goals?

Every time you don't ask someone for help, you're depriving them of a moment to feel seen, important, and valued. When you ask for their assistance, you're telling them that you trust that they are gifted enough to help you with something that you couldn't possibly accomplish alone, and you're giving them an opportunity to feel fantastic for helping you.

BECOMING A MASTER ASKER

I make no secret that one of my biggest goals in life is to be the greatest motivational speaker of all time. But let's get something straight here: the massive wave of imposter syndrome that radiates through me as I write that statement still makes me feel like I wanna puke a little. But I know that the more I put my goal into words (no matter how petrified I am of failing or looking stupid for making such a massive proclamation), the more comfortable my subconscious mind will be with thinking of it as reality. And, as we discussed already in Chapter 5, the more your subconscious mind believes you've already achieved your desired outcome, the more clearly the path toward accomplishing the goal will become. I also want you to keep in mind that the more people who know your goal, the greater the chances that someone will connect you to someone who can help you, or even directly give you the opportunity. You never know who's listening (or reading! Hi there, event planners, I'm available!).

So I've been putting that biatch fear in the passenger seat of the car and doing all the things I'm teaching you in this book to create the ultimate vision that I see for Jen 2.0. I really mean it when I say we are in this together! When it comes to taking action toward my specific goal of being the best speaker in the world, the biggest needle-moving strategy so far has been investing time and money in building relationships. I know what you might be thinking—investing money in relationships? Does that mean like "buying friends"? No, I like to refer to it as paying to get in the room.

Let me explain. I invest over six figures a year on joining masterminds. Before you visualize a group of futuristic space cadets with huge brains meeting on a spaceship in the middle of a far-off galaxy (when I first heard the word *mastermind*, that was my visual), know that a mastermind is a group of business owners who gather a few times a year to connect and help each other. Motivational speaker and best-selling author Tony Robbins says it best, "proximity is power," and masterminds are a great way to get in proximity with the people who can help you get where you want to go.

One of the masterminds that I invested in had the greatest impact on my business (and life) so far, and it cost $100,000 for the year. Yes. I know. That's a lot of money, and yes, you better believe I was absolutely terrified to bet that much of our company's hard-earned cash on me making magic happen in 365 days with this clique of uber-successful people that I didn't know. When you drop that much coin to be part of something though, you know that the people beside you—who are also investing that much in themselves—are going to be super high level. Or to put it in the words of my limiting beliefs at the time, I was probably going to be the least successful person in the room. And while I was scared shitless, I knew that if I wanted to push through my Upper Limit and continue growing, I needed to be around people who were thinking and doing bigger than me. The financial investment was accountability on steroids that would force me to show up even when fear was throwing a rager in my mind. Speaking of fear, I felt so nervous and out of place during the welcome dinner that I could barely stand up and say my name in front of everyone. My imposter syndrome was a 10 out of 10 and I started feeling like I had no right to be there amid all those millionaires and successful entrepreneurs. What value did I have to offer them? Who the hell was I to be in that room?

But I'd made an investment, and I had no choice but to show up even if fear was in my passenger seat screaming profanities. I had six figures riding on our business getting a return on this investment, so there was no room for fear's bullshit symptoms to get in my way.

So I gave fear the finger, channeled Jen 2.0, and made a commitment to allow myself to be seen by every member of this mastermind. I sat in the front row of every session; I raised my hand and asked questions even if I secretly thought I might sound totally stupid. I engaged with the speakers and made it a point to introduce myself to the members I didn't know. I kept showing up, making myself visible, and taking action. And as we know (thanks to Chapter 3!), action is what initiates the tiny wins that give you momentum and confidence over time. So the more I showed up, the quieter fear's voice became, and I slowly started to feel like I truly belonged in the room.

As time went on, I noticed every speaker I ever saw at that mastermind was a man. I asked around and learned there had never been a woman keynote speaker on that stage, so I made it a Dare of the Day to get myself up there and be the first. The only way to do it was to ask, and thankfully, I knew if the answer was no, it wasn't going to kill me—thanks, Chapter 8! So with my fingers shaking, I texted Dan Fleyshman, who ran the mastermind, and asked if I could speak on his stage. His response? An overwhelming yes!

But before I get any further in the story, let's rewind, because—and I need to be clear on this—this was *not* as easy as shooting him a quick text to say, "Hey, can I speak at your mastermind?"

Nope, absolutely not. In order to convince Dan that he should help me when I asked, I had to make sure I provided value to him first. Dan wasn't going to let just anyone on that stage—some of his past speakers were people like Tony Hawk, Mike Busta Rhymes, Cedric the Entertainer, and Alex Rodriguez. Since I'm no Arod, I needed to (a) figure out how I could prove to Dan that I could serve up value to his audience like nobody's business, and/or (b) help *Dan* so much that he would be open to me making an ask because of the Law of Reciprocity (we will talk about this amazing concept in a few minutes). So I went to work on both, providing as much value to Dan as I possibly could. I engaged with Dan's content online, referred new members to the mastermind, gave a fabulous testimonial about the experiences he puts together, and when he referred new clients to our agency, I always hooked them up on his behalf. I'd provided so much value to Dan that by the time I asked him for help, he was excited to finally reciprocate all I'd been doing for him.

After I felt confident that the value I gave was more or equal to the level of the ask I was about to make, the next part of the equation was just as important: pitching my ask to Dan in a thoughtful, intentional way by taking into consideration what he needed. He needed his mastermind members to get a lot of value from a keynote speaker, and those mastermind members needed to learn how to get themselves in front of the media. Go figure—this was my specialty! I had my angle.

When you're pitching the media, pitching to be on a podcast, or pitching your living room to host next month's book club, you need to think about what that person wants. What is their goal, and how can *you* help them get there?

In my message to Dan, I barely mentioned myself. Instead, I angled my ask entirely in terms of how I could provide value to his mastermind members by teaching them how to get in front of the media. I made sure Dan knew I had a talk that I'd used before, and sent him a video so he could see it for himself, and then I asked, "Is that something you'd be open to?" I didn't say a word about me or my personal goals. The best part? When Dan replied "Yes, absolutely!" we were both getting something great from the experience.

I crushed that talk, by the way. So not only did I make Dan look great by providing a ton of value for his members, I also achieved my goal of being the first female speaker at the 100 Million Mastermind, and then followed it up by speaking at Dan's other mastermind for real estate professionals. Both those opportunities led to me being seen by other influential people with masterminds, who then asked me to speak at their events. Not only did this one stage lead to other stages, it also led to millions of dollars in revenue for our agency. The success built on itself again and again, but only because I had the guts to make the ask.

GIVE A LITTLE, GET A LITTLE

The sad truth is, not everyone you ask is going to be excited and willing to help you right away and that's okay. Sure, you could get lucky and land an ex-photographer in front of the Santa Monica Pier, but most of the time, you're going to have to put in some work in the form of relationship capital to get the enthusiastic "hell yes" you're looking for—give a little to get a little.

Think about it. When someone does something kind for you, you're that much more inclined to want to return the favor, right? If you receive a random DM from a stranger asking you to promote their page, you don't have a lot of incentive to lend a hand. But if that same stranger has been sharing your posts, responding to your Insta stories, stitching your TikToks, driving new followers to your platform, and leaving reviews for your products, you're a lot more likely to recognize their name and want to help out in return.

That's called the law of reciprocity, a concept of social psychology that basically stops humans within shared communities from being dicks to each other all the time. We've been taught this since childhood ("Treat others the way you want to be treated") and all throughout human history, good or bad ("An eye for an eye").

Countries literally go to war to repay favors to other countries from decades or centuries ago, and our entire system of economics ("You give me this item and I will give you this money, which has equal worth to you") is based on exchanging value.

Reciprocity relies on connection, trust, and mutual respect. In his book *Influence: The Psychology of Persuasion*, Dr. Robert Cialdini lays out example after example of how reciprocity is an integral part of human interaction. Back in the caveman days, humans exchanged food, supplies, and skills, creating a tight-knit weave of obligation to one another because they recognized that one person couldn't do it all. They needed help to get everything done, and to get that help, they had to share their own skills in return. What's more, humans have proven again and again that while asking for help provides better results the more someone likes you, the sense of obligation to repay a favor completely overpowers everything else. What that means for you is that providing value to the people around you is, quite possibly, the best way to get help in return.

Now, I know how this sounds. Angling for a specific result risks making any help you offer feel transactional, and I'm warning you now, people can smell that shit from a mile away. Have you ever received a cutesy DM from someone you haven't talked to in years? From the second you get that first "hey you :)" notification, I bet your bullshit alarm is ringing off the hook. Sure enough, within minutes they probably try to sell you something.

Keep that feeling in mind when the shoe's on the other foot. When you help people in a sincere way, it's going to come back to you—but it might not come back the way you think, and what's important is that you don't start to expect certain results. In fact, it's important to not expect *any* results. Providing value needs to be an act of service, not an act of expectation. Your giving has to come from the heart because it's then, and only then, that you'll build that relationship into something authentic and powerful— something that yields long-game value for everyone involved.

In the game of reciprocity, you need to shift your mindset from a sequence of "give, give, give, give, expect" to "give, give, give, give, ask."

Let's talk about that asking.

THE TOP 20 TOOL

What would you say if I told you I have a powerhouse exercise that will help you get anything you want in 20 days or less all while helping you build powerful long-term relationships? My husband, Chris, designed this system, which I—and thousands of our clients—have used to book dream stages, land major podcasts, get featured in mega publications, and even meet their soulmates!

We're going to do this right here, right now, so get yourself a pen and paper.

Start by believing this: you're only one connection away from That Thing you want, that big hairy audacious goal of yours. Somewhere in your network is a link that will get you there. Write that goal at the top of your paper. I'll give you an example:

Goal: Be featured in *Forbes*

Next, you're going to draw four columns on your paper, and label them like this.

For a printable Top 20 Chart, head on over to beseenbook.com/goodies

Now, in that leftmost column, under People, list 20 people in your life network who have a connection to your goal. Not just your Instagram network or your business network; I'm talking your *whole* life network, aka anyone you've ever met who has any kind of connection with your goal—in this case, the media, or more specifically, *Forbes*. Aunts, uncles, cousins, your sister's ex-boyfriend. Their connection to your goal doesn't have to be a great one. It can be wimpy or tenuous, or the person can be someone you haven't spoken to in years. Don't worry about any of the details yet; just focus on those people. Look at your phone contacts, social media connections, and high school yearbook if you need to.

Got your 20 people? Great, now it's time to move over to the second column, influence. On a scale of 1–10, you're going to rate each of the people on your list in terms of how influential they are. How many followers do they have on Twitter? How much

PEOPLE	INFLUENCE	HELP	TOTAL
1.			
2.			
3.			
4.			
5.			
6.			
7.			
8.			
9.			
10.			
11.			
12.			
13.			
14.			
15.			
16.			
17.			
18.			
19.			
20.			

power would they have to get you featured in *Forbes*? Let's say your sister's ex-boyfriend is a writer at *Forbes*, so you rate him a 10. Your best friend has 100,000 followers on Instagram, but her audience is way different from yours—she'd be rated more like a 4.

In the Help column, you're going to think about your relationship with each of those people. In this column, you're going to rate each person on a scale of 1–10 based on the following question: *How likely is this person to help me?* Think in terms of your relationship and how much value you've provided to them in the past. Your sister's ex? Probably a 1 or 2, especially if you haven't spoken to him since their breakup (oof, and you'll probably need to take into account whether it was a messy one, and who was the dumper vs. the dumpee . . .), but your best friend (hopefully) scores a 10. Likewise, a new co-worker you met just a week ago probably scores a lot lower than a professional contact you've been helping to promote for years.

In the final column, add up the scores from the middle two columns, and then sort these scores in order, so the highest totals are at the top, and the lowest are at the bottom.

Congratulations, friend. You've just created the most powerful networking tool you'll ever use.

The people at the top of the list, with totals of 18–20, are your golden geese. These are the people who both have influence and are likely to want to help you on this specific goal, so you can reach out to them for help—right now if you want! Because you've hopefully already been working the law of reciprocity and providing either personal or professional value to them, they're probably pretty likely to say, "Yeah, I love the work you do in your field, and our readers would love to learn from you. Of course I'll talk to my editor at *Forbes*!"

But those people a little further down the list, especially the ones with lower "help" scores, aren't well positioned for you to ask them for help. So instead of asking them for anything, what I want you to do is find a way to do one thing that provides value for them. Do they have a book coming out? Buy a copy and share a picture of it in your stories. Do they have a podcast? Leave a five-star review, take a screenshot, and send it over to them. Are they getting married? Send them a gift or a thoughtful card. I don't care what it is, but what's important is that it provides value that helps them achieve *their* goals. It's your job to figure this out. Asking someone, "Hey, how can I help you?" takes what should be help and turns it into a homework assignment for them. Instead, consider this *your* homework. Slowly and consistently start to do things that help provide value for them—it absolutely *cannot* be a "one and done" deal. Over time, that number in the Help column is going to increase.

By using this Top 20 tool as a guide, you can start asking for help *and* helping others, bringing those numbers up until you have a strong, powerful network that is not just able, but practically begging to help you achieve your goal.

Our network is the most powerful tool at our disposal because it's like an endless web. Everyone we're connected with is connected to their own entire network; it's like the *Six Degrees of Kevin Bacon* game, only in this case, "Kevin Bacon" represents your goal. It's up to you to ask for help and leverage your network to get you there, but those network members aren't going to help you unless you make yourself seen as a crucial member of *their* network. Being seen *is* being connected; you can't create connection (a human need, remember!) if you're not being seen, and people can't find or help you if you're hiding. So stop hiding, because in the next chapter, you're going to learn all about how to recognize and build those valuable connections so you can completely own the room when you're around them.

MIC DROP MOMENTS

- Asking for help *helps* others.

- Being asked for help makes us feel seen, so asking someone else for help makes *them* feel *seen*.

- Before asking for help, you need to put in the work by

    o Showing how you can provide value

    o Asking strategically and thoughtfully

- What is the other person's goal? How can you help them get there?

- The Law of Reciprocity is a human imperative, and it's what our interpersonal society is built on. It's also what you'll use to ask for help—though it's important to remember that while you will get positive results, they may not be exactly the results you expected.

- Entering into a season of giving and providing value needs to be an act of service, not an act of expectation.

- People who see your value and like you as a person are more likely to help you, so it's up to you to build meaningful relationships with people who can lift you up on your climb to your goals.

👏 A QUICK WIN

- Assemble your Top 20 List (head over to beseenbook.com/goodies for your printable chart!)

- Start providing value to the people on that list so you can raise those scores.

- Ask them for help when you need it—in a thoughtful, strategic way.

✎ PUT IT ON A POST-IT

- Every time you don't ask someone for help, you're depriving them of a moment to feel seen, important, and valued.

CHAPTER 10

BECOME A NETWORKING NINJA

Saying no, hearing no, and asking for help are things that a lot of people would file under "uncomfortable," but they're all 100 percent necessary when it comes to building a community that's worthy of catapulting You 2.0 into the spotlight. While we're on the topic of doing uncomfortable things in order to grow here in Part III, we might as well segue into something that, when done right, can unlock the opportunity floodgates and change your life by helping you create the amazing community you've been learning about. The caveat is that, for many people (including myself), it is more painful and anxiety-inducing than a trip to the dentist.

Networking.

There aren't many things I find more draining than small talk. Just the thought of having to do it makes me want to stop writing right now and take a nap. I'm just gonna say it—I couldn't give two shits about how you feel about it being a Monday or how it's slightly more humid today than yesterday, and I most definitely don't want to see a video clip of your kid's last soccer game. Networking is necessary when it comes to building your community, but if you're nodding with me as you read this and maybe even screaming at the page, "Same, Jen! Same!" then you're in luck, because we've all been lied to when it comes to networking, and it's time to take a different approach from what you've been told.

I hate networking.

I'm so bad at making friends.

I always feel so awkward and never know what to say.

If you've ever had any of these thoughts, then you're going to want to bookmark this chapter. I'm going to teach you how to tell your imposter syndrome exactly where to shove it all while showing you that networking doesn't have to be shallow chit-chat about the latest traffic update. No matter how scared you are or how much you despise small talk, you can create powerful, win-win relationships that can get you past your introvert tendencies and toward your goals, building a powerful network in a way that you might actually enjoy. Yes, I just used the words *enjoy* and *network* in the same sentence—and I meant it!

Though most people wouldn't know it by looking at me, I am a mega-introvert. This doesn't mean I'm not great at building connections, public speaking, or making people I interact with feel seen when I'm "on." In fact, I will take this opportunity to toot my own horn and let you know that if you bump into me IRL, you will think I'm as extroverted as they come. My secret? I've gotten really good at utilizing the tools I'm about to teach you.

What I mean when I say I'm an introvert is that being out with people can be incredibly draining for me, and I always prefer sweats and a messy bun over a dress, full glam, and heels. Me at a party or networking event is like an iPhone with all its apps open at once. My battery starts to deplete super fast and I need to get home, be silent, take off my bra, and wash my face to charge back up to a full green bar.

So yes, I dislike networking—but I love the magic that comes as a result of it. So, like most things I find uncomfortable, I do the damn thing anyway, and each time, it gets a little easier. I'm always reminded that while I hate the thought of going, I'm *always* happy I went.

TEARING DOWN THE PEDESTAL

A great lesson I've learned from both producing and speaking at events full of influencers, celebrities, and major media execs is that the moment you put somebody high up on a pedestal is the moment you invite them to look down upon you. When you meet someone for the first time, whether it's a celebrity or your latest Bumble date, *your* confidence and self-worth is what dictates how the other person will see you.

Let me give you an example. I didn't realize this at the time, but my lack of knowledge about heavy metal music back in my VH1 days really helped me when it came to making awesome relationships with rock stars. Since I didn't know who the hell most of them were, I never treated any of them like they were anything special. As far as I knew, we were all just humans on a set with a job to get done. I didn't feel nervous to talk to any of them, and I certainly didn't put anyone who stepped backstage wearing a cool leather jacket and combat boots onto some invisible throne. This made the rock stars feel really comfortable with me and open up deeper than they typically would in an interview. Not fangirling over these musicians helped me to see the human behind the celebrity and—bonus!—gave me a massive gift for my future networking endeavors. It reminded me again and again that we're all human, and the only reason anyone is up on a tall pedestal is because we're the ones who put them there.

So when you do get the opportunity to meet someone who is a little further ahead of you professionally, please remember that when you remove the designer clothing, Instagram followers, and fancy vacations, they are human beings that need help with something just like you, and chances are, they probably feel just as uncomfortable with networking. If you can remember that and treat them as such, you will instantly go from being just another fan to a potential new friend.

Another super eye-opening example of this is the phenomenon that happened every single time Chris and I hosted one of our Media Mixers during Unfair Advantage Live, where we gathered some of the most influential media gatekeepers to mix, mingle, and—here it comes—*network* with our mastermind members and attendees. I'm talking producers of all the major national TV shows, editors of the top publications, and some of the biggest influencers in the world. And they were all at one cocktail party ready to meet and discover the next expert guest for their shows and articles. Are your palms sweating just thinking about entering a room like that? Don't worry, mine always do too, and it was my own party!

We spent the entire second day of every event arming our attendees with the skills they needed to make the best first impressions possible with these media superstars. But here's the mind-boggling thing: the media guests were always just as (if not more) nervous and uncomfortable to meet the attendees! It's a total "grass is greener on the other side" kind of situation, but what it all boils down to is that we all get nervous to meet new people! Never underestimate someone else's insecurity, even when it feels like your own is raging out of control. While you might be desperate for someone else's help to get an opportunity to be seen, that exact person might be just as desperate for the kind of help that only *you* can offer! Finding that person and connecting with them is how you create a win-win relationship.

Take Paige, who came to one of our Unfair Advantage Live events feeling super nervous about our Media Mixer but excited to try out some of the tactics we'd been teaching. At the bar, she saw a man whose name tag told her he was a booker for *Good Morning America*, and so after a good ol' Dare of the Day, Paige worked up the courage to say hello. They struck up a conversation, and Paige asked him what Chris and I always refer to as the magic question: "What do you need help with right now?"

He started talking to her about his struggles to find a guest for a segment he was working on for GMA with Barbara Corcoran and Robert Herjavec from *Shark Tank*. "I'm driving myself crazy," he told her. "I need to find a parent whose child is about to enter into the workforce, and if the parent could be a business owner and an entrepreneur, that would be even better."

Little did he know, he couldn't have been talking to a better person—Paige fit every single one of those criteria. She shoved her fear into the passenger seat and told him, "I might be exactly who you're looking for. I'm a business owner, and my son is graduating college this week."

The very next day, Paige was on *Good Morning America* with Barbara Corcoran, Robert Herjavec, and her son. Not only was she able to provide value for the show, but she also had an opportunity to promote her business on national television. She found the perfect person at that mixer to create a win-win relationship, all because she got over imposter syndrome and spoke to the GMA booker like he was a person, without putting him on a pedestal.

FOUR HACKS TO OWN ANY ROOM

I know Paige's story sounds almost too ideal, but she didn't just luck her way into that amazing opportunity. She used four concrete, incredible hacks that I'm about to share to help you get a little more comfortable with the uncomfortable-ness of networking at an event. It's time for you to stop hiding at home on your couch and start making the connections you need to be seen.

1. Acknowledge the Elephants

This first hack is all about getting a little vulnerable and capitalizing on the obvious or awkward to build connection. A lot of times, announcing the elephant in the room looks a lot like saying what everyone's thinking.

"Am I the only one who's a little out of practice when it comes to networking?"

"Welp, there's that awkward silence we were all worried about!"

"Is anyone else *starving* right now?"

Sometimes, but not always, acknowledging the elephant will draw a laugh. Sometimes you'll say it to the whole room, while other times you'll say it to just one person (and possibly make a new bestie for the rest of the event). But the one thing that being vulnerable always does is break the ice and make other people think, *Oh thank god, I thought I was the only one!*

I discovered this trick completely by accident, and all thanks to a cute pair of kicks. Let me explain.

I love getting glammed up when I speak onstage. My style—usually complete with sky-high heels—has become a big part of what's helped me build the confidence to be seen as the best combo of Real Jen and Jen 2.0 on these big stages. Buuut you already know that I prefer the comfort of sweats and flats to skirts and pumps any day. So the second I step offstage, the heels come off, and my skirt and crop top set with the Nikes I wore at the gym that morning usually becomes the number-one topic of conversation.

"I was going to ask how you stood up there in those shoes!" is a refrain I hear every time. "I could never wear those heels onstage!"

And do you know how I respond?

I tell them, "My feet are fucking killing me! I wear those heels for 30 minutes, maybe an hour, when I'm up there, but they come immediately off afterward."

It always brings a laugh, especially when I'm talking with people who have worn heels themselves, because then we share a commonality. (I dare you to find me someone who really, truly *loves* wearing tall heels for long periods of time!) Just like that, a connection is sparked. This interaction brings me closer to the person I'm talking with. It takes me off that stage and down to their level—where I belong—because remember, we're all people. We're all *real.* And when you draw attention to that realness by announcing your vulnerability—in this case, my poor aching toes—you're bringing everyone to the same level. You're hopping down from that pedestal or taking the other person off of it so the two of you are at eye level with one another.

Remember back in Part I when we talked about being Real You? It's just as important when you're trying to make connections. Nobody wants to see that fake, perfect version of you. That person is untouchable and unapproachable, and other people can smell it from a mile away. They want to see the version of you who wears beat-up tennis sneakers with your designer dress. Whether you're an introvert or an extrovert, a total newbie to networking or an old pro, showing your vulnerability is an amazing trick to fast-track a new connection, wipe social anxiety off the board, and get past the awkward small-talk portion of any new social situation.

2. Be the Most Interested Person in the Room

The best way to make somebody walk away from a conversation with you and think, *I love that person, that was one of my favorite conversations ever*, is to simply ask them about their favorite topic. And I'm not talking about the decor at the event you're at, the hottest bingeable show on Netflix, or the satay chicken skewer you just grabbed from the waiter. Whether they consciously know it or not, everyone's favorite thing to talk about is themselves!

Neuroimaging has shown that our brains light up like the Rockefeller Christmas tree when we hear our own name mentioned.[1] And when we talk about our accomplishments, a Harvard study discovered that we stimulate the mesolimbic dopamine system—the same area of the brain that gets activated when we have sex, eat a delicious meal, or take part in anything we find pleasurable.[2] These parts of the brain are also associated with motivation and reward, so doesn't it make sense that you'd want to activate that motivation in someone you're trying to network with?

As an introvert, I love this trick. The cool thing about being the most *interested* person in the room rather than trying to be the most *interesting* is it's a hell of a lot easier on your social batteries. When you're asking questions and letting the other person do most of the talking, you don't have to think about what to say. Instead, all you have to do is be interested in what they're saying and ask them to talk about themselves. I have been to so many conferences, dinners, and cocktail parties where I have said almost nothing and people have followed up later telling me, "I love you, Jen. You're the greatest conversationalist." But I said nothing! I just asked them a million questions, and they loved it. Like asking for help, asking questions gives the other person an opportunity to feel seen.

When Paige went into that conversation with the GMA booker, she got what she needed by first being interested in his work. She asked him what he was working on and used her detective skills to follow up with thoughtful questions until she understood how she could be of value to him.

The biggest mistake anyone can make going into an event, a job interview, or even a first date is trying too hard to impress people. Do you know how many dates I've been on with guys who just talked about themselves the entire time? It's such an easy mistake to make. It can feel like there's so much at stake if you don't put your best foot forward, and humble-bragging about your accomplishments doubles as a great way to make yourself feel worthy. But when you focus too much on what *you're* going to say, you make the biggest rookie networking mistake there is: you stop listening to the other person.

Nobody wants to feel like they're not being seen and heard. But if you can stop worrying about whether you're interesting enough (maybe by announcing your vulnerability, hey?) and go into a new conversation thinking of all the questions that you could ask that person and actually listening to their answers, you're going to have a better shot at having a memorable conversation, which is key to kickstarting a powerful connection.

You can take this even further if you like, especially if you're a nervous introvert. If there's someone you really want to connect with, do some research before the event or before your conversation so you can make them feel even more special. (I recommend following this rule: if it's on their public social media accounts, it's fair game. Otherwise, you're crossing into creepy territory, and I never want you to end up there.) Have they made any announcements they're super excited about, or posted recently about getting married, or having a baby, or a recent trip to Greece? Find connection points that already exist between you. Whenever I find out that someone else has a Maltese, I always talk about Dexter, and when someone has recently posted pics from a place I've been wanting to visit, I take that as an immediate in! I can ask questions about their trip. When I'm going to a dinner with someone and I find out through social media that their company was recently acquired, I can confidently walk into that room and tell them, "Congratulations about your company! That must feel freaking amazing. Tell me more!"

I bet those people will be impressed you actually took the time to find out about them. I know I am! When I go to an event and someone asks a thoughtful question about a recent podcast interview or one of my keynote speeches, they always stand out to me. They're the people I remember most clearly, and when their names pop up in my DMs or inbox later, they're the people I'm most excited to answer. Like I always say, the extra mile is never crowded, so don't be afraid to walk it.

3. Go In with a Goal

There's a game I play with myself at networking events, interviews, speaking engagements, and even parties. Any time I have to go out and be around people, I give myself a goal. It could be something like:

- Get five people's Instagram handles and follow up with a DM

- Take three selfies with different people

- Find the most successful person in the room and strike up a conversation

These goals vary depending on the event, and sometimes they're extremely vague, but they always ensure that I make at least one great connection before I go home. You've known for some time now that collecting wins builds momentum, and I hope you've been implementing the Confidence Continuum in your own life so you can see it in action. This trick accomplishes that same sense of achievement because when you go to that networking event and achieve your goal, you're creating the ability to walk into the next one with a hell of a lot more confidence in yourself.

Having a goal for a specific event or gathering also means you're giving yourself a plan of action with a clear ending, because you know that once you've accomplished what you came to do, you have permission to get out of there! You can go home and put your sweatpants on knowing you've made at least one new friend. Hell yeah!

I'm the queen of disappearing from a party once I've achieved my goal. If you're thinking, *But wait, I have to say good-bye to people!* that's totally fine. But just know that your sweet plan to say a "quick good-bye" will probably leave you at the event for another hour, which will completely negate the reward of being able to leave once you've hit your goal. Believe me, no one has ever cared or held it against me when I quietly slipped from a crowded room. Leaving without saying good-bye also gives me a great opportunity for a follow-up, which we'll talk about in just a sec.

Tackling networking through a goal-based approach gives you a sense of focused purpose, which can sometimes be hard when you're feeling out of place at an event where you don't know anyone or your imposter syndrome is making an appearance. It creates more trust within yourself that you have the capability to go in, do the job, get the win, and leave. Then, after the event (when you're safely back home on your couch), you'll look back and tell yourself, "That wasn't bad at all! I can do that again." Another coin in the bank!

4. Follow Up with Value

Time for a bold claim: I'll argue, right here and now, that 99 percent of people are following up incorrectly. And if I'm being totally honest, people with shitty follow-ups piss me off. I want to scream every time I see an e-mail that says, "Just bumping this to the top of your inbox," or "I just wanted to follow up with you about XYZ . . ."

Whew. Deep breaths, Jen.

Okay, look, I appreciate the follow-up, and if you're following up your new connections this way, you haven't ruined your chances of making a meaningful connection. But you could be a lot smarter about how you continue the conversation. When it comes to the media, I always tell my clients that 20 percent of the value is the actual media segment, and 80 percent is what you do with it afterward. This makes it extra important for you to pack that follow-up opportunity with so much value the other person can't ignore what you have to say.

How can you provide personalized value in your follow-up to make someone really remember you? One way I love to do this is with photos. When I take a selfie with someone at an event, I always DM it to them later. When Chris and I host events, we hire a professional photographer so we can send gorgeous, high-quality photos to our guests. This acts as a confidence booster for them (because who doesn't love receiving a good photo of themselves?) as well as an opportunity for me *and* the other person to post the photo on social media and tag each other in it, allowing us both to be seen by each other's audiences. Win-win.

Let's put this in the context of a networking event. You attend the event in the hopes of making a connection with someone who can help promote your new product. The event goes great, and you even accomplish your goal of getting a selfie with that person and following each other on Instagram (social media is the new business card, and I will absolutely fight you on this). In the Uber home that night, you take a few notes about your new connection, including a restaurant recommendation they gave you when the conversation turned to your mutual love of sushi. Well, the next day, you could follow up like this:

> *Hi there!*
> *I just wanted to follow up after meeting you last night. If you're still interested in promoting my new product, let me know!*

Or you could say:

> *Hi [name],*
> *I'm so excited we connected last night. I got this adorable picture of us and thought you'd like to see it—we look great! I'm also sending over a link to this podcast episode I did last month, which is all about imposter syndrome. I know you mentioned you were struggling with that yesterday, so I think it might be a great listen during your workout! Let me know if you find it helpful, or if you need any suggestions.*

I'm still thinking about that sushi restaurant you were talking about, by the way. (The omakase looks incredible!) I'd love to go there for lunch next week and talk some more about working together. What night of the week works best for you?

The latter method does a couple of things:

1. Reminds them who you are and what you talked about together

2. Shares a picture of the two of you, which either or both of you can share on your socials

3. Provides credibility about your expertise and how you specifically can help them with their problem (this could be a podcast, article, blog post, or any other resource)

4. Creates an opportunity for future connection

Overall, what you're doing is making the other person feel seen while providing value, which will make them much more likely to remember you.

You don't need to accomplish *all* these things in every follow-up, and you can follow up in other ways too. Some of the most memorable follow-ups I've ever received were thoughtful, creative gifts from people who clearly listened to what I had to say when we met. But it's important to be careful, because a bad follow-up gift is almost worse than no follow-up at all. I once received a box of personalized cookies after an event, and they were gluten-free and vegan, which made me feel so seen since the person sending them clearly knew about my dietary restrictions. That was an amazing follow-up gift! But I've also received flowers and bottles of wine, which we always end up having to throw out or give away because Chris is massively allergic to flowers and neither of us drink. Those generic gifts weren't well-researched or thought out, even though those facts about us are pretty well-known. See the difference?

Just like when you're asking for help, following up requires thinking about what the other person wants, needs, and enjoys. A good follow-up will position you for success because it will strengthen your connection. If, on the other hand, you don't take steps to bolster the relationship, meeting that person in the first place doesn't matter. Following up is the most important piece of the puzzle, and how you do it is absolutely crucial.

YOU'RE ALWAYS HAPPY YOU WENT

Introvert confession time: I'm always secretly hoping my friends will cancel plans on me so I can stay home and watch a Netflix docuseries, and when I have to make a phone call to a new contact, somewhere in the back of my mind I'm always chanting, *Don't pick up, don't pick up, don't pick up.* It's the exact same with networking events (multiplied by a million!), and I feel confident saying I'm not alone here. There's nothing quite like the relief of suddenly having an entirely free evening, of being able to slip into my comfiest clothes and not have to be "on" or accountable to anyone.

But look—and I'm saying this as someone who *really* gets how great that feels—it's always better when you do the thing. Even when I'm tired or not in the mood, I always end up happy I went. Something good will come of every networking event, no matter what. Even if you come home at the end thinking, *Well, that was the worst night of my life,* you can now tell the story of that awful night forever as a great "elephant in the room" icebreaker! Maybe you learned something, even if it's as simple as *I'm never gonna hang out with that person again* or *That's the last time I ever wear white pants to a carnival.* That sounds a lot like a win in my book, and it turns even the worst night into a gift.

You might love networking, and if so, good for you. I'm officially jealous. But I know I'm never really going to want to network, and if you're like me, that's 100 percent okay! You're not always going to want to go, and you're not always going to feel comfortable while you're there. But just keep coming back to this mantra: *I will be happy I went.*

Even if it was the worst night, and especially if it was the best night, there will be a reason it was worthwhile. At the bare minimum, going to that event means you stuck to a commitment you made with yourself. You got through the discomfort, and you put another coin in your confidence bank in the process. With practice, you'll begin getting a lot more bang for your buck because you're learning how to make powerful relationships in the environment you're in with the time you have.

That's what it's all about, really—making the most of your time.

Chris and I always joke that we work really hard to make our lives easy. In order for me to continue building on the momentum I've created, I have to consistently surround myself with reminders not to take my foot off the gas pedal or start hiding or self-sabotaging. I still spend a lot of time and effort building my confidence muscles and using the mindset strategies I've taught you in this book to make sure I'm consistently working toward becoming and being seen as Jen 2.0. I owe it to myself, because this time is all the time I'm going to get.

Reality check: just because you've reached a certain level of success doesn't mean the work stops. (And you know as well as I do by now that reaching that Upper Limit just means it's time to find a sledgehammer and smash through it.) Even when you do stop, *time* never does. In fact, the more successful I become, the more I know I need to double down on investing in my confidence bank. As we discussed in depth in Chapter 3, that means practicing discomfort regularly. That's why my one very tiny, very adorable tattoo is the word *Time* on my wrist in thin black script.

The word *time* has saved me in hundreds of instances where I've felt debilitating discomfort and awkwardness. It's gotten me through moments of utter embarrassment, physical pain, and even extreme boredom, like waiting at the DMV or watching 10 consecutive episodes of *Dora the Explorer* with my stepdaughter when she was eight. One thing I know for sure is all discomfort is temporary. Time never stops, and no matter how difficult or painful something is, it will eventually end. You will end up looking back at that moment as a stronger, wiser, more equipped person *because* you experienced it.

It's what I think about every time I look at that tattoo on my wrist. Time. Doesn't. Stop. You will be at this networking event for only a couple of hours of your entire life, and before you know it, those hours will be over, and your social anxiety or imposter syndrome will be gone along with it. But so will the *good* stuff, like being around people who could promote your brand, take your business to the next level, or become your new best friend. Believe me, you don't wanna miss that.

When you remind yourself that discomfort is temporary and those hours are all you have, you'll allow yourself to be in the present moment, taking all the photos, engaging in meaningful conversations, and soaking up every last second of your experience. It's up to you to make sure you're doing everything in your power to be able to wake up the next morning knowing you made the most of your time.

The network you build is such an important piece of the puzzle because at the end of the day, it's almost impossible to build influence and visibility on your own. In order to be seen and create influence with your target audience, you need to be able to leverage other people's audiences—and not just anybody's going to let you leverage their audience. It's your powerful connections and win-win relationships that help get you to that next level. Those relationships you form when you take advantage of your time and make yourself do the damn thing are what move your dreams forward. And just like you've learned in this book again and again and again, the more you do it, the easier it gets.

🎤 MIC DROP MOMENTS

- Time never stops. Discomfort is temporary, but the growth on the other side of your discomfort is permanent.

- Shallow networking conversations are draining for everyone involved. Treating people—even hugely successful ones—like people allows you to get past the discomfort and into a real connection.

- The moment you put somebody up on a pedestal is the moment you invite them to look down on you. Everyone, and I mean *everyone*, gets nervous when it comes to networking.

- People love talking about themselves—so pay attention and listen!

- 20 percent of the value is in the original interaction, 80 percent of the value comes from what you do with it.

- You'll always be happy you went.

👏 A QUICK WIN

- Go to an event by yourself and practice being the most interested person in the room!

PUT IT ON A POST-IT

- You're always happy you went!

PART IV

BE VISIBLE

CHAPTER 11

THE SIMPLE SECRET TO MAKING YOUR STORY SHINE

"I am SD nertvous I cvould puke!"

Thank god for autocorrect, I thought as I texted Amanda. She was, as always, my biggest cheerleader, and she'd been instrumental in getting me to this moment: pacing the carpet in the green room for *Life & Living with Joanna Gagis*. This PBS lifestyle show highlighted New York–based individuals and businesses that were making an impact, and Amanda had gotten me booked as a featured guest.

At this point, JLG Fitness was fully booked with a waitlist of potential clients. Business was booming, and I was ready to take it up another notch by appearing on national TV for the first time. But in the back of my mind, there was a slight (okay, *major*) problem, and it was making me nauseous.

My brand was all over the place.

Publicly, not many people knew yet that I had made the shift from "Miss Box of Junk" to "celebrity fitness trainer." Unless they did their Google research or spent a lot of their downtime listening to Black Sabbath, none of my fitness clients knew about my pleather-pants-wearing past life—and I planned to keep it that way.

If they knew I hadn't always been a personal trainer, would clients even want to work with me? Worse, if they knew my previous life had been *so* radically different from my present, would they take me seriously as someone who could help change their life?

In spite of how far I'd come, I was still not 100 percent ready to be myself. In the heavy metal world, I was somebody. But in the fitness world, among the audience I was *actually trying to reach*, I was a total nobody. Since my current following was still tuning in for the studded cuffs and cleavage, DMing me asking to buy a pair of my socks or the cut-up shirt I wore in episode 26, I knew I needed to officially transition my brand away from "sexy metal chick" to a strong, positive motivator who could lead people to their fullest potential. It was clear—and absolutely critical—that I start building a new audience that resonated with my new message.

Sound familiar at all? If so, welcome to Part IV, Be Visible, where we're going to take everything you've learned in the past 10 chapters and start getting you out on that stage—or in front of that camera—so you can start standing under the spotlight to be seen by the audience who needs you. Here's the part of the book where you're going to learn how to pitch yourself to the media and tell your story in a way that's going to make your audience think, *I have to know more!* I'm not gonna lie to you and tell you it's easy, but believe me, it's doable. You can build your brand from the ground up. You can pivot your brand when an old one stops serving the interests of You 2.0. But you absolutely cannot do it without Real You right there under those lights, no matter how messy the view might be.

It's a lesson I had to learn the hard way in that PBS dressing room. I was stuck in another spiraling internal showdown. Tonight's contenders were Real Jen and—at the opposite end of the ring—her best frenemy, fear. The bell hadn't even rung yet, but my opponent was already winning this match. Fear was a master when it came to trash talk, and it had convinced me I wasn't worthy of the future I wanted to create. It whispered in my ear that I wouldn't be accepted if I publicly owned my imperfect past, so I dug Miss Box of Junk a grave and packed up her studded fingerless gloves, chain belts, and concert tees into an under-the-bed-box from the Container Store. I tried to erase her from my resume and my memory. *That was then and this is now*, I told myself. *Nobody needs to know.*

"What's wrong with me!?" I continued to text Amanda in a massive panic. I mean, I had worked on a professional TV set for over four years! This should have been a breeze. But this time felt totally different. There was no mask of heavy makeup to hide behind, no teased-to-the-sky hair. Just me, in my new Lululemon leggings and highlighter-yellow Nike running shoes, about to be seen on camera as Real Jen.

But I had been in showbiz long enough to know the past is never truly past. Somewhere deep in my psyche, a part of me was freaking out because it knew the whole "I'm a celebrity fitness trainer and always have been" schtick was liable to fall apart the moment I walked onto that set. What I could never have seen coming was how embracing my story and allowing the truth to finally be seen was the best possible thing I could have done.

UNPACKING MY BOX OF JUNK

The topic I had pitched Joanna Gagis was "Small Steps You Can Take to Start Losing Weight." My plan was to talk a little bit about some healthy food choices viewers could start making and then get Joanna out of her seat to teach her squats, chair push-ups, and, of course, forward lunges. I could see it all in my head, crystal clear. It was going to be epic!

So you can imagine my shock when I walked onto the set and the host was clad in a beautiful white dress. This was no Hoda-in-Athleta moment! I immediately realized we were *not* going to be working out together like I had thought. I instantly went from adoring the new Lululemon outfit I was wearing to feeling like I wanted to rip it off my body in embarrassment. It got worse when the first words from Joanna's mouth were, "I'm so excited to talk about *That Metal Show!*"

What!? My stomach did a backflip.

I was supposed to spend this segment doing jumping jacks and talking about putting the salad dressing on the side. Instead, she had outed me publicly about a previous life I was trying to move past. *Oh no!* Luckily, that very past had set me up well for this moment. Even though I was having a mini-meltdown internally—my thoughts were racing, my fingers were vibrating, and fear had officially moved from the passenger seat of the car to sitting on my lap—externally, I held it together (thanks, acting school!).

"I'm so excited to be here!" I said, sounding like everything was going according to plan.

We went on to have a conversation that changed everything I thought I knew about connecting to the media. It turned out, the interview *she* had planned to do was "How Jennifer Gottlieb Went from Being a Broadway Actress and Co-Host of *That Metal Show* to a Celebrity Fitness Trainer." Yes, I know—*so* much juicer than salad dressing and squats! Thanks, Joanna! She dove right into questions about how my acting career started and asked me all about my journey to landing my dream role in *The Wedding Singer*'s Broadway tour. Without missing a beat, she brought up *That Metal Show.*

Based on the wreck I'd been in that green room before the show, you'd think this would have completely derailed me. But strangely enough, from the moment I sat down in that chair, all my fear completely disappeared. Poof! I didn't feel nervous to talk about it anymore! So without hesitation, I dove right in about how I actually didn't know much about rock-and-roll until I started listening to a ton of songs by a badass female rock musician, Lita Ford, in preparation for my role in *The Wedding Singer*. And it all came full circle when Lita ended up being the very first guest I got to interview on the set of *That Metal Show*!

The story flew from my mouth as if I were just shooting the shit with one of my best friends, but you have to understand, this is something I had never told anyone before! I was open and honest with someone for the first time about what had been my big secret for four years: I was not an actual "metal girl." The more I shared, the more I connected the dots of how "Miss Box of Junk" Jen had been deeply connected to Real Jen all along. The journey from the VH1 set to that very moment *was* the story that was going to differentiate me from everyone else. In that chair across from Joanna, I discovered how to tell the story that would eventually land me hundreds of media placements and hundreds of thousands of dollars.

I discovered that what I thought was my mess was, in fact, my message.

LEANING ALL THE WAY IN

Not all of us get to play back our life-changing moments on our phones or computer screens, but since this one of mine is publicly available, let me share my revelation with you. When I rewatch my interview with Joanna, something wildly important stands out to me. As I shushed my fear and shared my story, my posture began to relax, and my voice grew more animated. But I wasn't the only one whose demeanor started to change! In the seat across from me, *Joanna* became more engaged too. She nodded along, laughing with me, her eyes brightening whenever I said something she liked. The more Joanna became interested, the more she *leaned in.* This story, the one I'd been embarrassed about, was so interesting to her that she physically leaned toward me because she was totally invested in what I had to say! That realization handed me a powerful tool that I now teach my clients so they can connect more deeply with their audience and the media. I call it the *lean-in story.* I bet you're leaning in right now, ready to learn how it works.

When I was first building my audience as a fitness trainer, I wasn't getting the response I wanted when I sent media pitches or posted content. If you're experiencing this too, you're probably doing what many media people like to call "burying the lede." This means you aren't beginning with the part of your story that's the most interesting to *other people*. Instead, you're hiding it behind other noise that, for whatever reason, *you* think is more interesting, appropriate, or flattering. I hate to break it to you, but when it comes to using messaging to attract your ideal audience, it can't be about your priorities—it's about what other people find interesting!

If you're wondering how you missed that obvious point, don't worry, my friend. You're not alone. Most of us bury the lede because we simply don't see our stories for the gold that they are. We're too close and can't see them from the viewpoint of someone who didn't live it. As a result, we often undervalue and underappreciate our most badass stories.

Let's use the story I just told about my interview with Joanna as an example. I went into the interview thinking about my audience, just like I was supposed to. I thought that the *Life and Living* audience wanted to hear about how to start exercising and eating healthier. A great message to be sure, but it's one that we've all seen countless times. There's nothing memorable about vegetables and squats! What made me stand out is that, unlike the other millions of fitness professionals out there, I used to be in a Broadway show and on VH1. It's a fact that makes people say, *Wait, what? Tell me more!* instead of just flipping the channel. That was my Lean-In Story, not the same old "how to lose weight" pitch I'd made. The exact thing I was hoping to hide was *why* they booked me on the show!

When I teach my clients about writing powerful pitches that the media will want to book, I always remind them that perfect is boring and unrelatable. Think about it—wouldn't you hate watching a movie or reading a book that has no conflict, where the characters have no relatable flaws and don't grow or change throughout the story? When connecting with your audience, share a story that helps them see you as a human being. When you're on the same level they are, they will feel seen by you. In case you haven't noticed, none of us are perfect. (If you really *haven't* noticed this, do me a favor and revisit the last chapter!) No matter how hard some people try to seem perfect on social media, behind the filters we are all beautifully messy—and thank god for that! Our fallibility makes us relatable.

One thing people often get wrong when creating content is leading with a story that's completely bland simply because it's what they see other people doing. Let's say you're an expert in gut health and you're looking to share some tips. Look around you! Everyone is writing articles and creating TikToks and doing segments with titles like "Three Ways to Heal Your Gut" or "Gut Health 101." You could throw a rock in the dark and hit a freaking gut expert these days, am I right?

In order to differentiate yourself from every other gut expert in the world, you need to find what makes you and your story different, something that makes your dream client want to work with you and not all those other gut experts out there. Find a memorable story—preferably a messy story. Maybe your gut health was so bad you almost pooped your pants once, and you had to run off the stage where you were speaking to go find a bathroom. Mortifying! Why the hell would you want to tell that story in a public setting, let alone in an interview?

Step out of your shoes and think of how you'd feel if you were experiencing bad gut health and heard that story. If it were me, I would think, *Oh my god, she's so real. I've had a moment like that, and I thought I was the only one!* I'd DM her, thank her for sharing her story, and ask her how she fixed her problem—maybe she has some tips for me. And—here's the kicker—I'd *always* remember her! In that packed field of gut health experts, she shared something more vulnerable and scarier than any of the others, and it made her relatable. It made her stand out.

Keep in mind, your mess doesn't have to be physically messy (though pooping your pants *does* stand out!). If that's not your vibe, your Lean-In could be sweet and simple, like the story of how you became an expert in the space you're in now.

From what I've seen in my years representing some of the most successful entrepreneurs and thought leaders in the world, the brands and business owners that embrace the messiness or quirkiness of their story are always the most relatable. Relatability is key when it comes to connecting. It's similar to acknowledging the elephant when you're networking—the point is to remind people that you're human, just like they are.

In the end, people want to feel like you understand what they are going through. They want to know you've been there and that's why you can help! And here's a majorly important reminder—there is always going to be someone else who does the same thing as you. So if you stick purely to the topic and say nothing about yourself, you're just going to be another voice lost in a crowd. But I can promise you that there is only one *you*—nobody else has your story, your voice, and your point of view. So if you want to stand out in the field of competitors and be the expert that people want to feature, the surest path is to tell more stories that only *you* can tell—in the way that only you can tell them.

THE LEAN-IN STORY LIBRARY

So how do you find your lean-in story? It's easier than you think: Talk. To. People.

I know, I know, that sounds way too simple, but think about it: When was the last time you really took a moment to think about the stories you tell? Most of us don't. But if you start to really pay attention to your "audience" in your everyday conversations, you'll see that different stories land differently. For example, pay attention to when people give you the "meerkat"—that is, when you're talking to someone and they are constantly looking over your shoulder to see if there is someone else more interesting to talk to behind you. Ouch! If this is happening, please, for god's sake, retire that story! But, if your conversation partner leans in, lifts an eyebrow, and genuinely gives you their undivided attention, *that's* the story you want to focus on. Once you have it, you can develop and fine-tune it until it's as powerful and fascinating as you are!

Take my SCM client Todd Herman. We were working on the book launch for his book *The Alter Ego Effect*, which is about creating "secret identities" that help you unlock your heroic self and transform your life. (I *highly* recommend you read it!) My team wanted to get him a spot on the *Today Show*, but we were having trouble finding the Lean-In Story to use for the pitch.

"Todd," I told him. "Just talk to us. Just start telling us some of your favorite stories about using your alter ego."

So Todd began to speak, and for a while, we just listened. He told us stories about how using an alter ego had changed his business and how he'd created some incredible opportunities. We nodded along, but nothing quite sparked until he shared about his three adorable kids. Todd's daughter once made him a beaded elastic bracelet, and he keeps it hanging outside the door. Every day when he comes home from work, he puts the bracelet on and snaps it against his wrist. And *bam*, he goes from "Work Todd" to his alter ego, "Dad Todd." He's able to set aside one version of himself and become the version his family needs him to be with one simple trick.

"Well, *that's* the cutest story of all time," I told him. Everyone in the room was leaning in like crazy! So we pitched that story to the *Today Show*, and guess what—it got him booked. But that's not all. Jenna Bush Hager loved his story so much that she made a bracelet for her own alter ego and even wore it a few episodes later. So not only was Todd able to get exposure for his book on the *Today Show*, but going forward he was able to talk about how Jenna was using an alter-ego bracelet. Talk about a bonus detail that embellished his lean-in story for the future!

My homework for you today is to start your own lean-in story library. This will be an ever-growing document of your most interesting stories. Remember—these are stories that you've discovered are interesting to *other people*, not just to you! Get on the phone, hop on Zoom, or meet a friend for coffee and simply start paying attention to their body language when you talk. If they are physically leaning in and asking questions about your story, write that sucker down and shelve it in your library! If they start to look at their phone, zone out, or meerkat over your shoulder, cut that one from your repertoire.

There's no magic formula for what makes a great Lean-In Story, but I'm willing to bet you've got some ideas already. Here's a hint: Start with stories that are authentic and personal. The ones that make you feel vulnerable, messy, and even a little mortified. The ones that illustrate who you were *before* your breakthrough and showcase how you got from there to where you are today.

Let's talk about one of our event attendees, Jessica. When she came up onstage for a hot-seat session with Chris, she had no idea what her Lean-In Story should be. She was a life coach who taught people to increase their sales through spiritual practice, but she didn't understand what was most interesting about her or her story.

"How did you get into that business?" Chris asked. "I bet you weren't always a life coach."

Jessica smiled and told him she used to be a teacher at an inner-city school. She taught her students yoga and meditation to help them with math. So cool, right? Chris and the rest of us thought so too. Right before the eyes of the crowd, Jessica had discovered her Lean-In Story: how she transformed from inner-city math teacher to spiritual sales coach. It was authentic and unique and totally personal to Jessica. Once she fully leaned into her story, her success blew up. Eventually, she was featured in *Forbes*, and wouldn't you know it—the headline was: "How This Teacher Left the Classroom and Started a Seven-Figure Coaching Business"!

Both Todd's and Jessica's Lean-In Stories allowed them to home in on what made them special. This was not necessarily their achievements or businesses—as amazing and unique as those were for both of them—but the fascinating personal journey that got them to those successes.

THE SIMPLE STORY STRUCTURE

So now you have a story library in the works, but don't stop there! How can you best leverage these amazing anecdotes to capture attention and wow potential clients? Through the Simple Story Structure. Whether you're pitching yourself for a media interview, having a discovery call with a potential client, or just connecting with someone new, the most important skill you need to master is how to make a memorable introduction.

When connecting with someone for the first time, either in person, virtually, or through written or recorded content, research has found that you have about 27 seconds before they decide if they want to "swipe right" and continue connecting with you. This means you want to make sure you can succinctly explain who you are and what you do in a way that makes them want to stick around to learn more. Basically, you want to "have them at hello," *Jerry Maguire* style.

If you love talking about yourself (it's okay to admit it!), you probably think you have this in the bag. But if you're anything like I used to be, the "succinct" part is where you need help. When someone asked me what I did when I was just starting out, I always ended up prattling on for 20 minutes, forgetting key details, or telling things out of order. I was anything but short, sweet, and captivating. If, on the other hand, you loathe talking about yourself, this technique takes all the pressure off. Once you have your structure down, you won't have to feel your belly drop 10 flights when someone asks that dreaded question, "So what do you do?"

Luckily the simple-structure story technique will package your lean-in stories in a way that will free you from ever having to say, "It's so hard to explain!" There are three components to a Simple Story Structure:

- Conflict

- Resolution

- How you fit in

The *Conflict* is the moment in your lean-in story that initiated a change. It's usually a messier moment in your life or a personal "breakdown" that led to the "breakthrough" of starting your business or discovering the angle from which to approach your brand. Aim for one to three concise sentences.

The *Resolution* is how you found a solution to the aforementioned conflict, and what happened as a result. Again, this should be brief and concise, about one to two sentences long.

How You Fit In is a short sentence about what you do now as an outcome of experiencing this conflict and discovering a resolution.

SIMPLE STORY STRUCTURES IN ACTION

Let's use Anna's story as an example. Anna is a client who was once a member of a cult that had a strict, gray-and-black-only dress code. She wasn't allowed any sort of freedom to express herself through her appearance. She lived by the rules of the cult until the day she received a terminal cancer diagnosis. With nothing to lose, Anna left the cult and started wearing colorful clothes, releasing herself from years' worth of confinement. When she went to the doctor for her next appointment, she discovered that her cancer had magically vanished! To this day, no one knows why, but since then, she's dedicated her life to helping women use their wardrobe as an expression of their most beautiful and vibrant inner selves.

Anna's story is simple, succinct, and deeply personal. Many of us know someone who had cancer, and I'll bet we can all relate to feeling unable to express our true selves (although hopefully fewer of us can relate to being in a cult!). Her story stands out because of the unique angle of her past, but it also feels universal. The fact that we've all overcome different conflicts throughout our lives means that regardless of content, the simple-structure story speaks to our emotions and makes sense to our brains. People love hearing about change and transformation, and we're wired to connect deeply and quickly to the emotional journey of overcoming an obstacle and finding a meaningful resolution.

Let's break down how Anna might tell her story at her next event:

> **Conflict:** *"I spent many years in the 1980s living in a cult that had a strict dress code, but everything came to a halt when I received a terminal cancer diagnosis in 2013."*
>
> **Resolution:** *"I left the cult, and used my remaining time to reinvent myself, transforming my wardrobe, appearance, and ultimately, my life. My cancer mysteriously vanished, and doctors to this day can't explain why."*
>
> **How She Fits In:** *"I now help other women over fifty use wardrobe reflection to transform their lives!"*

Voila! I don't know about you, but I am definitely leaning in!

Let's look at another example. One of our clients, Amy, was a mom whose favorite family tradition was making pizza with her kids on Friday nights. When she was diagnosed with lupus, it came along with a million shiny new dietary restrictions. Among them was a major prohibition on gluten. Well, *crap*—that meant no more pizza nights for Amy and the kids. But Amy wasn't willing to take no for an answer. She figured out a way to make pizza crust using cauliflower to make it gluten-free and healthy, and started making it every week for her family. Soon, she decided she could actually sell this pizza crust to other families like her own. Because of Amy's ingenuity, she's now the mastermind behind a multimillion-dollar company, a best-selling cookbook, and a brand-name product—Cali'flour Foods—which you can find in grocery stores across the US. She's living the dream!

What's great about Amy's story is that it can work in two different ways. First, we have Amy's personal simple-structure story:

> **Conflict:** *"My lupus diagnosis meant I could no longer enjoy my favorite tradition of Friday pizza nights with my kids."*

> **Resolution:** *"Through months of experimentation in my home kitchen, I created a new way of making pizza with cauliflower that adheres to my dietary needs, plus it tastes really good!"*

> **How She Fits In:** *"Now my kids and I can continue spending quality time together—and my company, Cali'flour Foods, helps families all over the world have healthier pizza nights together through my products, recipes, and best-selling cookbook."*

But Amy's Simple Story Structure has a business side too. Remember—Amy looked at her own family's needs and applied them to an entire industry, and it led her to mind-blowing success. Take a look at her story again, but from a business perspective:

> **Conflict:** *"Everybody loves pizza, but it's loaded with carbs, and if you have dietary restrictions like a gluten intolerance, it's going to wreak total havoc on your body."*

> **Resolution:** *"Through experimenting in my kitchen with my family, I found that making pizza crust with cauliflower instead of traditional flour is great for people with dietary restrictions or those who are health conscious."*

> **How She Fits In:** *"Now my multimillion-dollar company, Cali'flour Foods, sells healthy gluten-free alternatives that actually satisfy your pizza cravings and taste delicious, so you can maintain a healthy lifestyle while still enjoying one of your favorite indulgences!"*

Depending on who she's talking to, Amy can use either her *personal* or *industry* Simple Story Structure to get her audience to lean in. At its heart, Amy is telling the same exact story, but when she shifts the focus and showcases different details, she can make the story work for her in different ways. Amy's personal story focuses on the founding of her company and is going to be interesting to everyday people who might be watching her do a TV interview. Her industry story, on the other hand, would be appropriate if she's trying to pitch Cali'flour Foods to a potential investor or vendor. Rather than appealing to their emotions or desire to eat healthy, she's going to want to focus on why her products are valuable and marketable.

Now it's your turn! Take one of the lean-in stories from your library and turn it into a Simple Story Structure by filling in the three parts below. I've given you a sentence starter for each, but feel free to write your own.

> **Conflict:** *When I . . .*

> **Resolution:** *Then I . . .*

> **How You Fit In:** *Now I . . .*

Once you've written your story down, it's time to practice. It may seem silly to practice telling your own story, but remember how you only have those 27 seconds to make a first impression? In show biz, they call this the elevator pitch, because it's designed to be used if you find yourself sharing an elevator ride with a movie producer and want to pitch your ideas before the elevator doors open and you part ways. No matter how captivating your story is, if you can't tell it in a clear and concise way, you're going to lose attention, and fast. Plus, once it's second nature, you won't ever have to stumble over this crucial introduction to who you are and what you have to offer. You'll always be putting your best foot forward.

Start by telling your Simple Story Structure to yourself in the mirror, making a recording of yourself on your phone, or test-driving it with a supportive friend or loved one. Don't be afraid to mix things up during this process: experiment with which details to include, change up where it begins and ends, and don't forget about *how* you tell the story—what kind of inflection are you using? Where are the pauses? Eventually you'll find just the right combination and your story will flow effortlessly through the three parts of the structure. Once you've got a prototype lean-in story, start over with a different one from your library. When you have a few stories ready to go, take a test-drive. At your next coffee date, dinner party, or school pick-up, tell your story. (Keep a close watch for your nemesis, the meerkat!) Eventually, telling your Simple Story Structure will begin to feel like second nature, and you'll be ready to roll it out to your audience—whether it's in a social media post, at a networking event, or for an interview.

And here's the kicker: making your audience lean in isn't just about self-promotion. It's about getting past any fear of talking about yourself and continuing to build that confidence we talked about *waaaay* back in Part I. When you hone your Simple Story Structure, what you're doing is honing your message. You're taking what's most important and fascinating about what you do and distilling it down to its purest, most authentic form. When it's really working, you'll be able to see—and feel—when others connect to you.

MIC DROP MOMENTS

- If you're not getting the response you want from your audience, you're probably burying the lede.

- When we're too close to our own stories, it's hard to see which parts other people find most interesting.

- In order to stand out from the crowd, you need to discover what makes your story different and unique from everyone else in your niche. The answer to this often lies in your failures, face-plants, and detours on your journey to get to your goals.

- A good Lean-in story is authentic and personal. Often, the best ones are the stories that make you feel vulnerable, messy, and even a little mortified. The ones that illustrate who you were *before* your breakthrough and showcase how you got from there to where you are today.

- Embracing your messiness or quirkiness is relatable and memorable, because it reminds your audience that you're human and allows them to feel like they're being seen.

 ## A QUICK WIN

- Write out your Simple Story Structure and create a post using it to reintroduce yourself to your audience on social media.

PUT IT ON A POST-IT

- No one is perfect. Perfect is boring, unrelatable, and uninteresting.

CHAPTER 12

YOUR FOMO IS FOR YOU

"You've got to get down here!" Our friend Donnie, the owner of a comedy club on the Upper West Side, sounded excited over the phone. "Don't tell anyone, but Jerry Seinfeld is going to be on-stage for a surprise set in ten minutes."

"Holy shit." Chris and I looked at each other, our eyes wide with excitement. By the time we hung up the phone, we were al-ready tripping our way out the door, tugging our shoes and coats on as we went.

Donnie's place is a tiny hole-in-the-wall on the corner of Broad-way and 75th Street that features a lot of new and rising talent as well as, yes, occasionally, some of the biggest names in the game. On this particular night, we rushed over and grabbed a table just as one of the greatest comedy legends of all time took the stage. Now, I feel like I don't really need to give the man an intro, but I'm gonna do it anyway. Not only is Jerry Seinfeld a household name in stand-up, but *Seinfeld* the show is a cultural zeitgeist. He's the kind of guy who made it so big with observational comedy that starting any joke with the right tone and the words "Did you ever notice . . ." or "What's the deal with . . ." is immediately recogniz-able as a Seinfeld impression.

What's the deal with airline food?

What's the deal with lampshades?

What's the deal with how damn easy it is for aspiring perform-ers to FOMO the crap out of a major celebrity like Jerry Seinfeld? It is sooooo easy to look at a famous person, or anyone who is suc-cessful in a field where you're trying to make a name for yourself, and think, *Ugh, I should be doing that. That should be me.*

FOMO is one of those sneaky symptoms of fear that stalks us like a serial killer in a true-crime documentary, always waiting in the bushes for a chance to strike. We talked a little bit in Chapter 2 about how defining it as "fear of missing out" is, well, missing out on the real point! For me, FOMO, isn't about sitting at home while your friends are at a party and wishing you were there with them. Yes, that's definitely a version of FOMO, but I'm talking about something a little different. My version is more like that feeling of scrolling through social media and seeing someone who does something similar to what you're doing, but they're getting more opportunities to be seen. They're being featured on podcasts or up on some stage with other amazing people, and there was a huge feature on them in *Fortune* last month talking about the same topic you talk about in your business.

Why isn't that me? you think when you see their post. *That should be* me *being featured as the expert on this!*

Soon you're down the rabbit hole, worrying that you're not good enough and you'll never get anywhere in life or business, and before you know it, you're stuck in a comparisonitis trap and endless cycle of analysis paralysis until all those symptoms of fear flood your brain and keep you at a standstill. Yeah, no thanks. You know by now that this result has been fear's evil plan all along, and when you play into FOMO over another person's success, you're letting your fear keep you from success. That's why I always say you're not afraid of missing out, you're afraid of missing your moment—your *opportunity*—to shine as brightly as someone else. So say it with me, bestie: FOMO: Fear of Missed Opportunity.

That night at the comedy club, I watched Jerry Seinfeld—one of the highest-paid celebrities of all time, who has sold out international tours, and who comedians everywhere FOMO over—get up on a tiny stage and perform. I was totally shocked to see that he wasn't doing some polished act that had us all bent double with laughter. No, my friends, the great Jerry Seinfeld read his jokes to us from a freakin' piece of paper! He was working out new material, making notes in his little book about which bits landed well with the crowd and which ones fell a little flat. As I watched him up there, I realized something: Jerry Seinfeld is exactly like the rest of us (just another reminder that everybody poops!). We always see these big celebrities doing their finished routines on their Netflix shows or some huge stage, and they're so funny and amazing. But what we *don't* see is those same comedians in practice mode: trying things out and refining bits over and over until it becomes the hilarious, polished end product we're used to FOMOing over.

I'm gonna be honest—some of Jerry Seinfeld's jokes absolutely shit the bed that night. But watching Jerry suck was actually one of the most beautiful things I've ever seen. I was getting a glimpse of his Chapter 1 instead of the Chapter 20 people are used to seeing from him. Watching him read his jokes from a sheet of paper was such a perfect reminder that we all start somewhere, and that "somewhere" isn't always all that good—even if you're Jerry fucking Seinfeld. It takes courage to get from the starting line to the end point, but it also takes a process. That night was another one of those moments that helped me realize how to use someone you're FOMOing over as a tool in your own success kit.

A ROAD MAP TO SUCCESS

When I started my podcast, I found myself FOMOing over my friend's podcast, which gets millions of downloads a month, scores massive celebrities as guests, and has major brands as paid sponsors. I had *just* launched *I Dare You* the week before, and my podcast obviously didn't have the momentum of some of the shows that had been working out their kinks for years (yet!). I completely understood that my friend had spent multiple years and thousands of hours of hard work to get to where he was, but that didn't stop good ol' FOMO and comparisonitis from swooping right on in and before I knew it, I was comparing my Chapter 1 to his Chapter 20.

My podcast will never get to that level.

I should have started this years ago.

I'm so far behind.

All these thoughts and so many more flooded my brain, making me feel like total crap when, hellooo, I had just accomplished something huge by getting my podcast up and running! I should have been overwhelmed with pride, not inferiority! Luckily, I have lots of practice in this arena and was able to catch this symptom of fear and use it before it used me! You see, FOMO can take you down a slippery slope of self-sabotage, but it can also be a powerful tool to supercharge your clarity. It can even become your road map to success if you let it. You get to choose! Chris reminds me daily that I'm not responsible for my first thought, but I *am* responsible for the thought that follows and the actions I take as a result. So, after a few shitty first thoughts, I made a conscious choice to use my FOMO as fuel. How can I be grateful for it?

Here's the thing: not only is my yucky feeling of missed opportunity showing me what I desire—to have a top podcast—but it's also showing me what's possible. If I lean in to studying what my amazing friend did to build the success that I desire, it will lead me to the exact steps I should take for a similar result! Success leaves clues, and the first step to discovering those clues is to experience that feeling of, *Ugh, that should be me.*

So in the case of my podcast envy, I back-scrolled to the very first episode of my friend's show. I took notes on what topics and guests he featured in the beginning—back when celebrities wouldn't give him the time of day. I also checked out the different ways he marketed the show throughout the years. I got so many ideas from this quick bit of research, plus it made my comparisonitis lessen because it forced me to remember that everyone starts somewhere. Just like that, I went from FOMOing my face off to experiencing an overwhelming amount of gratitude for my friend, his podcast, and everything I learned from my good ol' frenemy fear.

When it comes to starting to be seen in the media as the recognized expert in your niche, your FOMO is going to become your greatest asset! One of the most popular questions from our clients and mastermind members when they first get started is, "Where should I be featured in the media?" The answer is a lot closer than you think, because, yes, you guessed it, it lies in the person you're FOMOing over! While your first (and very normal) thought might be, *Ugh that should be me* when you see Hannah featured in a top publication, make the second thought, *I'm so grateful I saw Hannah in* Inc. *magazine because this proves that the media wants my expertise and shows me that I could be featured there too!* And if you go down the Google rabbit hole and backstalk all of the media that Hannah got up until the *Inc.* magazine feature, you'll most likely find many other publications, podcasts, and shows that are perfect for you too.

RECOGNIZE YOUR OPPORTUNITY

> *And so it's best we end this*
> *Before we even start*
> *Signed, your pal Linda*
> *The 'i' is dotted with a broken heeeeeart . . .*

My foam fat suit covered in several layers of "old lady" garb had me sweating like I'd just finished a Peloton ride though I was only standing there in the wings, watching April, the actor who had my part, perform my song in *The Wedding Singer*. (I know you know how this story ends already, but step back in time with me for a moment!)

That should be me, I thought, watching the way her fingerless-gloved hands clutched the bouquet and glaring at her legs in those thigh-high white boots. Jealousy flooded me until I was practically choking on it. *I should be singing that song. I could do it better than her, couldn't I?* I went home every night and compared myself to her, performing the song in front of my mirror and letting comparisonitis trample all over me. Still, I couldn't get a handle on my FOMO until I realized what wiser people than me have realized for a long, long time: my jealousy was doing nothing but bringing me down! Nelson Mandela is quoted as saying, "Resentment is like drinking poison and hoping it will kill your enemies." I was chugging bottle after bottle of toxic waste every night in those wings, but my negativity wasn't hurting April, it was only hurting me! I had to flip this around.

Instead of being jealous and pissed off, I started putting my energy into studying her every move. She'd been cast as Linda instead of me, so she must have done something better than me—and now that I was in detective mode, I was going to figure it out so I could improve myself and get to her level. I made it my mission to master everything she was doing right—the choreography, the intonation in her voice—as well as everything she was doing wrong. I started using my time in the wings not to glare at her and wish she'd trip and break her ankle, but as an opportunity to determine what I liked and disliked about how she played Linda. I was going to prepare my ass off for my opportunity. That way, when it was my turn to get up there and put that costume on, I'd be able to fucking *rock* that role.

Refocusing my energy this way had an added bonus: As I studied and analyzed her every move, my fear of missing out on my opportunity began to lessen. I began to turn all that FOMO into better focus, and, to paraphrase Wallace D. Wattles from his famous book *The Science of Getting Rich*, I began to detach myself from the competitive plane and get on the creative plane instead. That's where all the magic happens.

My energy shifted so much that I found myself wanting to befriend April! So I started sitting with my new buddy at lunch and taking walks with her between shows all while asking the questions that flooded my mind as I watched her perform. "What was your objective in the scene with Julia after 'Let Me Come Home'?" I asked. "How did you rip the skirt off without tearing the Velcro? Can you show me so when I do it, I can do it right?"

As you and I both know by now, people love helping other people (even when it's your understudy who, until recently, might have been lowkey plotting your demise). Asking April for help made her feel really special and seen because I made it clear that I looked up to her and wanted to learn from her expertise. We ended up becoming good friends and I ended up bettering my own performance—all because I was able to recognize my own FOMO and flip it from jealousy to curiosity and gratitude.

THE SHOULDERS OF GIANTS

Sir Isaac Newton once said, "If I have seen further, it is by standing on the shoulders of giants." So many other well-known people have used variations of this phrase—philosopher Bernard of Chartres, author Mary Shelley, self-help coach Tony Robbins—to make the same point: success doesn't emerge fully formed from a vacuum.[1] We all have something to learn from those who came before us. We can take their knowledge and experience and apply it to our own specific circumstances, even steering those lessons to a different destination if we want. But the point is that looking up at the "giants" of our field and climbing onto their shoulders to see further than we could on our own is one of the best ways to learn and grow.

It's also exactly how I want you to flip your FOMO.

My clients tell me all the time, "Someone else is already doing that." They use it as an excuse not to pursue a new idea, but hearing this always makes me want to flick them on the nose. Someone succeeding at what you want is actually really amazing news because it means it can and should be done and, further, that people want it.

In my own entrepreneurial journey, there is absolutely no better story about FOMO being *for* me than my friendship with best-selling author and top podcast host Lori Harder. Back when I was rebuilding my life after the Rob breakup and brick wall breakdown, I spent most days trekking around New York City going from casting to casting with a rollie bag full of audition dresses in one hand and my iPhone connected to Apple Podcasts in the

other. The very first podcast I became hooked on was Lori Harder's *Earn Your Happy*. I was still flirting with the idea of entering
the fitness industry, and I immediately started girl-crushing (and
FOMOing) hard over this amazing, inspiring woman who rocked
the cover of fitness magazines, ran a successful coaching business,
and hosted a top podcast all about mindset and being your best
self. She had an Instagram page with hundreds of thousands of
engaged fans, a beautiful website with courses and e-books on fitness and nutrition, and most importantly, she was cool, vulnerable, real, funny, and wise. These were all the things I wanted to
create and the qualities I possessed. The problem? Nobody saw
any of that because I was still known as "Heavy Metal Jennifer." I
so desperately wanted to shift the inauthentic narrative I had created and start building something that came from Real Jen, but it
never felt possible until my FOMO for Lori's career slowly helped
me develop a new belief. I would walk around the city for hours
listening to her, and with every step, I became clearer about what
I wanted to create and how it was totally achievable.

I leaned in to my FOMO and discovered there was a big need
for empowering female creators who shared a message of positiv-
ity, collaboration, and personal growth. Researching what Lori did
and how she did it gave me the road map and the confidence I
needed to build JLG Fitness into a super successful multi-six-figure
business that made a huge impact on thousands of people's lives.
Lori had no clue at the time, but she was my virtual mentor, and
my FOMO for her changed my life.

FLIP YOUR FOMO

I need you to go through an exercise with me right now. Take a few
deep breaths and think about someone in your life or your field
who you're seriously FOMOing over. This should be someone who
eats at your insides with jealousy when you see them succeeding
at something *you* should be doing instead. Someone who is maybe
five years, or one year, ahead of you in your climb to the top. If
you're writing a book, choose someone who already has an agent

or a book deal, and if you're launching a new brand or business, choose someone who's been in your field for a year or two already. Scroll through their Insta grid or read a few of their blog posts on their website, then put on your Sherlock Holmes trench coat and ask yourself the following questions:

- Who are they connected to?

- What topics are they talking about?

- What media outlets are featuring them?

- Who has been talking about them?

- What makes them stand out?

Now go ahead and repeat the exercise for two or three more people, then look at the answers you've written down. Do you see any trends?

Those people you're FOMOing over have been paving the yellow brick road, showing you exactly how to get to the Emerald City. Those answers you wrote down are a road map to that same destination. Congrats, friend! You've just built yourself a step-by-step travel guide full of actionable, achievable goals to get you to your Oz.

When I realized how much my own business goals aligned with Lori Harder's, I got to work. I searched Google News for "Lori Harder," and listened to every podcast she was a guest on. What publications featured her? Which Instagram accounts did she follow, and how did she engage with them? Who did she collaborate with? Because she worked in the same field as me, it was like I'd suddenly opened up a step-by-step instruction manual. I learned about blogs I'd never even heard of and thought, *I could pitch myself there*, and then followed the writer who wrote about Lori on social media so I could start to form a connection. Using my Top 20 list and my lean-in story, I found TV shows and media outlets interested in what I had to offer and built relationships with people who could help me book a guest spot. Over time, I provided value to writers and producers and increased my Top 20 score with people who could help create opportunities for me. I flipped my FOMO into curiosity and traced the steps of Lori's success to see how she'd done it. Armed with the map she'd written for me as my virtual mentor, I began walking a path toward success that I hadn't even known existed.

The cool thing I want you to remember about all of this is that me building success in the same industry as Lori took nothing away from her. In fact, my success provided me the opportunity to pay it forward in some majorly impactful ways. Let's skip ahead to when Lori and I eventually met and (shocker) became best friends. We have traveled the country together, spoken at each other's events, and referred one another to speaking engagements. We've recorded multiple powerful podcast episodes together, promoted each other's programs, and danced the night away at my wedding. One of my proudest moments was when I was able to give back to her financially and become an investor in her new company.

STOP WAITING TO BE "ORIGINAL"

Maybe you're saying, *But I want to be original, Jen! I don't want to follow in any footsteps; I want to do things no one has ever done before!* Well, I promised I'd always give you the hard truth. So my friend, here's an important (but maybe difficult to swallow) truth: your idea is never going to be completely original. There's *always* going to be somebody else who, to some extent or another, has done what you want to do. I'm sorry, but I mean it. *Always.*

Even revolutionaries like Steve Jobs built upon the foundations of the people who came before him. We like to think of inventions like the iPhone as completely revolutionary, and while it's certainly an achievement that advanced the world of technology, Jobs didn't create that first phone from nothing in 2007. The first touch screen was invented for air traffic control decades earlier in 1975, and the iPod was built on the example of the Sony Walkman.[2] That doesn't make any of his inventions less groundbreaking, but it serves as an important reminder that everything we create builds on research and ideas from a long line of people and innovations throughout history.

The good news is that you're far from the only person who wants to do it all on their own. It's so prevalent that there's even a term for it. Not-invented-here syndrome is a psychological bias that makes us not want to buy into ideas or use products that exist already or come from an outside perspective.[3] When applied to branding, this generally means we're intent on making our own way so we can feel like our ideas and success are completely original, and even if a solution to our problem exists already, we're apt to reject it simply because it was "not invented here." We want to pull ourselves up by our bootstraps, and like stubborn toddlers matching a tutu to a pair of overalls, we're obsessed with doing things on our own. This is even why studies have shown consumers are ready and willing to pay, on average, 63 percent more for furniture they have to assemble themselves, also known as the IKEA effect.

But what's wrong with someone having done what you want to do first? Not-invented-here syndrome sometimes stems from concerns about copyright infringement or being accused of stealing ideas, but let's remember, without standing on the shoulders of giants, human civilization wouldn't have progressed much at all! It's our nature to build on the ideas, inventions, and people who came before us, and addressing your FOMO is absolutely no different.

So while you'll never be completely original, someone else succeeding in an arena you aspire to doesn't take anything away from you or what you have to offer. When you launch your new product, it's okay that it's inspired by or descended from someone else's idea. It's okay that your business isn't the only one in the world to do what you do. Maybe you will do it better or maybe you won't, but I know for certain you'll definitely do it *differently*, because the one thing that you can count on is that there's only one you.

There are a bajillion life coaches out there but if you're a life coach, that doesn't mean you should just throw in the towel.

There is only one person on this earth who speaks the way you do and brings together the exact combination of experiences and knowledge that you do, and that person, my friend, is *you*. Maybe other coaches use the same quote as you in their talks, but they don't say it the way *you* say it. We've already talked about your lean-in story and how your mess is your message, so you know that those vulnerable moments make you unique and help other people feel connected to you.

Maybe other fitness coaches could have gotten on that talk show with Joanna Gagis and helped her audience learn how to better their lives, but none of them had my history of being Miss Box of Junk. So I promise that if you're seeing somebody who is doing what you want to do, it's not a bad thing. It's a fantastic thing because they're showing you that it can be done. Now all you have to do is go and do it in your own way. The people you are helping need to hear what you have to say directly from *you*, and that's why you owe it to your audience to get past your FOMO and use it to reach them.

THE HIGHEST FORM OF FLATTERY

If you grew up with siblings or have kids, I bet at some point you've heard the phrase "Imitation is the highest form of flattery."

In the land where I used to live (the Wild West known as the acting world), I had a mindset of *If they get this part, then there are fewer parts for me.* If someone else succeeded, it meant I couldn't. It bred a sense of one-upmanship and competition that became a cesspit of negativity that only took away from my own experience, just like when I let my jealousy get the best of me in the wings of *The Wedding Singer.*

I don't live in that world anymore. Now I've come to understand that an opportunity for someone else does not mean a lack of opportunity for you, and when you're focused on creation instead of competition, you're creating opportunities for yourself and for those around you. I've gone from a mindset of pulling others down to bring myself up, to building others up so I can build myself up too. A rising tide raises all the boats, as the saying goes.

I believe with all my heart that understanding how to use your FOMO *for* you is the shortcut to achieving your goals, like a secret bookshelf door hidden out of sight unless you know exactly which book to pull. After all, a trail that's already been blazed by someone else means you don't have to spend all your time hacking and slashing at thorny branches on your way to your destination.

This is why I 100 percent believe in the power of mentorship, masterminds, and putting yourself in rooms with people who are doing what you want to do. Whether you're FOMOing over Brené Brown, Jerry Seinfeld, or someone who's well known in your specific niche, I invite you to stop being jealous and start being a detective. Follow the path they've laid out for you, and you will eventually find your very own, very unique version of success. It can start here with me! I've laid out in this book everything I've done to get to where I am, and I'm inviting you to use my story as your road map. If you backstalk my YouTube or Instagram or even take a moment to Google me, you will see the messy breadcrumbs I've left for you. Many people pay tens of thousands of dollars to scrub old videos and photos off the Internet, but not me. I purposely leave my imperfect mood board of life chapters up for the world to see. Because no matter how messy, off brand, or (incredibly) embarrassing they might be, they are all puzzle pieces that make up who I am today and, more importantly, who I'm continuing to become.

Please learn from my mistakes, copy what's worked, throw away what didn't, and tag along for the journey as I continue to try new things. I hope it will help you discover what I did: that my FOMO was never actually a problem; it was my solution in disguise the whole time.

🎤 MIC DROP MOMENTS

- Your FOMO (fear of missed opportunity) is for you.

- Don't compare your Chapter 1 to someone else's Chapter 20.

- Success leaves clues, and it's important to follow the footsteps of the people you're FOMOing over to see how they did it—and how you can do it too.

- We all stand on the shoulders of giants—even the most famous, successful people in the world built off of the ideas that came before them.

- An opportunity for someone else does not mean a lack of opportunity for you.

A QUICK WIN

- Identify someone you're FOMOing over in your field and ask yourself:

    - Who are they connected to?

    - What topics are they talking about?

    - What media outlets are featuring them?

    - Who has been talking about them?

    - What makes them stand out?

- Now look at your answers and find one of them that you can replicate right now.

✍️ PUT IT ON A POST-IT

- Success leaves clues, and it's up to you to follow them.

CHAPTER 13

VISIBILITY IS YOUR RESPONSIBILITY

Now, I'm no doctor, but when a holistic child psychologist came to us looking for help, it was easy for me to immediately diagnose Dr. Norah with one of the most serious cases of imposter syndrome I'd ever seen. Dr. Norah is an incredible woman who helps adolescents and young adults with mental illness and behavioral disorders heal through the power of nutrition and functional medicine, but because of her own symptoms of fear, she was hiding and not allowing herself to be seen.

"I hate talking about myself," she told me when I met her at an event. "I just feel like I'm bragging, and what if people don't agree with my ideas around healing mental health through nutrition? What if people call me a fraud?" (Um, hello, as a reminder, the woman has a Ph.D. in child psychology and is certified as both a psychologist and a nutritionist!) Even though she was one of the leading doctors in her field, literally saving lives, she was still terrified of people thinking she wasn't the real deal. This kept her from putting herself out there and being seen by the people who needed her. Dr. Norah was petrified to be on television, but she knew this fear was only hurting the families that desperately needed her help and weren't getting it because they didn't know she existed. So she put fear in the passenger seat of her minivan and signed on to work with Super Connector Media for her PR. Because Dr. Norah was so qualified and her messaging points were so timely, she started booking TV spots right away. Our team was thrilled, but her? Not so much. Her fear of being seen was so bad that she made herself physically sick with anxiety and didn't show up for one of her segments.

"Norah," I said in a coaching session, using my no-bullshit New Yorker voice. "Does what you do help people?"

Without hesitation, she looked up at me with utter certainty and said, "Yes. One hundred percent."

"Then this is not optional," I told her. "It is your *responsibility* to be seen."

She'd never thought about it that way. That the families and children who needed her might continue to suffer or go get the wrong treatment simply because the woman who had their solution was too scared to make herself known. Thankfully, this angle hit home for her. That next week, Dr. Norah dove headfirst into the Confidence Continuum, took that first scary action step and did her debut TV segment on a local news channel. Honestly, this story is a great testimonial for the Confidence Continuum too (refer back to Chapter 3 for a refresher!), because getting that tiny win of doing the segment even though she was scared gave her the confidence she needed to do it again, and again, and again! Before she knew it, she was making a real name for herself, all because she shoved her fears aside, did something scary, and built on her own momentum.

"You know I've had major resistance to being in the spotlight," she told us in a DM later. "But the second time I was on TV talking about food, nutrition, and kids' health, a mom of an acutely suicidal teenager saw the segment, looked up my website, and contacted my office. Her daughter had been to every treatment center and practitioner in the area and was on every drug—and she was still symptomatic and suicidal. They came into the clinic, and I started treating her. I uncovered some critical nutrition and other issues no one else had found. She is no longer suicidal, she's back in school, and she's continuing to improve. You pushing me to share my gifts, get over my own fears, and share what I know with more people literally saved her life."

Whoa.

Let's let that sit there for a second.

I don't want to think about what might have happened if Dr. Norah didn't get over her fear of being visible, do you?

That's the power of visibility. When you have a service, product, story, or message that has the potential to help people, it is your *responsibility* to be seen. Every single day that goes by that you're not being seen is another day that the people who need your help are going to go hire someone else, or listen to someone else, or follow someone who's maybe not as good as you are, can't provide the value that you can, or doesn't care as much as you do. Your audience—the people who need you—are going to hire them instead simply because they can't find you. So, not putting yourself out there because you're scared or worried about what you look or sound like or how it will come across to others?

That's an act of pure selfishness.

Yes, I said it, and I will fight you on this.

If you're not being seen, you're being selfish. Can I get a mic drop on that? Because guess what? Self-promotion isn't gross. It's (say it with me now!) your responsibility.

Most of us who don't want to be seen are worried because we care about what they think about us (and who the hell is *they* anyway?). We care because we're human, and it's human nature to care about what other people think. But what if we stopped letting those other people live rent-free in our heads? What if we loved ourselves and believed in our mission so much that other opinions couldn't touch us? What if we took all the time and energy we put into caring about what other people think and put it into loving ourselves and the message we are serving the world with? What if we stepped into the spotlight and started owning our main-character energy? What would happen then?

In this chapter we're going to totally reframe the way you look at being seen, because at the end of the day it's honestly kind of hilarious how little it has to do with you at all! Being seen is about serving the people who need you most, and right here, right now, we're going to take the ego out of being visible. It's not about you and how you look; it's about the person reading that magazine article or watching you on the news or bookmarking that Instagram reel so they can revisit it again and again. It's about helping one person, just one, in a way only you can, like the mother who saw Dr. Norah's segment on TV and made a call that saved her daughter's life.

GETTING YOUR NERVES DOWN
AND YOUR H.O.P.E. UP

These days, you can't get away with avoiding the camera. Many of us are on Zoom all day for work, and when you're trying to grow your business, that means you need to get real comfy with showing your face on Facebook Live, TikTok, Instagram, and good old TV. The truth is, you're going to connect to your audience better on video because they like seeing you and feeling like they know you. But understanding that fact and getting in the spotlight are still two different things. Being on camera can be so scary even for me, but one thing that always, *always* helps me press record with more courage is H.O.P.E.

H.O.P.E. stands for Help One Person Every day, and it's a concept that helps me be seen onstage, in front of the camera, and in interviews. When I get nervous (and believe me, I still get super-duper mega nervous all the time!), I can imagine I'm talking to just one person instead of thousands of people. For the longest time, I kept a cute li'l photo of Chris right next to my camera when I did media segments, because a lot of what makes us nervous on camera is talking to a lens instead of a human being. (Where's the connection in that, you know?) Having a photo of my love next to my camera allowed me to take a scary conversation with a blinking red light and turn it into a comfortable chat with someone I never feel nervous around.

Who needs to hear your message most? Is it your best friend? Your 13-year-old daughter? Your partner? Your favorite client? An old co-worker you still think about? Start talking like you're speaking directly to them when you make your content, and I'm willing to bet you're going to have a much easier time talking to that camera—*and* serving your audience.

If you're having trouble thinking about who you're speaking to, I want you to consider this: we are most equipped to help the person we were 10 years ago, or the person we were when we first started. When I feel fuzzy about my audience or my content, I ask myself, "Who would I have needed to talk to? What did I need to hear?" If you're reading this book right now, you probably had to go through a hell of a lot to be in a place where you can teach a concept or provide a service that you, at one point in your life, really needed. More likely than not, your original inspiration came from a place of not having this all-important thing.

I think a lot about teenage Jen who cried herself to sleep in shame after throwing up her birthday dinner because she was obsessed with fitting in with the cool girls, and about depressed, dumped, post–Miss Box of Junk Jen staring at that brick wall, so unsure about her next steps in life. A lot of my content is like a magic, time-traveling DM addressed specifically to me. I talk directly to those past versions of myself because I know exactly what she wants and needs to hear most. I know there are others out there who need to hear it too. And, you guys, it makes it so, so, *so* easy to speak my message.

I speak to one person when I'm onstage too, thanks to a trick I learned when I was an actress neck-deep in auditions. Before my speaking events, I'll talk to people attending and start up some conversations. I don't have a set list of criteria, but I'll choose one person every time who I really connect with and draw energy from them while I'm up there speaking. I'll think about that person, and in my head, I imagine my presentation is for nobody but that one person. Thinking of any speech as a one-on-one conversation completely takes away my nerves, and as a bonus, everyone in the room always seems to think that one person I'm pouring into is them. This is the exact secret sauce that standing ovations are made from.

If you can just pretend you're talking to one person, it also helps you stop worrying about what you look or sound like, because it's not about you anymore; it's about that person who needs your help. With H.O.P.E., you can just show up and serve, like Dr. Norah did when she made herself visible to that teenage girl's mom.

Helping others in the way only you can is the name of the game. It is why being seen matters. You have been given a gift, not so you can hold it inside, but so you can share it with the world and provide value to other humans and the planet we call home. That's why it's yours, and that's why you need to take your visibility seriously.

Some of the most famous people in the world are people who knew they had a gift from a young age and fought tooth and nail to get themselves where they could be seen and use that gift to help people. Oprah Winfrey knew what her gifts were from the time she started interviewing her dolls as a young kid. She took those gifts to a job as a local news anchor, but she found it too restrictive—when she was reporting the news, she had to be completely objective, but her gift lay in her empathy and her ability to connect with the people she was interviewing. Oprah realized she wasn't able to help people the way she knew she could by reporting the news and said she felt misplaced and inauthentic in that position. She wasn't making herself visible in the right way or to the right people! After being fired from that anchor job (and turning that rejection into her bestie!), Oprah continued to make herself be seen by any means, leading her to talk radio, and eventually her own show where she was able to change millions of lives.

Oprah once told Reese Witherspoon, "People just want to be seen. They want to be acknowledged. They want to know that they were understood. And if I could help people do that I'd feel really, really proud of the work I've done in this world."[1]

First of all, Oprah gets it. Second of all, what would have happened if Oprah had given up? What would have happened if she'd dimmed her light when her news manager told her, "You're too emotional when you interview people"? Oprah knew what her gifts were, and she knew her audience needed her to be seen so *they* could be seen. So she set her doubts (and the haters) aside and climbed her way to the very top. If Oprah never made that pivot and started being seen for her true gifts, we might have missed out on all the incredible authors she made famous through her book club, the recurring guests on her show who went on to host their own, and the impactful people who call her a mentor and got where they are today by FOMOing over her and following in her footsteps.

Practically every influential person in the world has a story like this. The most successful CEOs of the world's biggest companies would never have gotten where they are today without sticking to their guns. Serena and Venus Williams's family fought to help make them visible by moving across the country so the girls could attend a tennis academy. Elizabeth Gilbert fought to make her writing visible even after six *years* of nonstop rejection. Jeff Bezos, Ruth Bader Ginsburg, Sara Blakely, Martin Luther King Jr., Elon Musk—they're not names you'd expect to see in the same sentence, because they all made their mark in very different ways, but the one thing they all have in common is that they knew their product, service, or message had the potential to make an impact so long as they could make themselves visible by the right people.

Remember Lori Harder? I found Lori when I needed her most, and now that she and I are besties IRL and not just in my head, I always like to joke that I manifested my best friend. But the funniest part is, Lori says the exact same thing about me! Back when I was listening to her podcast, living in a horrible little closet bedroom, Lori was using the H.O.P.E. method without even realizing it. She was thinking to herself, *I'm talking to this one girl out there who just really needs what I have to say.*

We hadn't met yet, and she didn't know it, but Lori was talking to me all along. She helped me grow and learn and expand my business, and now that we're friends, I've been able to provide value to her as well by being a guest on her podcast, speaking on her stage, and becoming part of her personal and professional support system. She had no idea that spilling her thoughts on her podcast would come back to her in this way! We've done amazing things for one another, and she changed my life, but none of it would have happened if Lori hadn't made herself visible!

If she'd gotten in her own head and thought, *No, I don't want to be braggy,* where would she be? Yikes—where would *I* be?

Because Lori made herself visible, I was able to learn from her content and see an example of what I could achieve if I took action consistently. Now, in part because of her, I help thousands of people too, because that's the thing about helping one person every day—it creates a snowball effect, and before you know it, your reach expands more than you ever thought possible.

SHINE BRIGHT LIKE A DIAMOND

In Part III, you learned all about assembling the group of people who are going to support you when you share your wins, and now that you've made it to this part of the book, it's time to start sharing those wins with your squad. This is where I usually start to see discomfort on my clients' faces, and then the usual refrain of excuses starts rolling in:

I don't want to sound braggy.

I don't want to be that *person.*

Posting new content every day feels icky.

Be honest with me. Have you ever had one of those thoughts? Do you see me raising my hand high over here? Because I definitely have! Back in the day I used to be petrified to share any of my wins online for fear of triggering my very-competitive friend group. I knew they would think that if I shined too brightly, it would take the shine away from them. Then they would become resentful and bitchy. Dimming your light to make others feel comfortable is something that a lot of people do without even realizing it. Ladies, this goes double for you because historically, a confident woman who is proud of her achievements has been thought of as bossy or stuck-up when a man acting the same way is not held to the same standard! This feeling comes from a fear of not being liked by everyone, aka the disease to please, which we talked all about in Chapter 2.

Just so we're clear, it's totally normal to have these thoughts. It's scary as shit to put yourself out there! I'm gonna be real with you—it's not easy. But you've gotten to this point of the book, so you're well aware that Easy Street is not on your Waze route toward your extraordinary future. Remember, discomfort is temporary, but growth is permanent, and here's the thing: *actual* braggy people don't think those thoughts. They're not worried about posting too much or sharing their achievements because they don't care how it comes across. So what I always tell entrepreneurs who come to me worried about stepping into the spotlight is that if you're worried about being braggy, then you're not a bragger—that's number one. Number two is that keeping yourself small does not serve your audience.

Marianne Williamson said in her book *A Return to Love*, "Our deepest fear is not that we're inadequate. Our deepest fear is that we're powerful beyond measure. It is our light, not our darkness, that frightens us most. We ask ourselves, 'Who am I to be brilliant, gorgeous, talented, fabulous?' Actually, who are you not to be?"

WHEN NOT TO BE SEEN

With all that said, I couldn't possibly write a book about being seen without warning you about the dangers of oversharing before your story is fully baked. Yes, you heard me right, there are times when you *shouldn't* be seen, and sometimes it's hard to decipher between a story that's ready to be told and one that should remain in the wings until it's ready for its debut.

We all have that one person we follow on social media who reminds us of a car crash. I know you know exactly who I'm talking about. You probably spy on them with one eye open, cringing from what my chief of staff, Liz, calls "secondhand embarrassment," as they cry hysterically on camera every other post and infiltrate your feed with morbid images of a weird rash or eye infection that no one wants to see. You might not be this extreme, but I would be doing you a disservice if I didn't tell you that being unnecessarily vulnerable just to get attention—what I like to call "vulnerability porn"—makes your audience more likely to smash that Unfollow button instead of the Like button.

Helping people through making yourself visible is your responsibility, yes, but visibility doesn't mean you need to share every dirty detail of your life experience as it's happening in real time. Not only could this damage your engagement and destroy your credibility, but it could hurt others as well. When a story, post, or message doesn't have a clear point, it's because it isn't finished yet. Just like 20-something Jen scribbling "One day I'll know why this happened" in my journal, not everything makes sense until it comes to its natural conclusion and you have a bit of space from it. Even then, sometimes it takes time for the wound to close before you want to show it to the world.

That's the question I want you to ask yourself when you're worried about whether or not to share something (especially when it's a vulnerable story). *Is this wound open or closed?*

An open wound is fresh and still painful, and you might not be able to talk about it yet without tearing it wide open. But a closed wound creates a scar. It doesn't hurt anymore (but it looks pretty badass!), and sharing the story of how you got that scar comes from a place of power: you know that you got through to the other side. These days, I can talk openly about my eating disorder because it's a closed wound, and I've Neosporin'd the shit out of that scar to the point where I can use my experience to help people. But if I tried to share about my journey when I was knee deep in it or when talking about it triggered me back into destructive habits, I'd know that wound was still open and I had some healing to do before I could make that story—that wound—visible to my audience.

Sharing open-wound stories doesn't just risk causing you a dip in followers, credibility, and engagement, it can also hurt the other people who are involved in that particular experience. Some stories aren't completely yours to share, and bringing to the surface something private that involves other people can open up a whole other can of worms that you don't want. So once you've made the decision that your wound is a sexy scar, do some due diligence to make sure that sharing your story won't cause any harm to others.

I want you to use your mess as your message, and yes, I want you to be visible and use your experiences to help other people, but never before the cake has been baked, the dough has risen, the goose is cooked, and it's ready to be served to your audience.

There might always be loose ends, even in closed-wound stories, and maybe a little bit of soreness. That's life! And determining which is ready to share and which isn't is deeply personal. But if you tap into Real You and ask yourself what's right, you'll know the answer. I trust you. If my story has taught you anything, I hope it's that the hardest things you've ever been through have the potential to lead to some of the greatest moments of your life. So when you look back at your wounds and you can see that, you'll know you're ready to make those scars—those beautiful, meaningful, messy, powerful scars who made Real You who you are—visible.

What I want you to remember in terms of visibility is that your audience is always growing, and you're going to be slowly building it over time. This is why it's so important to keep talking to that audience, keep sharing your message. Remember that shining your light doesn't dim anybody else's; it just makes the room brighter for everybody and gives *them* permission to shine too.

🎤 MIC DROP MOMENTS

- It is your responsibility to be seen. Every single day that goes by that you're not being seen is another day that the people who need your help are going to listen to someone else who's maybe not as good as you are, can't provide the value that you can, or doesn't care as much as you do. Your audience— the people who need you—are going to hire them instead simply because they can't find you.

- If what you do helps people, not putting yourself out there (even if it's because you're scared) is an act of pure selfishness.

- Being seen has very little to do with you at all!

- H.O.P.E.: Help One Person Every day.

- We are most equipped to help the person we were 10 years ago.

- Ask yourself, "Is the wound open or closed?" to know if you're ready to make a new part of yourself seen.

👏 A QUICK WIN

- Create and share one piece of content today that can help the person you used to be.

✍️ PUT IT ON A POST-IT

- Visibility is your responsibility.

CHAPTER 14

BECOMING A CIA AGENT

Nowadays, anyone can create a social media account and say that they're awesome. Joe Schmo who's never built a business can literally go online and create a fancy website calling himself a business guru and charge thousands of dollars for his services. Anyone can say they're the greatest real estate person or coach in the world, and there's nothing stopping them from making that claim. There's nothing to stop the pizza joint down the street from putting up a sign that says "BEST PIZZA IN THE CITY" or the car dealership near your office from saying "YOU WON'T FIND PRICES THIS LOW ANYWHERE ELSE" even if it's not true. (In fact, there's even a name for this—"puffery"—and it's perfectly legal under the Federal Trade Commission! Scary, right?)

The good thing is, lots of people are onto this and need a hell of a lot more convincing than a colorful banner or a pretty IG account to smash that Buy Now button or even just to hit Follow. So how do you cut through the noise and show that you're a credible, trusted expert with a legitimate product or service that helps people? Pay attention, because I'm gonna give you three letters that will take you and your brand from being the "best-kept secret" to a household name. Ready for it?

CIA.

No, I'm not asking you to become a secret agent—or at least, not in the way you think. Remember, the whole point is to *stop* keeping your business a secret! But I am going to ask you to start going undercover as you're making yourself more visible, because these letters represent three magical words that will separate you from the fakers and, ultimately, help you build a profitable brand. They stand for:

- Credibility

- Influence

- Authority

When you have these three things under your belt, you will go from just another person on the Internet to the recognized expert in your niche. I know you're leaning in, so let's talk about how you can add them to your toolbox.

CREDIBILITY

Your credibility is, to put it simply, your trustworthiness. Your stamp of approval.

When your customers are looking to work with somebody, whether they know it or not, they're going to be subconsciously looking for your credibility markers. Imagine you're looking for a copywriter for your new website and you get two referrals for people who both happen to have the same name and charge the same rate and both happen to be awesome. What's the first thing you're going to do? You're gonna Google them, right?

Now, copywriter A has a nicely designed website with a great headshot, and his About Me page says all the right things. Copywriter B has all this too, but with one major difference: at the top of his homepage is an "as seen in" banner full of logos from *Business Insider* and *NBC* and *The New York Times*.

Which one are you going to choose?

Without even speaking to either of them, it's a total no-brainer, because copywriter B has credibility from some pretty trustworthy sources. If *The New York Times* can trust this guy, then so should you! That's why you need to make your credibility instantly visible to your audience. "But, Jen," I can hear you saying. "What if I don't have it to begin with? How do I start to build it?" It's simple. You need to start getting featured by credible media sources as the "expert" in your space.

A while back, I got a bunch of Instagram DMs from followers asking about how to get over their introverted tendencies when it comes to connecting with people in real life. At the time, we were all still reeling from being locked inside during the pandemic, and I realized that a lot of my followers were having trouble networking in the real world again. I did an Instagram Live about networking in person and making powerful belly-to-belly connections with other people. I was so sure I was tapping into something that people needed that I could practically see the numbers flying through the roof as it went viral. In reality, though? That IG Live pretty much shit the bed. I got a couple of good comments, but nobody shared it, and I didn't get any DMs or sales leads from it. But I still really believed in the power of this topic, and I had a connection to a writer from *Forbes*. So I reached out to her and told her, "This topic is powerful and timely. Let's write an article." (That e-mail cost me nothing, for the record!)

The writer agreed, and suddenly my dinky little Instagram Live was now a *Forbes* article. Exact same content, but can you guess what happened when it said *Forbes* on top of it?

Hundreds of shares from people all over the world, and even some influential entrepreneurs.

DMs coming out of the woodwork from ex-boyfriends and old friends and—most importantly—new connections.

People like my parents, who have no idea what Instagram Live is, could finally appreciate and understand what I do, and the ones who knew me shared the article with everyone they knew! A post on social media is one thing, but a post in a publication like *Forbes* is another one entirely.

My article gained *credibility*, and because of that, it gained *visibility*.

And I gained clients. Leads were pouring into my inbox to ask if they could work with me, and in 72 hours, I'd taken my $0 investment into that article and turned it into $370,000 of profit. Why yes, thank you, I *will* take a round of applause for that one!

Now it's your turn. How can you take some content that you've created and turn it into instant credibility by getting it onto a well-known platform? What Lean-In Stories or popular posts could you turn into an article, podcast episode, or TV segment? Who needs to hear that story, and what publications or media outlets would allow you to connect to that audience? Once you've become clear on where you want to be featured, use your Top 20 tool to find the people to pitch to and use the lessons you learned about your Lean-In Story to find what people actually want to hear. Are all those puzzle pieces falling into place now? I hope so!

INFLUENCE

People love to throw around the word *influencer*. Becoming a social media influencer is a pretty popular career path for Gen Z'ers, and I don't blame them. There are influencers out there getting paid up to seven figures for one social media campaign. Huge companies like Calvin Klein, CÎROC, and even Walmart are taking their marketing dollars out of traditional publishing and pouring them into influencer marketing. They know that just one post or mention from a top influencer with their ideal audience can turn into millions of dollars in sales. As of 2022, the market value for global influencer marketing reached over $16.4 *billion* dollars, with no indication of dropping anytime soon.[1]

In the world we live in today, the more influential you and your brand are, the more money-earning potential you have and the more impact you can make. Why? Because you can influence people to do things, and when you're in business, that usually translates directly to sales. But it's not so easy to build influence on your own. (Remember, literally anybody can get on the Internet right now and say they're awesome!)

It's okay to admit you're having a hard time building your following on social media. Don't be shy—we've known each other for a while now, so you can be honest with me (and with yourself). Did you have lofty plans for your TikTok account only to realize you'd only gained 100 followers after your first 30 days? Do you plot and plan a Facebook Live for hours beforehand, only for a grand total of three people to watch it?

Building *anything* from the ground up is a process that takes years of consistency and lots of patience, but there is a way to fast track your growth in this area. It has to do with what we talked about in Chapter 12: standing on the shoulders of giants. Why try to build an audience on your own when there are people and accounts out there that have already gathered your ideal followers? The key is to get featured on those platforms and get in front of OPA (I know, I know, more acronyms! I'm full of them in this chapter!), which stands for "Other People's Audiences." Using OPA means leveraging influence from other people who are already trusted in the space you want to grow in. This makes getting your message out there to the *right* people a *hell* of a lot more efficient.

We're going to keep using my *Forbes* article as an example here, because honestly the wins didn't stop in those first 72 hours. I woke up one morning a few months after the article to my phone ringing. It was my chief of staff, Liz (and she's a millennial who *does not call*; she texts!), so I knew it had to be important.

"Jen!" she cried into the phone, which was practically vibrating off my ear from her excitement. "Oh my god, you're on the radio. Elvis Duran just quoted you on Z100!"

If you're from New York City, you'll know why this was such a huge deal. Elvis has one of the most popular radio shows out there, along with more than half a million followers on Instagram, so I quickly joined the "Omigod, omigod, omigod" freakout dance party with Liz. I did some googling and found out that he'd quoted what I said about getting out of your comfort zone. So then I did what any normal person would do: I slid into his DMs.

Hey Elvis, I said in my message, *thank you so much for quoting me on your show when you were talking about your comfort zone.*

And Elvis responded and said, *Hi Jen, thank YOU for the jumpstart on this topic. I'm looking forward to taking this further.*

Okay, yup. I had my in. I said, *I'd be happy to come on and dive deeper for your listeners!*

And before we continue, I want to point out how I phrased this. I did not brag about myself and tell him I'd written a book and owned a business and yada yada yada, because Elvis wouldn't have given a shit. I was following up, and because you've read Chapter 10, you know that the follow-up isn't about me. It's about providing value to him, and the thing that would provide the most value for a major radio host would be to provide value for his listeners.

Long story short, Elvis booked me for a 20-minute segment all about my four tips to dusting off your networking skills and connecting at events, the topic of that *Forbes* article. We had an incredible conversation on the show where I got to be visible to his entire audience. His team also created a reel for the show's Instagram, so I got to borrow his influence and his audience there too. This is how you build your audience, my friend! That reel got over 120,000 views, and because they made me a collaborator on the video, I got some amazing kickback.

My "new followers" remained steady until the day Z100 shared that reel, and then, BOOM, a massive increase of new followers.

That made me pretty happy, but it didn't stop there. I got a hell of a lot of leads from this radio segment too, and that profit from my initial $0 investment continued to skyrocket now that I was combining Elvis's influence with the credibility I'd built.

With every Live, podcast, article, media segment, and post that you put out into the world, you need to be thinking about building your audience and your community. The more people who are listening to you, the more people you're going to have influence over and the more impact you're going to make.

So many of the tools you've already learned in this book are great for determining where you can start to build influence, and once again, I'm gonna lead you right back to our good friend the

Top 20 tool (bet you believe me now when I say it's a fucking powerhouse, right?). Who do you know who has a platform, and how can you leverage *their* audiences to build yours? How can you provide value to people whose platforms are more powerful than yours? How can you use this knowledge to build more influence for your brand?

AUTHORITY

One of my favorite movies to rewatch on airplanes (don't ask me why, but it's a great airplane movie!) is *Miss Congeniality* starring Sandra Bullock. If you haven't seen this classic gem, I'll give you a one-sentence summary: it's about an FBI agent who goes under-cover as a beauty pageant contestant to prevent some bad people from bombing the event. I'm sorry, but for context, I have to spoil the ending for you. (Look, it's from 20 years ago, so I don't feel too bad!) Sandra's character, Gracie, becomes the hero (and first runner-up!) when she solves the puzzle and arrests the real cul-prit onstage. But first, everyone thinks she's completely batshit because she looks like a jealous pageant contestant. It's not until the winner's crown explodes that anyone believes her, but what if she had flashed her FBI badge *before* trying to arrest the bomber? They would have immediately respected her authority instead of trying to escort her off the stage.

Authority equals power, and it comes from the combination of credibility and influence, or in this particular scenario, an FBI badge that says she means business and you have to listen. When you have authority and can show it, you have the power to make people take action, because they're listening to what you have to say and believe you're the expert on the topic. Just like anyone can get online and say "I'm awesome!" anyone can try to tell you what to do. But when a police officer (or Sandra Bullock) flashes their badge at you, you're a lot more likely to listen, right?

Let's take a look at a less fictional example. Not too long ago, I was featured on the cover of *Strong* magazine. Pretty dope, right? Well, yeah, it's definitely cool, but it would have been an extra-cool authority builder if I was still a fitness professional—but I'm not! Still, I was absolutely not going to turn down being on the cover of a magazine, so I had to find a way to spin the topic of the article to work in my favor. My challenge was finding a way to make sure it lent me authority in the business I actually *am* in, because that authority—that extreme expertise in my field that commands respect—would give me more influence and credibility.

So I thought to myself, *How can I make this happen? They want me to be on the cover of a fitness magazine, but I want to gain credibility, influence, and authority in business.*

And then it hit me. I spoke with the amazing team at *Strong* and shared a cool idea I had about an angle for the article that wouldn't cover workout tips. They absolutely loved it, and the cover and accompanying six-page spread was called "Why Health Is Literally Her Wealth." The entire feature was about my story as an entrepreneur, which gave me unbelievable amounts of authority as a business owner, even though it was a fitness magazine. Your goal is to be seen everywhere, but make sure you're always spinning the message from an angle that helps build CIA with your ideal audience. In this case, that magazine helped me be seen by people who wanted to become successful entrepreneurs, just like I did.

I got a message from an entrepreneur shortly after the magazine came out that said, "Congrats on the cover. If I sell my business, I really need your help elevating my personal brand. I want to speak on stages and be on magazine covers like you."

This wasn't someone who wanted my help training them in the gym. This was someone who was saying, "You're a successful brand and you're on the cover of magazines—I want to do that too."

The *credibility* of my story and the *Strong* fitness name, combined with the *influence* of the magazine's platform and my *authority* as someone who built a successful company and a powerful personal brand allowed me to reach that person. Even though by that point we'd already sold our agency, I was able to turn that conversation into a $30,000 VIP strategy session.

We're all about turning you into a CIA agent right now, but that's the thing about working undercover—no one will ever know you're a CIA agent until you flash that badge. So how do you flash your credibility markers to build authority in a way that makes people want to engage with you, share your message, and—most importantly—buy whatever it is you're selling?

Here's a little math equation for you that might sound a teensy bit familiar after Chapter 10: 20 percent of the value of the credibility marker (the media segment, podcast, article, or award) is the initial piece of content, and 80 percent of the value is *what you do with it* to increase your authority. (It's the magic of the follow-up again!) How are you flashing your badge? Can you share it on social media? E-mails? Ads? Your marketing materials? Building authority is all about amplification. So that means if you want to build authority in your space, you're going to have to figure out how to capture your audience's attention. One way to do that is with the perfect social media post that shares your credibility markers inside of a story.

HOW TO WRITE THE PERFECT POST

The more visible you and your brand become, the more wins you'll have to share. I mean, by the time I'm done with you, you'll have so many podcasts, articles, TV segments, and stages that you'll have content for years! But remember, it's not as much about the initial piece you're featured in as it is the CIA that comes as a result of sharing it with your audience.

Think about it this way: flashing your badge doesn't have nearly as much of an effect if you fumble it and let it drop into a mud puddle, after all. You want your moment to be smooth, compelling, and powerful. And you're in luck, because there's a framework I use to write a perfect post that makes this a lot easier, and it's going to help you craft content that is compelling, engaging, and profitable every single time.

Step 1: Use a Compelling Headline

You're creating content for your audience—that one person you're trying to help—but if you can't engage them from the get-go, they'll never click on the article, or they'll swipe up and keep scrolling two seconds into your reel. An amazing tagline, lead-in, caption, or headline is so important for every post you make, and an effective one should do the following four things.

Address a problem your audience wants to solve

What's a common problem your followers face? What mistakes do you see them making when they dip their toes into your world of expertise? What keeps them up at night? Finding your audience's pain point and then helping them solve it is a great way to build CIA. Put on your detective hat and start creeping on your audience. What questions are they asking the most in your comments, DMs, and e-mails? What kind of help do they need? Dog-ear the answers you uncover, because those are your customers' pain points. Then, make sure you're using a headline or opening line that starts right away with something that addresses that question, problem, or desire.

Pose a question (not always literally!)

I've found that opening with a line that creates curiosity always helps encourage my audience to continue reading. Headlines or captions that lead with questions make us automatically want to know the answer, and even when we think we already know, they make us click through just to check. A good headline will pique curiosity and make the audience want to know more or encourage conversation, thought, and engagement.

For good question-based headlines, think everything from FAQs to "Would You Rather . . . ?" or "Underrated or Overrated?" games to play with your followers. Questions are a super amazing way to start a conversation and engage with the people who follow you.

Don't bury the lede

I know it's super tempting to be cute, cliché, and clever when writing headlines. There is definitely a time and a place for play-on-words, sarcasm, and cutesy hidden meanings, but it's not when sharing a win in a post with the intention of building authority.

You literally have seconds to state your case to your audience before they scroll past the post you took hours to create, so make sure you're straight up and to the point with your opening line! Don't assume your audience is going to slog through your entire story before you get to the part you want them to read, because, reality check—they won't. Remember those 27 seconds to make a first impression from Chapter 11? When it comes to posts online, the number is even lower. There, the average human has an attention span of 8.25 seconds,[2] and I don't know about you, but that actually feels long to me. Data released by Facebook shows that the human attention span is even shorter—around 2.5 seconds on a computer, but only 1.7 seconds on a phone or mobile device.[3] Think about it, and I bet you'll find you do this too. I know when I'm on my phone, if I don't get pulled in within the first few words, I've already scrolled away! This eight-second rule also varies by generation, so if you're trying to appeal to Gen Z or a younger crowd, make sure you're paying extra close attention to this!

Even though I'm sitting here teaching you this, I still make this mistake sometimes and bury the lede. Here's the caption I used for a reel I made using footage of me seeing my cover issue of *Strong* magazine for the first time:

> *That moment when you see yourself on the cover of a magazine for the first time!*
> *Every birthday I write out wishes for the number of years I've been alive*
> *For the past decade, it's been on the top of my wishlist to see myself on the cover of a major magazine . . .*
> *Today that moment I used to see in my mind turned into a reality!*
> *Thank you,* Strong *magazine, for this epic experience!*

See that powerful, compelling opening line? I did not write that. Originally, when I posted, I started with the second line, but when Chris read it, he reminded me, "Jen, people only read the first line of a post before they scroll away. And if you don't say immediately that this is about the magazine, people are going to think it's about your birthday!"

I married a smart man. He was totally right.

If you're writing a blog post, tell your readers right away what they're reading about. When you're editing a video, throw some text in those opening seconds to make sure viewers know what they're about to learn. When pitching the media, be sure to open with a timely news hook in the first sentence. Always, always, *always* make sure the thing you want people to know most is right there at the top in clear, specific language. Even if they glance at it and look away, you want that first line to be what they remember.

Be specific and unique

Vague and clichéd language is not your friend! Include relevant keywords so you catch your audience's eye, and use numbers and statistics when possible to give a sense of how long or involved the post will be (*3 Lessons I Learned from Being on TV for 14 Seasons* sounds so much more specific and interesting than *Tips for Visibility*, doesn't it?). People love certainty, so the more information you can give them about the amount of time and attention that they're about to invest in your content, the better. I would be irresponsible not to add that if you're having trouble coming up with compelling headlines, you can always engage the help of ChatGPT. Simply type in the prompt: You are the greatest social media marketer of all time. Give me 10 compelling headlines for a social media post about [insert your topic here].

Step 2: Tell a Story

Since the beginning of time (or at least as far back as people have been communicating) we humans have been conditioned to love listening to and telling stories.[4] Think about it: all of our religious literature—the Bible, the Torah, the Quran—are full of stories. Each day we spend billions of dollars as a culture on stories in the form of books, movies, TV shows, theater, or even just catching up with friends. We love a good story because it's entertaining, but also because we often relate to it. You already know from constructing your Lean-In Story that the right story makes people connect with you emotionally. Stories make us laugh, cry, and fantasize. They allow our brains to connect more deeply with a message and remember details more clearly. Most importantly for writing the perfect post, they make us pay attention. People are way more apt to read your entire post and actually engage with it if you're telling a story rather than just announcing something. Let me give you an example. Which of the below posts are you going to be more excited about reading and engaging with?

> So excited I was featured in *Forbes* today! Check out the link in my bio for the full article.

OR

> Wanna know what's totally nuts about this feature of me in @forbes? 👇
>
> The first time I went to a "networking event," I totally sh*t the bed. 💩 🙀 ♀
>
> ✔️ I forgot the name of the host (in front of her!)
>
> ✔️ I finally got to speak to someone I had been wanting to meet and I was so nervous that I actually FORGOT my own phone number! 🙍 ♀ 🙍 ♀
>
> I was so bad and it was so traumatic that networking became one of my top five least favorite activities, alongside camping and water sports (another story for another day).
>
> Years later I decided to squash this fear, rewrite my limiting beliefs around this, and make networking MY thing.
>
> So even though I'm actually an introvert (even though no one believes me!) and it's not natural for me to enjoy working rooms full of people (unless I'm on a stage!) I committed to finding a way to "network" without "networking"!
>
> I have four badass hacks that anyone (even the most introverted) can use to totally rock any in person event with ease and dare I say . . . while having fun!

> Check out this dope *Forbes* feature written by the talented @heystephanieburns and share it with someone who needs it! 🖤

I don't know about you, but number two has me hooked. And just so you know, I've tried both ways. The story always wins when it comes to engagement! So instead of just telling your audience something, share a story that they can relate to instead and watch what happens.

Coming up with a story to tell might not always feel easy. When your well of inspiration dries up and you're thirsty AF for new content ideas, hit up ChatGPT to give you some inspiration and then co-create with it to make your ideas come to life. If you want to go at it solo, try some of these prompts to get you started:

Top tips for . . .

What NOT to do when . . .

The biggest mistakes I see people make are . . .

Things I wish I knew before I . . .

How (something you did in your past) helps me (something you do now) today . . .

Yesterday I read that . . .

A letter to my younger self . . .

I'm looking for advice about . . .

The thing most people miss when they . . .

All these prompts share one thing in common: they're not just about what you have to offer—they're about your very real, very human experience, which will connect you to your audience in a very real, very human way and provide valuable information in a format that will speak directly to your followers.

Step 3: Provide Value

Steve Martin, the amazing comedian (and star of another one of my other favorite airplane movies, *Father of the Bride*), once said, "Be so good they can't ignore you."[5] Before I put my thumbs to screen or fingers to keyboard to write a caption, I always remind myself of Steve's words. You see, if you're consistently giving your audience golden nuggets with each piece of content (especially ones where you're sharing a win, aka flashing your badge), it will be almost impossible for your reader to not double tap, share, and/ or eventually convert into a customer.

In Chapter 10, we talked all about the law of reciprocity, which states that when someone does something for you, you immediately want to return the favor. Inserting these value bombs into your post—whether it's making them laugh, entertaining them, or giving them a mic drop business tip—will not only be a way to Help One Person Every day, it will also incentivize them to reciprocate the favor by liking, sharing, and commenting.

Step 4: Call to Action

Without a call to action, what's the point of your post? Really think about that question for a second. Even if you're just posting an inspirational quote and a pretty image to go with it, you would be doing the person on the other end a disservice by not encouraging them to take some sort of action. What do you want them to get from that quote? For example, if you genuinely just want to make someone's day by posting a saying you love, ask them to reshare it and pass the message along. Not only will that potentially help you get more eyeballs on your post, but it will help that person feel good because they helped someone else.

The term "call to action" is a loaded one because I feel like it immediately makes people think they need to be selling something. But a call to action is simply encouraging your audience to do *something*. You could ask viewers of a video to drop an emoji in the comments or stitch the video with their own. You could ask them to share your article, DM you with questions about your next event, check out the link in your bio, or follow you on another platform for more content. Always have something in mind that gets your audience to engage with your post. That way, you're not just pleasing the pesky algorithm gods; you're creating the opportunity to engage right back and create a relationship with your followers (but more on that in just a sec!).

Even if your calls to action don't convert directly to sales, they will convert to a more actively engaged follower base and, more than likely, a big bump in that follower count. That will make you more and more visible to a wider audience that needs what you have to offer. Remember, at the end of the day, content isn't king—conversion is—and a call to action is the only way you're going to showcase to your audience exactly what you're trying to convert them to.

Step 5: NEVER Post & Ghost

I'm gonna ask you a question, and I want you to do some real, honest self-reflection here. Have you ever spent hours creating a super powerful piece of content, formulating an engaging head-line, pairing it with the perfect photo, and finally pressing Post at a strategic time when you know people are paying attention so you can get the maximum engagement . . . only to then not respond to any of the comments your audience took time to write? It's okay if you have. We are all friends here, and I'm actually happy we're calling this out so you can finally realize how counterproductive and flat-out rude "posting and ghosting" really is.

If your goal is to get people to see you and actually engage with your content, then there is nothing on planet Earth more import-ant when you pick up your phone than acknowledging those beau-tiful humans for taking the time from their busy lives to write a comment below your post. Think about it this way: when some-one takes time to comment on your content, they are giving you a gift of their attention and time (which is unbelievably valuable). If someone gave you a real-life gift wrapped up with a bow, would you just walk away without saying thank you? And if you did, do you think that person will give you a gift ever again? Honestly, I hope not. So if you want to build a fanbase of people that know, like, and trust you, *thank them* for their gift of engagement! Otherwise, they will spend their time and energy on someone who's grateful for it.

Bonus Step: Reuse, Recycle, Repurpose

Another important point I like to make is that your content doesn't always have to be completely new! In a perfect world, you'd have a new story for every occasion, and you'd always be able to give your followers something fresh. But news flash! We don't live in a perfect world. I want you to pay careful attention to my next words, because they're gonna blow your mind, okay? Never, ever, ever share anything only once, please. I mean, why throw away the orange when there is still so much more juice in there?

A year after that first *Forbes* article went live and single handedly skyrocketed my CIA, I decided to do an experiment and see what would happen if I shared it again just with a different caption, photo, and story this time. Using a new image with the *Forbes* logo and headline of the article, I posted it on my accounts. I didn't claim it was new or anything, and even though some of my followers had certainly read the article a year before, it still got an amazing response.

Here's a thought that just might set you free: people aren't paying nearly as much attention to you as you think! Not one person remembered that I had already shared this, including my parents, who congratulated me profusely both the first and second time I shared it as if they were completely different articles. In fact, this second version got more shares than the first time! I got another rush of DMs and congratulations e-mails from people, *and it was the same damn article!* Why is that, do you think?

Well, it's for a few reasons. We're all constantly getting new followers, which builds our own CIA and makes it more likely that our content will reach new people, but even our old followers aren't seeing every single one of our posts (foiled again by the algorithm gods). So repurposing content makes it visible to more of those followers. Even if they did see it the first time, some people need to read things a few times before it really sinks in. Timeliness is another factor—when something relevant happens in the world, content that speaks to that news is more likely to relate to your audience, who will already have it on their mind and be more likely to engage with it.

Sometimes, though, it just comes down to luck and timing. An influential friend who wasn't following you or didn't see it last time you posted might reshare it this time, lending their influence to yours and leading to a chain reaction. Someone who barely glanced at the first post and got pulled away to answer a call might be seeing it now while they're relaxing and have more time to engage. There are too many factors at play here to narrow it down to one cause, but all I can say is you're never going to know until you try it again.

All those shares and likes and DMs from my second *Forbes* post were still adding to my credibility. Repurposing my content was actually amplifying my message and giving me more authority. And as a fabulous bonus, more introverted people who needed to read that content got to benefit.

"Congrats, Jen! I feel like I'm seeing you everywhere!"

"Jen, you're crushing it!"

"Jen, thank you so much for sharing this. It helped me so much!"

I bet you're not surprised that my experiment worked, and I got several more speaking engagements and leads in my inbox from resharing. The real truth of this story is that good content is the gift that keeps on giving.

Are you getting this? 'Cause now it's your turn. What media or content can you repurpose? What do you have sitting around that you haven't shared in a while, or that didn't get as big of a response as you know it should have? Can you plop a new photo on that magazine feature from last year? Copy/paste the old post into ChatGPT and prompt it to change the story up to give it a new twist or call to action? Tell a story you haven't shared in a while? What will give you more credibility, influence, and authority in your field? Think about it, start jotting things down, and more importantly, go take action now and press Post!

START BEFORE YOU'RE READY

In 2022, I chose two "words of the year" that completely transformed my business. It was the combination of the two together that sprinkled the extra fairy dust on what would become an unbelievably successful year. Before I tell you what they were, let me explain how I chose them. At the end of December, I spent a few hours getting really real with myself by listing out all the ways I held myself back from achieving what I wanted the prior year. As I carefully analyzed 2021, and did some major, super-honest self-reflection, I realized that I had two blocks that were stopping my momentum:

1. My perfectionism and addiction to structure and certainty

2. My laziness around content creation (which, now that I look back, probably stemmed from a fear of showing the world a real, imperfect image of myself!)

Once I became honest with myself, I had no choice but to make a commitment to do whatever it took to break those limiting patterns and beliefs. So I chose two words to live by that would not allow me to hide anymore. They were—drumroll please—*content* (the noun, not the adjective) and *flexibility*.

I made a commitment to myself (and by now, you know I stick to the commitments I make to myself!) that I was going to post every single day and produce content that provided value and told a great story. I also promised myself that I wasn't going to care if it was perfect. I wasn't going to wait until the video or photo was retouched and had the perfect filter or if the font on the image was pretty. I was going to be flexible, easygoing, imperfect, and post it anyway.

Not gonna lie, it was hard at first. But you know this next part: confidence comes from consistently sticking with the commitments you make with yourself. Every single time you follow through and make yourself visible in that livestream video or on your YouTube channel, you're putting a coin in the confidence bank. Even though it was scary. Even if it sucked. Even if your hair looked terrible. And believe me, I have many videos and photos in the Googleverse with cringeworthy hair.

During my year of content and flexibility, I tried a gajillion new things. I became a content machine, even when I didn't feel ready. Even when it wasn't perfect. I posted on Instagram, TikTok, Twitter, Facebook, YouTube—you name it, and I posted consistently with all my fears and insecurities in the passenger seat. And you know what? The results were so amazing that my year of content turned into a new practice that I continue to this day.

Posting every single day brought my brand-new TikTok account from zero to 70,000 followers in less than six months. It also led to several reels of me speaking on stage going viral with millions of views, which led to me being chosen as one of the top 50 keynote speakers in the world by *Real Leaders* magazine. When I received the e-mail from them telling me I made the list, which also happened to include some of my personal heroes like Gary Vaynerchuk, Tony Robbins, Brené Brown, and Jay Shetty, it opened like this: *Hey Jen! It seems like every time I open my phone, you're droppin' that hot knowledge on me! We're honored to let you know that we've included you in our list of the Top 50 Keynote Speakers in the World for 2023!*

People see me everywhere because *I make myself be seen everywhere.* By creating consistent content, I'm ensuring that whenever someone who follows me opens any of their apps, they get a gift of value from yours truly as a reminder that I'm there for them. Being top of mind leads to more media features, more speaking engagements, and more opportunities. It doesn't matter that the content isn't perfectly shot using amazing lighting, filters, or microphones. In fact, more often than not, my messy, in-the-moment selfie videos perform waaaay better than the carefully curated professional ones! People love realness.

What helped me when I first started, and still does now, is reading this quote by Steven Pressfield to myself every single morning:

"Start before you're ready. Don't prepare, begin."

Remember, the enemy is not a lack of preparation. It's not the state of the marketplace. It's not the difficulty of your project, or the emptiness in your bank account.

The enemy is resistance. It's your chattering brain, and if you give it even a nanosecond of attention, it will start producing excuses, alibis, self-justifications, and a million reasons why you can't, shouldn't, *won't* do the thing you know you need to do.

So even if it isn't perfect, post it anyway.

Start before you're ready.

Start being seen. (I added that line!)

MIC DROP MOMENTS

- Anyone can say anything they want on the Internet, but to get your audience to trust you and believe you, you'll need the following three things:

- CIA: Credibility, Influence, Authority

- Leverage OPA (Other People's Audiences) to boost your message. Make connections with those people with bigger platforms by providing value to them.

- Don't be afraid to flash your badge. Remember, 20 percent of your credibility marker is your initial piece of content, and 80 percent is what you do with it to increase your authority.

- Key steps for writing a perfect post:
    - Use a compelling headline
    - Tell a story
    - Provide value
    - Include a call to action
    - Never post and ghost
    - Reuse, recycle, repurpose

A QUICK WIN

- Use the tips in this chapter to craft (and publish!) a perfect post. Right now—I mean it!

PUT IT ON A POST-IT

- Start before you're ready.

. . . .

CHAPTER 15

CONNECTING THE DOTS

I put my head on my dad's shoulder and my eyes welled up with tears, a few escaping down my cheek onto the fuzzy knit blanket where we were snuggled up on his leather La-Z-Boy couch. We were having a conversation about what it was like for him to see me give a keynote speech for the first time, and it was one of those moments where everything that had ever happened in my life until that point finally made sense.

"This was one of the most incredible days of my life," he said. "To see my daughter up there, so enthusiastic and realistic, and hear you teach people so many good strategies . . . it was wonderful."

Because of his multiple sclerosis, my dad, Al, hadn't been able to travel to experience any of my speaking engagements or events in person. For years, this had been hard for both of us because for my entire childhood, my dad held front-row season tickets to every performance, competition, recital, graduation, and every other major and not-so-major moment of my life. From those days as a wildly enthusiastic five-year-old who danced and flipped in front of his camcorder in the basement to my Broadway tour debut in *The Wedding Singer*, my dad has proudly held the title of President of the Jen Gottlieb fan club. We didn't have a theater in my high school, so we performed all of our shows in the hallway with metal lockers as a backdrop. But for every janky, fluorescent-lit production of *Chicago*, *A Chorus Line*, and *Guys and Dolls*, I could count on Dad being there, sitting on the cold tile floor with a bouquet of flowers and a proud smile that stretched from ear to ear.

"Jenny, you're going from hallway to Broadway," he always told me. "I just know it."

Now that I'm a speaker, he's had to learn how to use Instagram (and he's crushing it, btw!) to see clips of my "performances," but no matter how many IG stories and reels he responds to with hearts and fire emojis, it still isn't as good as seeing the real thing. Then, while writing this book, I got the opportunity to speak at a major real estate event at the Hard Rock Hotel in Hollywood, Florida, which is only 20 minutes from his house! He was so excited, and even though it was a stretch for him to walk through such a big venue with his cane, he told me there was no way in hell he was missing it. When I stepped onto that stage and saw him in the front row, I felt like little Jenny all over again in the best possible way.

This time, instead of glitzy costumes, a perfectly rehearsed script, and an audience of theatergoers with playbills in their hands, it was just me and my slides, sharing my expertise with a room full of real estate investors who were feverishly taking notes and physically leaning in with every word I said. Instead of my audience just watching the show and applauding after each scene, my crowd of bigshot moguls were standing up and visualizing their future selves as I led them through a meditation, many with tears in their eyes. For my dad to see that I did that for them made it extra powerful and fulfilling. I wasn't playing a character anymore. I was finally allowing myself to be seen as *me*.

In the car ride home, Dad was quiet for a minute, and then he said to me, "It all makes sense now."

"What makes sense, Dad?"

"I always knew you had a gift," he said. "I've watched you work so hard, and from the time you were a kid I always thought you'd be a performer. But I never saw you doing this with your life." A knot grew tight in my throat, and tears sprang to my eyes as he continued. "This is why it was the way it was for you. All of it was so you could be here, doing this. Helping people."

That day, my dad got to watch me onstage helping and inspiring people and using my own words instead of a script someone wrote for me. He got to hear me using my story for good, and he knew exactly how much it meant to me that I no longer had to stand in an audition room and wait for someone to pick me, because *I* was picking me. *I* was dictating my own future.

I looked out the car window and all of the pit stops of my journey started to flash before my eyes. Little Jen basking in the spotlight in bedazzled overalls, declaring that I would be a Broadway star. The all-lettuce "diet" with the mean girls at lunch. Stepping onto the stage as Linda for the first time. Playing the part of Upper West Side housewife to Rob. Becoming Miss Box of Junk and later getting rid of Heavy Metal Jennifer. Crying with my mom at that Italian restaurant. The bruise on my forehead from hitting it against the cement wall. My fight for that trainer shirt that kickstarted my entrepreneurial journey. Meeting my soulmate on a bench in Central Park. Starting, running, and later selling my agency. All that, and everything in between. I stared out that car window, and as the palm trees whizzed by one at a time, all the dots of my life up until that moment started to connect.

As a kid, all I ever wanted was to be seen—by Dad's video camera, by my figure skating coach, by the cool girls at school, by the audiences at my children's theater productions. Looking back now, I realize I spent years screaming at the world to look at me, but I didn't have the courage to showcase who I really was. That only led me to bulimia, a broken heart, and a bleach-blonde breakdown on the floor of *That Metal Show*. As we pulled into my dad's driveway, all those neon signs I'd followed, knowingly or unknowingly throughout my entire journey, lit up in full force like a field of light behind me. I looked into the rearview mirror and finally saw them for what they were.

They were dots, and they seemed random. But when I look back at my life now, I can see that they connect to form a constellation that is messy, mesmerizing, and so completely imperfectly *me*. I see it now, and I know that without all the twists and turns, the story wouldn't be half as good for you to see.

Before I leave you, I want to share one of my favorite quotes of all time:

> You can't connect the dots looking forward, you can only connect them looking backwards. So you have to trust the dots will somehow connect in your future. You have to trust in something—your gut, destiny, life, karma, whatever. This approach has never let me down and it has made all the difference in my life.
> — Steve Jobs

This quote hangs in the entryway of my apartment. It's my favorite quote because it reminds me that every single thing that's ever happened to me—every open wound and rock-bottom bathroom floor along with my dad watching me speak my truth onstage or walking down the aisle to marry the love of my life—has been a dot that led here to this moment, being seen on this page with you as you use my stories and the strategies that came from them to help you find your own voice and create the life you're dreaming of.

Many of us set off on this journey of life and business with a strict plan of what we think it "should" be like. We walk the path that others see for us and often people-please our way to an unfulfilled future, not allowing the world to see the gifts that make us truly unique, for fear of what others will think if it's imperfect. But if you keep walking in a straight line and ignore all your own neon signs and scenic detours—if you don't mess up and fail and try and try and try again—you'll never fully realize what this life could have been. When I was a personal trainer, I never could have imagined I was going to own a PR agency, and I never could have imagined I would become a personal trainer when I was a struggling actress and arm candy to Rob. To put it simply, I had to try (and fail at) a lot of different shit to get to where I am today.

But now, all those chapters are the stories that I can tell to connect me with the people I've been put here to help.

If I've learned anything at all from this wild ride thus far, it's that you have to allow yourself to courageously take action in the face of fear, embrace your failures when they try to crash the party, and allow people to really see you for who you truly are and who you're becoming.

When you're in the thick of it, it's impossible to know how your dots will all eventually connect, but when you look backward, it always makes sense! It might take longer than you'd like, and the lines probably won't be perfectly straight or what you imagined them to be, but you always figure out why it happened. Each dot is part of the story that people are going to want to read and share about, because it just might help them through a similar struggle. One thing I know is that the story you will tell on the other side of your own constellation of dots will be even cooler and more powerful than you could have ever imagined. Hey, it might just become a book.

Please remember, my dear friend, that life might get messy and it might be imperfect, but I promise you it's going to lead you somewhere truly special. Your personal stories are what make you uniquely you. They're what make you stand out in this crowded world of Paris filters and Facetuning. They're what make people want to connect with *you* instead of that other life coach, doctor, speaker, or interior designer. And if you can embrace all your dots—the good, the bad, and the ugly ones—and use them to connect to the people you can help, I promise you this: You *will* be seen.

Because of my past, I'm being seen in a way I never would have given myself permission to be seen. I want you to grant that same permission for yourself again and again and again, because remember, being seen is more than just a bump in your follower count—it's your responsibility to be visible to the people who need you. Every time I feel scared to put myself out there, I ask myself, *Where would I be without all those podcast hosts I listened to on my Wonder Walks and authors whose books I read on the floor of that Barnes & Noble if they never made themselves visible?*

Where will your audience be if you don't start building your brand into something that can help even that one person to grow and follow in your footsteps and make their life better? Who is that person who needs to see you in order to change their life? You owe it to yourself, and you owe it to your audience, to see where this road will take you.

I have no idea where the rest of my life will lead me, but I know it doesn't stop here, because I'm not done. Not even close. I'm just getting started, and so are you, because none of us are ever done growing. You've got the tools right here in this book, so now it's time to use them so you and I can continue growing together.

It's time to look around you and connect your dots.

Your real self.

Your real future.

Your real community.

Your real audience.

Connect those dots and see where they lead you. I just know it's somewhere great. And I can't wait to see.

EXTRAS

You know I couldn't just hand you this book without sprinkling in a little extra magic! This isn't just ink on a page, it's a tool for your transformation. So, I've crafted some game-changing, behind-the-scenes goodies just for you.

Ready to supercharge your path? Scan the code below and to get access to the extra resources, custom-made to help you BE SEEN in all your badassery!

ENDNOTES

Chapter 1

1. Cretian Van Campen, *The Proust Effect: The Senses as Doorways to Lost Memories* (Oxford University Press: 2014).

Chapter 2

1. "Why We Physically Feel Fear," UWA Psychology and Counseling News, June 21, 2019, https://online.uwa.edu/news/what-causes-fear/.

2. Jamie Ballard, "Women Are More Likely Than Men to Say They're a People-Pleaser, and Many Dislike Being Seen as One," YouGovAmerica, August 22, 2022, https://today.yougov.com/topics/society/articles-reports/2022/08/22/women-more-likely-men-people-pleasing-poll.

Chapter 3

1. "National Eating Disorder Awareness Week," Office on Women's Health, February 15, 2022, https://www.womenshealth.gov/nedaw.

3. Jamie Ballard, "How Americans Feel about Their Bodies," May 26, 2021, https://today.yougov.com/topics/society/articles-reports/2021/05/26/body-image-americans-feelings-about-bodies.

4. "Beyoncé on Her Alter Ego, Sasha Fierce," *The Oprah Winfrey Show*, OWN, August 17, 2019, https://www.youtube.com/watch?v=4AA5G8vCl9w.

5. Todd Herman, *The Alter Ego Effect* (New York: Harper Business, 2019).

6. David Robson, "The 'Batman Effect': How Having an Alter Ego Empowers You," LSA Psychology University of Michigan, August 19, 2020, https://lsa.umich.edu/psych/news-events/all-news/faculty-news/the--batman-effect---how-having-an-alter-ego-empowers-you.html.

Chapter 4

1. E. Kross and O. Ayduk, "Self-Distancing: Theory, Research, and Current Directions," *Advances in Experimental Social Psychology*, April 2017, http://selfcontrol.psych.lsa.umich.edu/wp-content/uploads/2017/04/SD.pdf.

Chapter 5

1. Christopher D. Green, "Where Did Freud's Iceberg Metaphor of Mind Come From?" *History of Psychology* 22 no. 4 (2019): 369–372. https://pubmed.ncbi.nlm.nih.gov/31633371/.

2. "How Reliable Are Eyewitnesses?" Constitutional Rights Foundation, https://www.crf-usa.org/bill-of-rights-in-action/bria-13-3-c-how-reliable-are-eyewitnesses#:~:text=Studies%20have%20shown%20that%20mistaken,errors%20resulted%20from%20eyewitness%20mistakes.

3. Anina Rich and Sarah Maguire, "What Is the Baader-Meinhof Phenomenon?" The Lighthouse, July 22, 2020, https://lighthouse.mq.edu.au/article/july-2020/What-is-the-Baader-Meinhof-Phenomenon.

Chapter 6

1. Mary Kate Lee, "Gratitude as an Antidote to Anxiety and Depression: All the Benefits, None of the Side Effects," Syracuse University Maxwell School of Citizenship and Public Affairs, May 28, 2019, https://www.maxwell.syr.edu/news/article/gratitude-as-an-antidote-to-anxiety-and-depression-all-the-benefits-none-of-the-side-effects.

Chapter 8

1. "Why Are We Likely to Continue with an Investment Even If It Would Be Rational to Give It Up? The Sunk Cost Fallacy, Explained," The Decision Lab, https://thedecisionlab.com/biases/the-sunk-cost-fallacy.

2. Geoffrey Abbott, "Exile and Banishment Law," *Brittanica*, updated September 6, 2022, https://www.britannica.com/topic/exile-law.

3. Liz Mineo, "Good Genes Are Nice, but Joy Is Better," *The Harvard Gazette*, April 11, 2017, https://news.harvard.edu/gazette/story/2017/04/over-nearly-80-years-harvard-study-has-been-showing-how-to-live-a-healthy-and-happy-life/.

4. Lindenfors, et al., "'Dunbar's number' Deconstructed," *Biology Letters*, May 5, 2021, https://royalsocietypublishing.org/doi/10.1098/rsbl.2021.0158.

5. Michael Miller, "The Life or Death Science of Community: Three Steps to Living a Longer, More Connected Life," Six Seconds, https://www.6seconds.org/2018/06/13/the-life-or-death-science-of-community-three-steps-to-living-a-longer-more-connected-life/.

Chapter 10

1. Dennis P. Carmody and Michael Lewis, "Brain Activation When Hearing One's Own and Others' Names," *Brain Research* 1116, 1 (October 20, 2006):153–8. https://www.ncbi.nlm.nih.gov/pmc/articles/PMC1647299/.

2. Frank Rose, "The Selfish Meme," *The Atlantic*, October 2012, https://www.theatlantic.com/magazine/archive/2012/10/the-selfish-meme/309080/.

Chapter 12

1. "Standing on the Shoulders of Giants," Farnam Street Media, https://fs.blog/shoulders-of-giants/.

2. "Standing on the Shoulders of Giants," Farnam Street Media, https://fs.blog/shoulders-of-giants/.

3. "Not-Invented-Here Syndrome," *Cambridge Dictionary*, https://dictionary
.cambridge.org/us/dictionary/english/not-invented-here-syndrome.

Chapter 13

1. "Reese Witherspoon on Her Mentor Oprah," *Fast Company*, May 30, 2018.
Video, 0:51. https://www.youtube.com/watch?v=Sxehc1Y0AAU.

Chapter 14

1. "Influencer Marketing Market Size 2016–2022," Oberlo, https://www.oberlo
.com/statistics/influencer-marketing-market-size.

2. Steven Zauderer, "Average Human Attention Span by Age: 47 Statistics," Cross
River Therapy, January 25th, 2023, https://www.crossrivertherapy.com
/average-human-attention-span#:~:text=Research%20has%20revealed%20
that%20human,seconds%20less%20than%20in%202000.

3. Tallulah David, "Attention Span on Social Media Is 2 Seconds. Turns Out,
That's Plenty of Time," CareerArc, June 2017, https://www.careerarc.com/blog
/attention-span-on-social-media/.

4. Paul J. Zak, "How Stories Change the Brain," *Greater Good Magazine*, December
17, 2013, https://greatergood.berkeley.edu/article/item
/how_stories_change_brain.

5. Maggie Zhang, "How to Become So Good They Can't Ignore You," *Insider*, July
17, 2014, https://www.businessinsider.com/become-so-good-they-cant
-ignore-you-2014-7.

INDEX

ACKNOWLEDGMENTS

Oh my goodness, my heart is overflowing with gratitude for the incredible people who helped make this book a reality! I couldn't have done this without each and every one of you.

First and foremost, I have to thank the love of my life and business partner, Chris. Your patience, honest feedback, encouragement, and loving nudges to dream bigger have been instrumental in helping me bring this book to life. You're my ultimate accountability buddy, best friend, personal comedian, and lifelong mentor. I'm so grateful for your unwavering support and belief in me, even during the toughest moments. You not only lift me up and help me shine, but you also showed me that I could be seen—that my voice and my story mattered. I couldn't have done this without you by my side, cheering me on every step of the way.

Next, I want to thank my incredible family—Mom, Dad, Glam-ma Thelma, Grandpa Gene, and my brother, Steven. You guys have always been my biggest cheerleaders, and your influence and impact on my life are woven throughout the stories that I share in this book. And let's not forget my amazing stepdaughter, Vivienne. Your sweet spirit and love have brought so much joy to my life, and I am beyond grateful for you. Your confidence and unwavering belief in yourself inspires me every day.

To my team at Super Connector Media—I am so unbelievably grateful for you! I feel blessed to work with such talented and dedicated rock stars. Your passion, creativity, and drive are truly contagious. Thank you for cheering me on during our "weekly wins calls" and for all the encouraging messages in Voxer and Slack that helped me stay motivated throughout the writing process. And a special shout-out to our Super Connector Mastermind family—you guys inspire me every single day!

To my incredible team at Hay House—thank you for making my first journey as an author so easy and fun! Patty Gift, Reid Tracy, and my fabulous editor, Anne Barthel, thank you for believing in me. I couldn't have asked for a more perfect home for *BE SEEN*!

Big thanks to my badass agents, Steve Troha and Jan Baumer—thank you for your guidance, support, and for helping me bring this book to life.

I have to give a special shout-out to my incredible mentors, Emily Krempholtz and Kelly Notaras. They helped me to take my stories to the next level and bring them to life in ways I never thought possible. But let's be real, all of that hard work we put in won't matter if we don't get this book into as many hands as possible, right? That's where my amazing book launch manager, Courtney Kenney, and my branding guru, Rory Vaden, come in. Your expertise, dedication, organization, and support have been invaluable throughout this entire launch. You helped me get *BE SEEN* seen!

And to my unbelievably supportive (and brilliant) friends—Lori Harder, Amy Porterfield, Gabrielle Lyon, Dan Fleyshman, Danielle Dimasi, Laura Belgray, Jenna Kutcher, Lindsay Schwartz, Randy Gam, and Kellyann Petrucci—I am so grateful for your love, encouragement, feedback, and support. You guys kept me inspired and sane throughout this wild ride.

Gabby Bernstein, you are a true queen! Thank you for writing the foreword and for constantly inspiring me to reach for the stars.

And to my brilliant creative team (and dear friends)—Annebet Duvall, Chris Eckert, Rachel Pesso, Jessica Mucumeci, and David Curcurito—you brought my vision to life in ways that surpassed my wildest dreams!

Last but certainly not least, a huge shout-out to my furry writing partners—Tammie, Teddy, King Arthur, and Dexter. Your snuggles, silliness, and love kept me going through the long hours of writing.

And to you, dear reader—I cannot express how grateful I am for you. You are the reason I wrote this book. The stories, the lessons, the strategies—they're all for you. I hope that as you read these pages, you feel seen, heard, and understood. I hope that you see yourself in my journey and know that you're not alone. You are worthy of being seen, of being heard, of being celebrated for who you are. And most importantly, you have something truly special to offer the world. Your unique gifts, talents, and perspectives are unlike anyone else's. The world needs them, and it needs you to step into your own spotlight with confidence and grace. So, my friend, I challenge you to take the lessons in this book and use them to BE SEEN in your own life. Whether it's in your career, in your relationships, or simply in the way you show up in the world, know that you have what it takes to shine. I believe in you, and I am cheering you on every step of the way.

ABOUT THE AUTHOR

Meet **JEN GOTTLIEB**—a power-house entrepreneur, author of the book *BE SEEN*, host of the *I Dare You* podcast, and co-founder of the award-winning Super Connector Media. With a successful five-year stint as a VH1 host and career as a Broadway actress under her belt, Jen now teaches business owners how to build profitable brands through her online education, events, and training company.

Her passion is helping entrepreneurs gain the confidence and skills required to make a splash in their industries. Through her sold-out events, online courses, and mentorship programs, she has helped thousands of business owners, experts, doctors, and coaches become "The Recognized Expert" in their field.

Jen is a sought-after speaker and has shared the stage with top thought leaders and celebrities, including Gary Vaynerchuk, Snoop Dogg, and Martha Stewart. Her work has been featured in major publications like *Forbes*, *Business Insider*, *Maxim*, and *Women's Health*, among others.

Jen was recently named one of the "Top 50 Keynote Speakers in the World" and her company, Super Connector Media, was listed on the Inc. 5000 Fastest-Growing Private Companies in America.

A true New Yorker at heart, Jen shares her Manhattan home with her husband, Chris, and their three adorable dogs, Tammie, Teddy, and King Arthur.

Hay House Titles of Related Interest

THE SHIFT, the movie,
starring Dr. Wayne W. Dyer
(available as an online streaming video)
www.hayhouse.com/the-shift-movie

***

HIGH PERFORMANCE HABITS: How Extraordinary People Become That
Way, by Brendon Burchard

THE GREATNESS MINDSET: Unlock the Power of Your Mind and Live Your
Best Life Today, by Lewis Howes

SUPER ATTRACTOR: Methods for Manifesting a Life beyond Your Wildest
Dreams, by Gabrielle Bernstein

TWO WEEKS NOTICE: Find the Courage to Quit Your Job, Make More
Money, Work Where You Want, and Change the World, by Amy Porterfield

UNFILTERED: Proven Strategies to Start and Grow Your Business by Not
Following the Rules, by Rachel Pedersen

All of the above are available at your local bookstore or may be ordered by
visiting:

Hay House USA: www.hayhouse.com®
Hay House Australia: www.hayhouse.com.au
Hay House UK: www.hayhouse.co.uk
Hay House India: www.hayhouse.co.in

All of the above are available at your local bookstore,
or may be ordered by contacting Hay House (see next page).

***

We hope you enjoyed this Hay House book. If you'd like to receive our online catalog featuring additional information on Hay House books and products, or if you'd like to find out more about the Hay Foundation, please contact:

Hay House, Inc., P.O. Box 5100, Carlsbad, CA 92018-5100
(760) 431-7695 or (800) 654-5126
(760) 431-6948 (fax) or (800) 650-5115 (fax)
www.hayhouse.com® • www.hayfoundation.org

———

Published in Australia by: Hay House Australia Pty. Ltd.,
18/36 Ralph St., Alexandria NSW 2015
Phone: 612-9669-4299 • *Fax:* 612-9669-4144
www.hayhouse.com.au

Published in the United Kingdom by: Hay House UK, Ltd.,
The Sixth Floor, Watson House, 54 Baker Street, London W1U 7BU
Phone: +44 (0)20 3927 7290 • *Fax:* +44 (0)20 3927 7291
www.hayhouse.co.uk

Published in India by: Hay House Publishers India,
Muskaan Complex, Plot No. 3, B-2, Vasant Kunj, New Delhi 110 070
Phone: 91-11-4176-1620 • *Fax:* 91-11-4176-1630
www.hayhouse.co.in

———

Access New Knowledge.
Anytime. Anywhere.

Learn and evolve at your own pace
with the world's leading experts.

www.hayhouseU.com